A Concise History of Canada

Margaret Conrad's history of Canada begins with a challenge to its readers. What is Canada? What makes up this diverse, complex, and often contested nation-state? What was its founding moment? And who are its people? Drawing on her many years of experience as a scholar, writer, and teacher of Canadian history, Conrad offers astute answers to these difficult questions. Beginning in Canada's deep past with the arrival of its Aboriginal peoples, she traces its history through the conquest by Europeans, the American Revolutionary War, and the industrialization of the nineteenth and twentieth centuries, to its prosperous present. As a social historian, Conrad emphasizes the peoples' history: the relationships between Aboriginal and settler, French and English, Catholic and Protestant, and rich and poor. She writes of the impact of disease, how women fared in the early colonies, and the social transformations that took place after the Second World War as Canada began to assert itself as an independent nation. It is this grounded approach that drives the narrative and makes for compelling reading. In the last chapter, the author explains the social, economic, and political upheavals that have transformed the nation over the last three decades. Despite its successes and its popularity as a destination for immigrants from across the world, Canada remains a curiously reluctant player on the international stage. This intelligent, concise, and lucid book explains just why that is.

Margaret Conrad is Professor Emerita at the University of New Brunswick in Canada. Her publications include *Atlantic Canada: A History*, with James K. Hiller (2010); *History of the Canadian People*, with Alvin Finkel (2009); *No Place Like Home: The Diaries and Letters of Nova Scotia Women, 1771–1938*, with Toni Laidlaw and Donna Smyth (1988); and *George Nowlan: Maritime Conservative in National Politics* (1986).

CAMBRIDGE CONCISE HISTORIES

This is a series of illustrated "concise histories" of selected individual countries, intended both as university and college textbooks and as general historical introductions for general readers, travellers, and members of the business community.

Other titles in the series are listed after the index.

A Concise History
of Canada

MARGARET CONRAD

Professor Emerita, University of New Brunswick

CAMBRIDGE
UNIVERSITY PRESS

CAMBRIDGE
UNIVERSITY PRESS

32 Avenue of the Americas, New York NY 10013-2473, USA

Cambridge University Press is part of the University of Cambridge.

It furthers the University's mission by disseminating knowledge in the pursuit of education, learning and research at the highest international levels of excellence.

www.cambridge.org
Information on this title: www.cambridge.org/9780521744430

© Cambridge University Press 2012

First published 2012

A catalogue record for this publication is available from the British Library

Library of Congress Cataloguing in Publication data
Conrad, Margaret.
A concise history of Canada / Margaret Conrad.
p.   cm. – (Cambridge concise histories)
Includes bibliographical references and index.
ISBN 978-0-521-76193-2 (hardback) – ISBN 978-0-521-74443-0 (pbk.)
1. Canada – History.   I. Title.
F1026.C6868   2011
971–dc23   2011021842

ISBN 978-0-521-76193-2 Hardback
ISBN 978-0-521-74443-0 Paperback

CONTENTS

ILLUSTRATIONS

ACKNOWLEDGEMENTS

I am indebted to almost every historian of Canada, living and dead, whose research made this book possible. *A Concise History of Canada* is dedicated to their hard work and scant acknowledgement in this and in many other publications. I owe more than I can adequately express to Alvin Finkel and James Hiller, coauthors with me of survey textbooks on Canadian and Atlantic Canadian history. Their wisdom and even their words are embedded in every chapter. In a lifetime I would be lucky to have had one happy collaboration; to have had two is nothing short of a miracle. It is also a miracle that I answered the life-changing e-mail that arrived on 24 September 2007 from Marigold Acland, Senior Commissioning Editor for Cambridge University Press. Given the unfamiliar name, I came mighty close to deleting it as just another piece of unwelcome spam. Her invitation to write the Canadian volume in the Cambridge Concise History series clinched my decision to take early retirement and get on with various writing commitments. It was the best decision I have ever made, and working with Cambridge University Press has been yet another happy collaboration. I am especially indebted to Janis Bolster, who saved me from embarrassing errors and bad writing, and what's more, agreed to everything I asked of her. It was a great pleasure to work with such an experienced and generous editor. Diana Witt, who developed the index, Joe LeMonnier, who drew the maps, and Joy Mizan, who pursued permissions for illustrations, endured with great patience my endless tinkering. I am also grateful to the anonymous reviewers of the manuscript, who read it so carefully.

As my friends can attest, I describe producing a history of Canada in ninety thousand words as akin to writing haiku. Sometimes the sentences are so freighted with nuance that an editor's change of one word throws everything off. Like aging, writing national history is not for wimps.

Marion Beyea, Gail Campbell, Gwendolyn Davies, Lyle Dick, Gerry Friesen, Don Fyson, Naomi Griffiths, Gregory Kealey, Linda Kealey, and Gillian Thompson – historians all – have helped me at one time or another with answers to questions. So, too, have people involved in several networks in which I participate: Jocelyn Létourneau and everyone associated with the Canadians and Their Pasts project; Penney Clark and others involved in THEN/HiER; my colleagues on the Advisory Board of the LaFontaine-Baldwin Symposium, spearheaded by John Ralston Saul and Adrienne Clarkson; and those working with me on the National Capital Commission Advisory Committee. Canada's History Society, especially the Chair of its Board of Directors, Charlotte Gray, and its President and CEO, Deborah Morrison, have kept me grounded on issues relating to Canada's past. Steven Schwinghamer, Research Coordinator at the Canadian Museum of Immigration at Pier 21, deserves a special thank you for finding the last photo used in this book. Finally, I want to acknowledge my ninety-five-year-old mother, who wonders what exactly it is that absorbs so many of my waking hours. She will not likely read this book, but she will be pleased that I have written it.

January 2012

Introduction
A Cautious Country

What is this thing called Canada? The second-largest country in the world geographically, it is a loose-jointed construction that seems to lack the cohesion that many other nation-states enjoy. So vast that it is difficult to grasp the whole, some provinces are nations unto themselves. One is at a loss even to establish a founding moment in Canada's past. While 1867 works for the four original provinces in "confederation," it serves less well for other areas of northern North America that were later induced to join the improbable experiment in nation-building.

Many scholars look to the conquest of Quebec by Major General James Wolfe's army in 1759 as a place to start for understanding a country that, in 1969, was proclaimed officially bilingual – French and English. People living in the Atlantic and Western provinces, with their own distinct historical narratives, would no doubt beg to differ on 1759 as the pivotal point, as would Canada's First Peoples and everyone living in Canada's three northern territories. Nevertheless, so prevalent is the province of Quebec in the nation's political landscape that "the rest of Canada" is now understood by its initials – ROC.

The term "Canada" is itself a slippery concept. Apparently a mistaken interpretation of an Iroquoian word for "village," it was applied by the French to their colony on the St. Lawrence River in the early seventeenth century. This space was enlarged and subdivided by the British Parliament into Upper Canada (Ontario) and

Lower Canada (Quebec) in 1791 and put back together in 1840 to form the United Province of Canada. The name was then affixed to the larger polity that took shape "from sea to sea to sea" in the second half of the nineteenth century.

In coming to terms with Canada, most historians have packaged it in several, essentially political, time periods: Pre-Contact to 1500; Natives and Newcomers, 1500–1661; New France, 1661–1763; British North America, 1763–1863; Confederation and Nation Building, 1864–1945; Modern Canada, 1945 to the present. Scholars have tried to move away from this template, but new turning points tend to fall roughly at the same temporal fault lines as the old ones. Gerald Friesen, for example, constructs his impressive narrative, *Citizens and Nation,* around four dominant communication systems – oral-traditional, textual-settler, print-capitalism, and screen-capitalism – but communications are so inextricably linked to economic and political transitions that it is difficult to determine cause and effect.[1] Economic approaches – hunter-gatherer, agricultural, industrial, and postindustrial – reflect similar overarching time frames. Intellectual and scientific innovations (Darwin's *Origin of Species* or the birth control pill, for example) have yet to drive a survey of Canadian history, but they, too, are part of a larger matrix of changes that accompany economic and political transformations. In this narrative, the chapters follow the conventional chronological framework with slight adjustments to accommodate my particular and, some may well argue, peculiar understanding of Canada's past.

No historian of Canada can ignore the tremendous geographical challenge of building a nation-state that spans the northern half of the North American continent. Canada's history is all about space, lots of it, and about weather, both hot and cold, but it is the winter that, until the twentieth century, determined how many people the land could support. Because Canada's climate and terrain have historically been inhospitable to human habitation, most immigrants – Aboriginal and newcomers alike – passed it by, preferring more salubrious southern climes.

While natural geological features (Appalachians, Great Lakes, Plains, and Pacific coast mountain chains) suggest that political boundaries might work more efficiently running north-south, other influences have prevailed. The boreal forest, the St. Lawrence–Great Lakes transportation system, and Aboriginal peoples eager to trade furs drew Europeans into the interior of the continent on an east-west axis. For better or for worse, North America was destined to produce three transcontinental nation-states – Mexico, the United States, and Canada – with Aboriginal nations embedded in each of them.

Space and weather have combined to make Canada a difficult place to inhabit and an even harder place to govern, but they have rarely impeded the exploitation of the area's rich natural resources. In the distant past, First Peoples harvested nature's bounty in their seasonal rounds, sometimes hunting species to extinction. Immigrants from Europe and elsewhere were even less likely to be good stewards of the environment. By the end of the twentieth century, it had become clear that there were limits to growth based on resource exploitation, but the habit was hard to break.

Contrary to the view that Natives were bested in the exchange with foreigners bearing trinkets, Canada's indigenous inhabitants were savvy traders and knew how to push their advantage to secure the European commodities – guns, knives, pots, blankets, brandy – that made survival in a cold climate much easier. This advantage disappeared under the assault, not of weapons in most cases, but of diseases to which Aboriginal peoples had little immunity. As microbes spread across the continent, sometimes in advance of European invaders, the population declined precipitously and social cohesion was undermined.

Canada's indigenous peoples have contributed greatly to the development of Canada, so much so that John Ralston Saul concludes that "we are a Métis civilization."[2] Originally a term applied to the offspring resulting from "country marriages" of fur traders and Aboriginal women, "Métis" captures the hybridity that increasingly defines Canadian society. During the first 250 years of European settlement, Aboriginal peoples dominated much of the Canadian landscape, and as settler populations continue to drift toward cities, it can be argued that they still do. Nearly 40 percent of Canadian territory is currently subject to Aboriginal land claims, and First Peoples are a force to be reckoned with on the Canadian political scene.

Although European nations were initially drawn to the eastern seaboard by the lowly cod, it was the beaver pelt that sustained two empires – French and British – that claimed much of the area now called Canada. Fishers and fur traders were mostly male sojourners, eager to return to their warmer homelands with "new-world" treasures. As one eighteenth-century observer noted with respect to Newfoundland, "Soe longe as there comes noe women," settler societies were unlikely to take root.[3] But women did come because the labour essential to human survival was deeply gendered and performed primarily in family economies before the Industrial Revolution transformed production processes. In colonial societies, women were responsible for preparing food; sewing warm clothing; caring for the young, the ill, and the elderly; and, in the case of communities dependent on the fisheries, managing the shore-based drying of the catch.

Canada as we know it today is the product of European and North American imperial rivalries and of the world wars that punctuated the long eighteenth century from 1689 to 1815. As such, Canada is heir to the Enlightenment and to the political currents that informed the Glorious, American, and French revolutions. Wars and negotiations in this period set the framework for continuing and often troubled relationships among the Aboriginal, French, and British populations of northern North America. Despite periodic efforts to transcend past transgressions, eighteenth-century treaties and parliamentary proclamations are still relevant to Aboriginal struggles for justice, and the legacy of the French regime remains deeply rooted, especially in Quebec and the Maritime provinces. Significantly, the colonies that emerged as "British" North America after the American Revolution consisted mostly of territory initially claimed by France. The thirteen original British colonies, meanwhile, enthusiastically cut the imperial apron strings.

Between the Treaty of Utrecht in 1713 and Confederation in 1867, British and American immigrants, many of them fleeing demons of poverty, oppression, and war, migrated to British North America. They brought with them modern capitalism, squabbling Christianities, a vigorous civil society, and hierarchical conventions relating to class, gender, and race. By the mid-nineteenth century, when railways made a transcontinental nation more than an impractical dream, settler societies from Newfoundland to Vancouver Island had much in common, including their governing institutions and political parties that drew heavily on the British parliamentary system.

Political leaders in the colonies, ever mindful of the freedoms experienced by the citizens of the United States, pioneered an evolutionary approach to self-government within the British Empire. After rebellions in Upper and Lower Canada (1837–38) and shabby political manoeuvrings everywhere, British North Americans achieved a limited parliamentary democracy, described as "responsible government" to distinguish it from the notion of full independence and from republican variants in France and the United States. Indeed, cautious colonials developed a whole new vocabulary to describe their ambiguous political condition, speaking of "autonomy" not "independence," adopting "dominion" instead of "kingdom" as their nation's status, and emphasizing "evolution" rather than "revolution" in their approach to reform.

The rebellions and responsible government set in motion what the historian Ian McKay describes as "the project of liberal rule."[4] In Canada, as elsewhere, the tenets of liberalism – individual initiative, democratic accountability, civil liberties, rule of law, property rights, separation of church and state, and a market-driven economy – have been hotly contested, but they served as the lodestar for many reformers and for the leaders of the Liberal and Conservative parties that have dominated the national political scene. In the twentieth century the social gospel and dreams of a more egalitarian society prompted farmers, feminists, intellectuals, and labourers to nurture a healthy strain of social democracy, still largely liberal in its essence, which is currently expressed most clearly by the New Democratic Party.

Confederation was a major step in the consolidation of the nation-state and a key factor in pushing the liberal objective of capitalist development. Undertaken in the context of a civil war in the United States, pressure from financial interests in Great Britain, and the rage for industrial growth in the Western world, three "responsibly governed" eastern colonies – Nova Scotia, New Brunswick, and the united Canadas (Quebec and Ontario) – came together in 1867 as the first "dominion" in the British Empire. By 1880, Rupert's

Land (the vast territorial domain claimed by the Hudson's Bay Company), the Northwest, and the Arctic, along with the colonies of British Columbia and Prince Edward Island, had been brought under the jurisdiction of Ottawa. The last holdout, Newfoundland and Labrador, joined Confederation in 1949.

This audacious attempt at nation-building by fewer than 4 million people was informed by the transcontinental model of the United States, blessed by the British government, and predicated on a communications network to tie the whole together. In his national policy, Canada's first prime minister, Scottish-born Sir John A. Macdonald, emphasized a transcontinental railway, agricultural settlement in the west, and tariffs high enough to cradle an industrial sector in the St. Lawrence–Great Lakes heartland, dominated by the emerging metropolises of Montreal and Toronto. By 1914 three rail lines spanned the continent and a new flood of immigrants from Europe, the United States, and elsewhere had expanded Canada's vast forest and mining frontiers, settled the "last best west," and contributed to the growth of the nation's industrial cities.

Under Louis Riel's leadership, Métis and First Nations on the Prairies twice (1870 and 1885) mounted unsuccessful resistance to the invading Canadians. The Métis were marginalized in the wake of the 1885 uprising, while First Nations, in the developing west and elsewhere, were controlled by the Indian Act and residential schools.

The challenge of surviving as a child of one superpower and the sibling of another is the key to understanding Canada as we know it today. At the time of Confederation, political leaders were deeply conscious of the role that Great Britain played in providing markets, military protection, and a countervailing force against the "manifest destiny" of the United States to dominate the whole North American continent. Imperial sentiment and self-interest determined that in the twentieth century Canadians would fight two bloody world wars on Britain's side, helping the embattled mother country to hold on until the prodigal sibling finally joined the Allied cause.

In keeping with their cautious approach to political change, Canadians were slow to assert their independence from Great Britain. Canada was a signatory to the Treaty of Versailles (1919) in its own right, and the Statute of Westminster (1931) confirmed the autonomy of dominions in the British Commonwealth of Nations. Following the Second World War, which greatly enhanced national confidence and productive capacity, the Canadian government began issuing its own passports, and in 1965 the government finally adopted, but not without noisy controversy, a distinctive flag sporting a red maple leaf. As improbable as it seems in retrospect, full autonomy remained elusive until 1982, when, by the Constitution Act, Canadians were able to amend their constitution without resorting to the British Parliament. Nevertheless, the British monarch is still officially the Canadian head of state, and Queen Elizabeth's head graces Canadian currency.

Despite foot dragging on constitutional matters, Canadians managed to reinvent themselves in the three decades following the Second World War. Emerging as a great industrial nation with one of the highest standards of living in the world, Canada embraced policies worthy of its newfound status. The federal government triumphed over defenders of provincial rights to implement a series of nationwide social programs, giving most Canadians a sense of personal security that was the envy of the world. In the 1960s Canada opened its door to immigrants of all cultural backgrounds to provide essential labour in the expanding economy, and in 1971 the country officially embraced a program of multiculturalism. The Charter of Rights and Freedoms, which was attached to the Constitution Act, reflects more than a century of struggle around individual and collective rights in a complicated country.

Canada positioned itself in the Cold War as a "middle power," participating actively in the creation of the United Nations and the North Atlantic Treaty Organization and emphasizing peaceful negotiation as an alternative to military approaches to conflict. First and foremost helpful fixers in the dangerous competition between capitalism and communism, Canadian diplomats in the postwar years had their hands full keeping Great Britain and the United States on track. In 1957 External Affairs Minister Lester Pearson won the Nobel Peace Prize for proposing a peaceful solution to the Suez crisis. Thereafter, "peacekeeping" became the brand of the Canadian military until the "war on terror" in the twenty-first century exploded this elaborate fiction.

Skeptics had long pointed out that, in most foreign policy initiatives, Canada served as handmaiden to the United States. Indeed, the new Romans had become so prevalent in Canadian development that Harold Innis, Canada's foremost political economist, proclaimed in 1948 that "Canada moved from colony to nation to colony."[5] Efforts to define a Canada that was more than a weak echo of the United States became a major goal of successive governments following the Second World War, but globalizing tendencies, defined largely in American terms, continued unabated. In 1988 the old national policy of protectionism, called into question by prevailing neoliberal orthodoxies, was swept away with the adoption of a comprehensive free-trade agreement with the United States. International developments that followed in the wake of the 9/11 attacks by Muslim extremists on the World Trade Center and the Pentagon further tightened the continental embrace. With unbridled greed, terrorist threats, the all-encompassing Internet, and climate change dominating the global scene in the twenty-first century, Canada's political leaders continued to pursue a cautious approach to public policy. Perhaps Margaret Atwood was right when she asserted in 1972 that "hanging on, staying alive," is the best ordinary citizens can do,[6] but many Canadians feel that we could, and should, do more.

Deep-rooted tensions – between Aboriginal and settler, nation and province, centre and periphery, French and English, Roman Catholic and Protestant, rich and poor, white and black, men and women – frustrate all efforts to present Canada's history as a story of triumphal progress. There are injustices in the nation's past so mean-spirited that they are difficult to believe. At the same time, it must be conceded that Canada is one of the most successful nations on earth, a country where people from all over the world have found opportunities for community and individual fulfillment. In any concise history of Canada, it is important to pay attention to the complexity that characterizes this rich and ever-evolving nation, which now seems to be experiencing yet another transformation in the way it represents itself in the world.

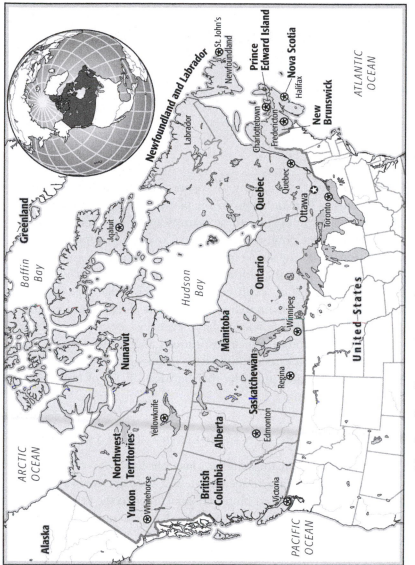

Map I.1. Canadian provinces and territories in the twenty-first century

I

Since Time Immemorial

Collective understandings of who we are and how we got here help to anchor us as human beings to the planet. What is remarkable is the diversity of thinking on these matters and how difficult it is to reconcile different points of view. The Canadian geographer Cole Harris argues that the single most important insight to guide us in our encounters with the "lifeworlds" of the distant past is recognizing the existence of localized fields of knowledge that enabled those who possessed them to live in particular places.[1] For the most part, these fields of knowledge have been lost or greatly altered as Europeans introduced their institutions and values on a global scale, but surviving evidence allows us to imagine how these long-ago societies operated and why their localized fields of knowledge remain relevant today.

THE ANCIENT HISTORY OF NORTHERN NORTH AMERICA

Aboriginal peoples maintain that their ancestors have inhabited the Americas since time immemorial, and they are correct in this assumption. While we can pinpoint, sometimes to the very day, the arrival of many of the first Europeans, the appearance of the first humans in the Americas, as everywhere, is shrouded in the mists of time.

In recent years, some archaeologists have argued, but not without being challenged, that human occupation of the Americas dates back thirty thousand, even fifty thousand, years and that people arrived by various routes across the Atlantic and Pacific oceans. The most common explanation is that the earliest Americans came from Asia across a land bridge connecting what is now Siberia to Alaska after successive ice ages that gripped the continent. Immigrants arrived this way, of course, but it is entirely possible that the peoples of the Americas have multiple origins, some skipping islands in the Pacific, others reaching the east coast of North America via Iceland and Greenland, still others sailing directly across the Atlantic from the Mediterranean. We may never know for certain, though geneticists have begun to match DNA from various regions of the world, a process that could help to solve the mystery of Aboriginal beginnings.[2]

The archaeological record is clearer that about thirteen thousand years ago, as the last ice age ended, migrants whom scholars call Paleo-Indians appeared out of Asia. Hunting species such as mammoths, mastodons, and longhorn bison, they moved rapidly across the continent as the retreating glaciers permitted, adapting to the changing climate, animal species, and vegetation. Paleo-Indian culture, based on chipped stone technology, gave way to a sequence of what are termed Archaic cultures, distinguished from their predecessors by the sophistication of their stone tools. Whatever their specific traditions, these early immigrants depended on a combination of fishing, hunting, and gathering. Their highly mobile communities consisted of bands made up of a few related families, thirty to fifty people on the average, who came together on a seasonal basis with neighbouring bands to exploit particular resources (a caribou run, for example), to seek marriage partners, and to engage in trade, diplomacy, ceremony, and conviviality.

As the climate improved about eight thousand years ago, boreal forest began to replace tundra, and animal and plant life flourished. People learned to catch fish in nets and weirs, to rely more heavily on smaller animals such as dear and beaver, and to use stones and mortars to grind nuts, berries, and roots. With a greater variety in their diet, people became more sedentary than in earlier times when the search for big game forced frequent relocation. Items found at grave sites suggest that a richer material culture accompanied this transition and that social rank was increasingly displayed through conspicuous giving.

This is not the end of the Asian immigration story. About four thousand years ago, the Tuniit (Paleo-Eskimos) crossed the Bering Strait, perhaps in pursuit of caribou and musk ox. They gradually adapted their hunting skills to the Arctic environment, increasingly depending on seals, walrus, and small whales, which they harpooned from the sea ice rather than from open boats. Equipped with bows and arrows tipped with stone, finely tailored clothing made of animal skins, and portable skin tents that provided shelter in all seasons, the Tuniit spread across the Arctic, reaching Labrador and the island of Newfoundland. Like many Aboriginal peoples, they were guided by shamanic spiritual beliefs and tattooed their face. Their culture evolved into what scholars call Dorset, named after the Baffin Island community of Cape Dorset where their remains were first identified in the 1920s (Image 1.1). Skilled in crafting stone, bone, and ivory tools and spiritual figures, the Dorset peoples produced distinctive soapstone lamps and cooking vessels as well as whalebone "shoes" to protect the runners on their sleds, which they pulled themselves.

About a thousand years ago, the Tuniit were overwhelmed by the Thule, a people based in Alaska, where they controlled the iron trade across the Bering Strait. Adept at catching bowhead whales with their large toggling harpoons and umiaks, and possessing dog teams to power their sleds, the Thule were an aggressive, highly mobile people who moved quickly across the High Arctic and crossed into Greenland. The Thule are the ancestors of today's Inuit, formerly called Eskimos – a derogatory term meaning "eaters of raw meat" – by the Europeans who encountered them.

The success of the Thule may well have been the result of environmental changes that temporarily brought warmer temperatures to the northern regions of the continent and also drew the Norse to Greenland and North America a millennium ago. Because of open waters, the Thule were able to exploit the resources of the Arctic more successfully than the Tuniit, who could no longer rely on the sea ice to support their hunting practices. The Thule amassed large quantities of food, which included caribou and sea mammals. In the summer they lived in campsites best positioned for catching seals and whales. During the long, dark winters,

Image 1.1. Ivory maskette from a Dorset archaeological site. As the Tuniit evolved into Dorset culture, it was characterized by the production of many small sculptures in ivory, antler, wood, and occasionally soapstone. This face probably represents tattooing that was practiced in many Aboriginal cultures. (Photograph by Harry Foster, Canadian Museum of Civilization, plate 8: 597-13698)

communities of fifty or more people lived in wooden houses banked with turf and snow and heated with ceramic lamps that burned whale or seal oil. Iconic features of current Inuit culture include the igloo – an easily-constructed dome-shaped shelter made of blocks of snow – and the inukshuk – a stone cairn that serves as a navigational aid and a marker for hunting grounds, shelters, and caches of food.

As the experience of the Tuniit and the Thule suggests, Aboriginal cultures were never traditional in a static sense. The pioneer inhabitants of North America adapted not only to enormous environmental changes that accompanied the gradual melting of the glaciers, but also to numerous localized crises, among them fires sparked by lightning or carelessness, volcanic eruptions and rising sea levels that submerged whole villages, landslides and earthquakes that destroyed favoured fish runs, and warfare, which escalated as populations grew and social structures became more complex. They also faced periodic failures in the hunt and resource depletion. Before European contact a great many species of animals disappeared, beginning with the mammoth and mastodon. While some of these extinctions were the result of climate change, others were caused by the routine overkilling of species in an effort to forestall famine.[3]

Technological innovation also brought major social transformation. On the western Plains, for example, the successive introduction of the spear-thrower, the bow and arrow, the buffalo jump, and the buffalo pound increased the standard of living and led to invasions by neighbouring tribes attracted to the abundant food supply. New technologies spread quickly, as did new cultural practices. More than three thousand years ago burial mounds similar to those found among the Adena in the Ohio Valley appeared in what is now eastern Canada. While it may be the case that the region was invaded by peoples who built such mounds, it is just as likely that the practice spread across the continent along with precious stones, metals, and other commodities that were widely traded. Less easily explained are three ritual burial mounds on the south coast of Labrador dating back seven thousand years, the oldest known of their scale and complexity anywhere in the world.

Archaeological evidence provides the broad strokes of various dramatic occurrences, and oral accounts document their impact on Aboriginal communities, but the details often remain elusive. With the arrival of Europeans, written documents, sometimes suspiciously one-sided but nevertheless thick with information, lift the curtain on the lifeworlds of diverse and well-adjusted North American societies.

ABORIGINAL PEOPLES IN THE AGE OF CONTACT

When the Europeans began arriving in the Americas in significant numbers five hundred years ago, the indigenous population was roughly the same as that of Europe at the time. The major cities in the Americas were as large as any found across the Atlantic, and, as in Europe, the cycle of empire-building, conquest, and destruction prevailed in the more populated areas of what are now Mexico and Central and South America. The small numbers of people on the frontiers of settlement inevitably lived with less elaborate institutional structures and often with more cooperative social arrangements. Because of its rugged terrain and cold climate, the area of present-day Canada was one of those frontiers of settlement.

Living on the periphery of, but connected to, the civilizations of the Mississippi Valley and Mexico, Canada's Aboriginal peoples south of the Arctic and east of the Rocky Mountains shared Mesoamerican beliefs and technologies. From archaeological evidence, it is clear that they were connected to a vast and intricate trading network that facilitated the exchange of ideas and practices. Products from the northern frontier, such as buffalo and moose hides, feathers, porcupine quills, red ochre, walrus tusks, and birchbark canoes, were exchanged for corn and tobacco from the southeast, shells from the Pacific coast and the Gulf of Mexico, copper from mines around Lake Superior, and precious stones from all over North America. As European explorers soon discovered to their benefit, Aboriginal peoples had clear mental maps of the terrain they travelled and had even charted trails through the formidable Rockies.

It is likely that many people living in what is now Canada in 1500 would have heard tales of the great city of Cahokia, located near present-day St. Louis on the Mississippi River. It rose to prominence about a millennium ago and supported at its height in the mid-thirteenth century a population of approximately twenty thousand – some estimates suggest twice that number. Its social structure was highly stratified, with commoners and slaves serving as the social base for a small class of privileged rulers, religious authorities, and warriors. Cahokia was centred on a vast plaza that featured markets, a circle of pillars probably used as an astronomical observatory, and a number of ceremonial mounds, some as large as the Egyptian pyramids. Although Cahokia's political dominance was limited to the central Mississippi Valley, its cultural influence extended broadly and continued after its abandonment in the early fifteenth century.[4]

Like most efforts to quantify developments in the past, it is difficult to say precisely how many people lived in northern North America at the time of European contact, or any time earlier. The best guess of scholars is that between five hundred thousand and a million, possibly as many as 2 million, people made their home in what is now Canada in 1500. While most people lived in small communities loosely connected to each other, we can better grasp the whole by seeing them as belonging to twelve major linguistic groups and more than fifty distinct cultures (Map 1.1).

Aboriginal societies at the time of European contact varied widely. At one extreme were the relatively egalitarian Inuit and Athapaskan living in the northern reaches of the continent; on the other were the highly stratified slaveholding communities of the Pacific coast and the agricultural societies of the Great Lakes–St. Lawrence Lowlands. In 1500 Algonquin peoples occupied much of the woodlands from the Atlantic to the Rocky Mountains, but their cultures differed, depending on available resources. The vast Canadian Shield that dominates much of Canada consists of ancient rocks that are resistant to agricultural production, but it supported wildlife in abundance, including deer and caribou that attracted hunting peoples, as did the western Plains where the buffalo sustained a rich livelihood. On the east coast, sea life, moose, and caribou provided an abundant subsistence.

In the Pacific region, the mountainous terrain encouraged diversity and yielded six of the twelve language groups identified at the time of European contact. Blessed with a warmer climate, towering cedars, and salmon and other marine resources, the Pacific coast peoples lived in permanent villages of up to a thousand individuals, enjoyed a high standard of living, and produced some of North America's most exquisite artwork, displayed prominently on their faces, masks, houses, totem poles, clothing, and storage boxes. Their rich material culture supported a hereditary social structure, which was sustained through elaborate gift-giving ceremonies, known by

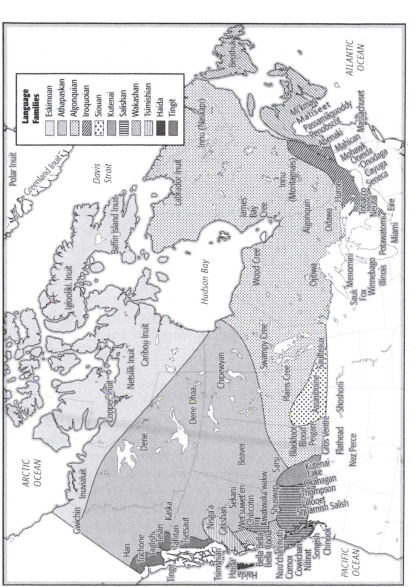

Map 1.1. Aboriginal peoples in 1500. (Adapted from Olive Patricia Dickason with David T. McNab, *Canada's First Nations: A History of Founding Peoples from Earliest Times*, 4th ed. [Don Mills, ON: Oxford University Press, 2008], 43)

the nineteenth century as "potlatch." Eager to secure material goods to enhance their status, the Pacific coast peoples were enthusiastic traders, exchanging their smoked and dried fish, fish oil, cedar boxes, and other products of their industry for such highly valued commodities as bear skins, obsidian, and ochre from their inland neighbours, and copper and small blades of iron from Alaska.

Around 1500 the Iroquois (known as the Haudenosaunee, or "People of the Longhouse") living in the Great Lakes–St. Lawrence Lowlands began cultivating corn, and later beans and squash, the staple crops of the Mesoamerican civilizations. They also grew tobacco, the drug of choice and of ceremonial occasions in North America. With agriculture accounting for as much as 80 percent of their dietary needs, the Iroquois built substantial communal dwellings in semipermanent villages, some as large as fifteen hundred inhabitants, which were relocated when the soil was depleted, roughly every ten to twelve years. One of the major ceremonies among the Iroquoian peoples was the Feast of the Dead, which usually occurred when they were locating elsewhere. Before leaving for their new territory, they buried the bones of their loved ones, along with precious possessions, in a communal grave to honour the spirits of the deceased and to establish harmony between the worlds of the living and the dead.

ABORIGINAL LIFEWORLDS

While change and diversity characterized Aboriginal societies in the pre-contact period, they shared the belief that humans were integral to a cosmological order in which all living, inanimate, and imagined things embodied their own spirit-powers. This perspective explained everything – there was no distinction between matters religious and secular. Spirit-powers were notoriously capricious, shape-shifting from a rock or tree, to a bear or raven, and then to a person, who might go by the name of "Bear Woman" or "Raven Man." A trickster figured in many cultures and evil lurked everywhere. In a universe where everything can change its shape as well as its intent, humans were obliged to tread carefully.

Creation stories centre on mythical figures with enormous spirit-powers. For example, the Iroquoian believed that Aataentsic, the mother of all humankind, fell through a hole in the sky and landed on an island that turned out to be a turtle with earth piled on its back. Other creation stories include floods and migration experiences. Whatever the narrative line, Aboriginal beliefs obliged individuals to acquire their own spirit-powers and the ability to change their shapes and minds as circumstances required. Only by communing with the spirits on all planes and maintaining harmony among the whole could people ensure worldly success and happiness. Communion with the spirits could be accomplished in a number of ways – through elaborate rituals; dreams induced by dances, drugs, or a period of fasting; and mediation by shamans, who played a central role in most Aboriginal societies. Shamans were adept at spirit-flight, which enabled them to travel to the sky world or underworld as the need required. In most cultures, amulets, feathers, ivory, tattoos, and body paint served as armour against malevolent powers. Taboos, variously defined, were observed in all societies.

As their surviving artwork suggests, Aboriginal peoples were much taken with the sun, moon, and stars, as well as various animals and birds, which were perceived as possessing special spiritual powers that warranted ritual attention. On the western Plains, the annual sun dance emerged as a major ceremonial occasion, during which young men proved their prowess. The historian Arthur J. Ray notes what "making a brave" entailed at the time of European contact:

The men tethered themselves to the centre pole of the camp with lines attached to wooden skewers impaled under the skin of their pectoral muscles. They then danced around the pole until the skewers tore loose. Often the dancers also fastened buffalo skulls or horses [which appeared on the Plains through trade networks well before the Europeans who had introduced them to the continent] to their backs with skewers and ropes and dragged or led them around until they ripped free.[5]

Because of their strong spiritual beliefs, most of the surviving evidence of pre-contact Aboriginal societies comes not from monuments to the living but from burial sites, where treasured objects were placed to accompany the spirit of the deceased. The same spiritual preoccupations characterized European and Middle Eastern peoples, who built impressive churches and mosques in which to worship their God. In the Judeao-Christian and Muslim religions, human beings are represented as the superior species in the creator's plan, a view that puzzled early Americans, who believed themselves to be equals with other inhabitants of the natural world. When early European visitors asked them who they were, Aboriginal peoples often replied that they were "the people," thus distinguishing themselves from other occupants of the earth.

The implications of the Aboriginal worldview are sometimes difficult for twenty-first-century minds to grasp. By way of example, we can take the perspective of a pre-contact hunter who believed that his success in seeking out and killing his prey was due not to knowledge of the environment, and only secondarily to his hunting skills, which in any case came from carefully following prescribed rituals; rather, he saw his achievement as the result of an agreement between hunter and the hunted. The prey presented itself to be killed because it had selected a hunter who knew how to follow the rituals designed to please the soul of the dead animal, rituals that enabled it to be reborn and be killed again (Image 1.2). In such a worldview, animal populations disappeared not from excessive hunting but because hunters had not treated animals with the respect they deserved, which resulted in their avoiding the hunter in the future.[6]

No matter how they explained it, Aboriginal peoples at the time of contact were well adapted to their local environments. Before the arrival of Europeans, they had developed ingenious methods of transportation (birchbark and dugout canoes, snowshoes, and toboggans), practical housing (igloos, longhouses, tipis, and wigwams), cooking utensils (in stone, bone, birchbark, and clay), tailoring methods (needles of delicate bird bones, thread from sinew, and a variety of decorative techniques), and efficient weapons (the spear-thrower, the bow and arrow, and the slingshot). The peoples of the Americas had also calculated the movement of the sun and stars and understood the medicinal properties of plants.

While symbols inscribed on birchbark sometimes served as aids to memory, knowledge was usually passed down orally. Early European observers were often impressed by Aboriginal powers of recollection. Nicolas Denys, a French fur trader who spent several decades on the east coast in the seventeenth century, noted that

Image 1.2. *Indian Hunters. Pursuing the Buffalo in the Early Spring*, by Peter Rindisbacher. This early-nineteenth-century depiction of Assiniboine using dogs and arrows to slay buffalo captures one of the ways of killing these large animals before European guns were introduced. Another method was herding them off cliffs. (By permission of Library and Archives Canada/C-114467)

memory keepers in Mi'kmaq communities recited genealogical traditions that linked them to a line of "ancient chiefs" stretching back more than twenty generations.[7] In the past, scholars claimed that oral history was unreliable because it changed over time and with the teller, but we now recognize that written history, no matter how well researched, is subject to similar shape-shifting.

What we would today call leisure pursuits were integral to the lifeworlds of Aboriginal peoples. They played games of skill and chance, using sticks, stones, and bones in imaginative ways. In all societies, dancing to the beat of drums, rattles, flutes, whistles, and voices was central to ceremonial occasions. The Cree, for example, had a thirst dance, a chicken dance, and a buffalo dance, among others. On the west coast, music, under the direction of a song master, accompanied potlatch ceremonies. The Inuit became famous for their vocal games. Usually performed by two women, "throat-singing" tested the control and strength of breathing and often ended with one of the performers bursting into laughter or falling over in exhaustion.⁸ Warfare between neighbours seems to have occurred throughout the Americas and was especially destructive in areas where the Aztec, Mayan, and Inca empires emerged. On the northern frontier of the continent, most warfare was episodic, prompted by vengeance, competition for scarce resources, and rituals in which young warriors proved their prowess in battle. Notwithstanding the limitations to violence, the result of military defeat could be calamitous for the losers. Torture, enslavement, and the killing of captives were common, and some victims were subject to cannibalism. Young women and children were often absorbed into the culture of the successful warriors but rarely as equals. In Iroquoian societies, "mourning wars" were launched for the specific purpose of taking captives who could replace people who had died, thus maintaining their numbers.

By some European standards, the Aboriginal peoples of North America had relaxed attitudes toward sexual and child-rearing practices. They expressed their feelings about sex without shame, and could usually dissolve marriages by simply agreeing to do so. Whereas in Europe the young were often subject to strict discipline and corporal punishment, Aboriginal children were usually free of such ego-destroying practices, though research suggests that children of slaves in Pacific coast societies inherited the status of their parents and were sometimes sacrificed. Aboriginal peoples were also more tolerant of homosexuality than Europeans. In many American societies, people today described as gay, lesbian, and transgendered were regarded as belonging to a third gender that possessed both male and female spirits. As "two-spirited" individuals, they were revered for their greater vision and often held important ceremonial responsibilities.

The relative power of men and women in Aboriginal societies varied widely. In most cultures, women's power was recognized because they produced and tended to children, controlled the food resources, and fashioned the warm clothing essential to survival. Men gained status through their skills as hunters and protectors. In most Aboriginal societies the work of women and men was separate but interdependent, so that, for example, men caught the animals, which the women then skinned and used to produce food, clothing, and shelter; men made the wooden frames for snowshoes, while women produced the webbing. On the Pacific coast, women were the weavers of cedar fibres; men had the exclusive right to carve the giants of the forest. European men often commented that women in hunting and gathering societies were greatly overworked. In this judgment, they reflected their own class biases, but there is little doubt that most Aboriginal women worked hard, dressing large animals, making clothing and lodgings from hides, smoking meat and fish for winter sustenance, and lugging material possessions from place to place in the annual seasonal round.

Puberty was an important occasion in the lives of both women and men. Although women rarely experienced such painful ordeals as those required of young men in the sun dance ceremonies, they were not exempt from proving their ability to face the rigours of adulthood. Women usually marked the beginning of menstruation by a ritual of seclusion with other women, lasting for a month or more. In addition to being trained in sewing and other skills, they also experienced tests of endurance, such as being deprived of water and fresh meat for long periods of time.[9] Being "tough" was considered a virtue for everyone in the struggles for survival. In most Aboriginal cultures women nursed their children for several years, a practice that operated as an imperfect form of birth control. Aboriginal women tended to give birth to a child every three or four years.

Women's second-class status can be discerned in many Aboriginal societies. Among the Inuit and Athapaskan, for example, female infanticide occurred in times of famine, a practice that ensured that fewer children would be born to add pressure to scarce resources. In these and some other societies, men could also exchange or share wives without the women's consent. Polygamy was widely practiced. From the earliest days of contact, daughters of chiefs, through marriage, often became the link with European traders. As in marriage alliances in European societies, the brides often had little to say in the matter. The Salish peoples on the Pacific coast were among the most patriarchal in structure, with property held by men and passed on to sons. When European men, who were uniformly patriarchal in their laws and customs, arrived in North America, they established trading relations with male chiefs, further enhancing their status.

As the foregoing suggests, power in Aboriginal communities was variously assigned, but in most cultures it was loosely

Image 1.3. Iroquoian women preparing corn as depicted by Father François Du Creux in *Historire Canadiensis*, 1664. (© McCord Museum, Montreal, M11712)

structured. Men usually served as chiefs and shamans, the two major authority figures identified by early European observers, but women also held such positions. In many cultures, women figured prominently in creation narratives and had considerable political and religious powers. Because fatherhood could not always easily be established, hereditary rights often passed through the female line. This was the case among the Iroquois, where women's power was enhanced by their central role in agricultural production (Image 1.3). Only men served on Iroquoian village and tribal councils, but powerful matrons participated in the selection of chiefs and had the final word on many decisions. In addition to being matrilineal, the Iroqouis were matrilocal; that is, husbands lived with the wife's family.

The Iroquois were also untypical in that, around the time of European contact, they had established a confederacy. According to oral testimony, this was the result of efforts by chief Dekanawidah and his associate Hiawatha to end the rising cycle of blood feuds. Five Iroquoian groups – Mohawk, Onondaga, Oneida, Seneca, and Cayuga – smoked a peace pipe to confirm their commitment to detailed constitutional arrangements designed to discourage infighting. Surrounded by enemies, the Five Nations benefitted from their alliance-building efforts, which came into play when the French and their Native allies tried to establish their dominance in the Great Lakes–St. Lawrence region in the early seventeenth century.

CONCLUSION

Over millennia, Aboriginal peoples in what is now Canada adapted to a changing environment, creating lifeworlds that sustained them over generations. Most of them moved well beyond subsistence to enjoy leisure time that included games of skill and chance, spiritual practices involving elaborate rituals, and artistic expression of a high order. Their complex symbolic universe and well-developed narrative sense of who they were provided meaning and social cohesion in their lives. Beginning in the sixteenth century, this cohesion was challenged when people living on the east coast of North America began having chance encounters with men from an unknown world.

2

Natives and Newcomers,
1000–1661

In 1918 the Moravian mission ship *Harmony* arrived on the Labrador coast. It carried the deadly influenza virus, which killed nearly 80 percent of the 236 Inuit living in Okak and soon swept through nearby communities. According to one observer: "When the Harmony left Okak, people were beginning to fall sick.... the dogs played havoc with the corpses. At Sillutalik 36 persons died, but only 18 remained to be buried. The only visible remains of the others were a few bare skulls and a few shankbones lying around in the houses."[1]

This report of the impact of the flu on the Inuit of Labrador describes what must have been a common experience in North America in the early years of European contact. Lacking immunity to the viruses carried by the newcomers, indigenous peoples often succumbed to common European diseases such as smallpox, measles, and influenza. Nor was the Labrador tragedy the only twentieth-century example of such an occurrence in Canada. According to Inuit tradition and DNA evidence, one small community of Tuniit survived the aggression of the Thule by taking refuge on Southampton Island in Hudson Bay. A Scottish whaling vessel brought disease to the island in 1902, wiping out the last survivors of a people who had lived in northern North America for five thousand years.[2]

THE CONTEXT OF CONTACT

The expansion of European animals, plants, people, microbes, and systems of knowledge is one of the most significant developments of the past five hundred years.[3] While all areas of the world have now encountered "Western civilization," the impact differed greatly. Only in the Americas and Australasia were Europeans able to displace so many of the indigenous inhabitants. In China, India, and Africa, the local populations, seemingly immune to the worst consequences of European pathogens, managed to avoid such dire consequences.

The role of disease in opening the Americas to European occupation has been the subject of much debate among scholars, but a consensus is now emerging that the impact was catastrophic. Summarizing decades of research, Cole Harris concludes that "mortality rates from virgin-soil smallpox (that is, among populations with no previous exposure to the disease) were characteristically in the order of 50 to 75 percent, sometimes higher." Moreover, he reports: "Growing evidence from around the western hemisphere suggests that a hundred years after the first epidemics reached a certain area, it seldom had more than 10 percent of its pre-epidemic population."[4] In many regions of the Americas, Europeans managed to enslave large portions of the inhabitants, which further contributed to population decline, but on the northern frontier, this exploitive form of labour proved impossible to sustain on a grand scale. Deaths from unfamiliar microbes, more than any other feature of European contact, undermined the numbers, spiritual beliefs, and medical knowledge of North America's Aboriginal communities.

In assessing the early years of contact, it is important to keep several points in mind. First, the Europeans who arrived in North America after 1500 came from their own localized fields of knowledge, which varied widely. Most of the early arrivals were a select group of male explorers, traders, and fishers, looking for terra firma, fresh water, and sex, along with fish, fur, and captives to take back home. Sojourners on the make, they were not always the types to make a good first impression. Second, there were many points of convergence between European and North American cultures.[5] Both subscribed to gender norms that defined work and power relations, and both were governed by highly imaginative spiritual worlds that facilitated understanding, if not mutual respect. Warfare was endemic to both continents in the sixteenth century, and barbarous practices prevailed everywhere. As Europe expanded overseas, its political and religious leaders at home unleashed a reign of terror in the form of the Inquisition that took the lives of thousands of people. Disease ravaged Aboriginal communities, but Europeans also suffered from pandemics. The Black Death (its cause still debated) wiped out at least a third of the population of Europe in the mid-fourteenth century, and bubonic plague periodically ravaged communities well into the nineteenth century. Crop failures and rampaging armies were usually followed by famine among hard-pressed European peasants, for whom survival was always precarious, as it was for the peoples of North America.

It is also important to acknowledge the difficulty of transplanting European lifeworlds to North America. While contact became continuous after the voyages of Christopher Columbus and John Cabot in the 1490s, it took more than a century for Europeans to establish a tenuous foothold on the eastern coast of northern North America and even longer for settler societies to take root. Only a few thousand immigrants lived in what is now Canada in 1661, nearly all of them clinging to the shores of the Atlantic Ocean and the St. Lawrence River. Elsewhere, contact came much later. In 1818 the explorer John Ross encountered a group of Inuit who had no knowledge of Europeans. Thinking the Europeans were spirits from another plane, they are reported to have asked: "What great creatures are these? Do they come from the sun or the moon? Do they give us light by the day or by night?"[6]

EUROPE IN THE AGE OF EXPANSION

While sagas had documented the far-flung explorations of the Nordic peoples, it was only in 1960 that the physical evidence of their settlement, established around the year 1000, was discovered at L'Anse aux Meadows in northern Newfoundland. The site was abandoned after a few years, perhaps as a result of the hostility of the local inhabitants, but more likely due to the distance from Norse supply lines. Because this brief attempt at colonization seems to have had no long-term consequences, it is important primarily for the evidence it provides both for the long reach of the Norse in this period and for the possibility of other contact episodes as yet undocumented.

The Europeans who bumped against North America in the late fifteenth century had changed considerably in the five hundred years since the Norse initiative. Following the Black Death, Europe became the focus for a dynamic transformation of its feudal values and institutions. By the end of the fifteenth century, European society was a swirling cauldron of political ambition, mercantile enterprise, religious turmoil, technological innovation, and artistic expression. Other peoples in the world at the time – the Chinese in particular – had the technological capacity to engage in overseas ventures, but it was the Europeans who took the lead. In the process, they created a world in which Africa, the Americas, Asia, and Europe were increasingly interconnected by traffic in people, commodities, and ideas.

In the fifteenth century, primacy in commerce and culture began to shift from the Mediterranean to the emerging nations on the Atlantic. This reorientation was driven primarily by commercial priorities. As hostile Islamic forces seized control of the Middle East, Europeans searched for routes that would allow them to trade directly with Asia. Technological innovation made such options possible. With better maps, ships, and navigational devices, longer voyages became feasible, and the lure of economic gain prompted ambitious sailors to push their seagoing technology to its limits. European expansion was also driven by rivalry among European monarchs, each determined to best the other in staking claim to portions of their "new world."

Overseas ventures were part of a dramatic cultural awakening in Europe fuelled by the Renaissance, a rebirth of interest in the achievements of ancient Greece and Rome. Under the influence of Renaissance thinkers, Europeans began to reflect on broad areas of knowledge and ask troubling questions about the nature of the physical world and religious beliefs. Johannes Gutenberg's invention of the mechanical printing press in the mid-fifteenth century made it easier to disseminate new ideas, and Europe quickly became a hotbed of intellectual ferment. In 1517 Martin Luther set in motion a protest against papal authority that fractured Christendom into warring Protestant and Roman Catholic factions. This Renaissance and Reformation provided the impetus for Europeans to take interest in new peoples and places and rationales for conquering anything in their path.

DISCOVERING ANOTHER WORLD

The Portuguese were the first to undertake the systematic exploration of the Atlantic. By 1487 their sailors had rounded the Cape of Good Hope in Africa, opening a sea route to India. In 1492 the Italian Christoforo Colombo (Christopher Columbus), sailing under the banner of Spain, reached the Caribbean. The Spanish and Portuguese, with the blessing of the pope, divided the non-Christian world between them in 1494 by the Treaty of Tordesillas and quickly established themselves in Asia, Mexico, and Central and South America. France and England were left with slim pickings in North America.

In 1497 Zuan Caboto (John Cabot), a citizen of Venice, made a second attempt to cross the Atlantic, having failed in his first effort a year earlier. Equipped with letters patent from King Henry VII of England to "sail to all parts, regions and coasts of the eastern, western and northern sea," and authorized "to conquer, occupy and possess whatever towns, castles, cities and islands" he discovered, Cabot set out from Bristol, England's second largest port and the source of capital for many overseas ventures.[7] He reached "new founde landes," possibly around Cape Bonavista, in Newfoundland, where he raised a cross and the banners of England and Venice. He returned with the news that the waters in the region swarmed "with fish which can be taken not only with the net, but in baskets let down with a stone." Cabot failed to return from a third voyage in 1498, but his impact on the course of history had been established. Within a decade, Europeans were conducting regular fishing expeditions to the "new founde landes."

Documented expeditions sponsored by Portugal, France, Spain, and England in the 1520s mapped the eastern seaboard of the North Atlantic but yielded no treasure, no passage to Asia, and no surviving colony. Captains of fishing vessels seem to have ranged more broadly. When Jacques Cartier, sailing at the behest of the king of France in 1534, explored the Gulf of St. Lawrence, he encountered Mi'kmaq on the Gaspé Peninsula who were clearly no strangers to European contact.

On his second voyage, in 1535, Cartier sailed up the St. Lawrence to the Iroquoian village of Hochelaga, the site of present-day

Montreal. The onset of winter forced the expedition to set up camp adjacent to Stadacona, near present-day Quebec City. Twenty-five of Cartier's crew died of scurvy, a hideous affliction caused by a deficiency of vitamin C. Nevertheless, the possibility of riches beyond Hochelaga convinced Cartier to become involved in an ambitious attempt led by a nobleman, Jean-François de la Roque de Roberval, to establish a French settlement near Stadacona in 1541–42. Cartier led an advance expedition, but one winter was enough for the reluctant settlers, many of them convicts. Eager to return home, Cartier's entourage decamped in the spring of 1542 with a cache of what they thought was gold and diamonds but what proved to be pyrites and quartz. Roberval, who arrived with more settlers later that year, followed Cartier's example. While the climate contributed to the failure of the mission, Aboriginal hostility was also a factor.

It is easy to see why the newcomers became so unpopular. On his first voyage, Cartier raised a ten-meter cross on the Gaspé Peninsula, claimed possession of the territory in the name of the French king, and pressured the Iroquoian chief Donnacona to let his two sons accompany him back to France. In 1535–36 Cartier defied Donnacona's injunction that he not proceed upriver from Stadacona and then kidnapped the chief, who, along with nine others, were displayed to curious French onlookers. The Stadaconians attacked the would-be settlers in 1541, killing thirty-five, a clear indication that the interlopers were unwelcome.

Cartier's expeditions are significant primarily because they document the mind-set of early European colonizers and the problems they encountered in trying to live so far from home. Although later French colonization in the St. Lawrence region was in no way predetermined, Cartier is credited with laying its foundation. He also gave French names to the areas he explored. Mistaking the Iroquoian word meaning village for the territory around Stadacona, he called it Canada. The name was inscribed on maps.

COMMERCIAL INITIATIVES

For several decades, European monarchs, preoccupied by their own problems, abandoned settlement attempts in northern North

America. Private undertakings nevertheless produced a growing European presence.

As an enterprise, the cod fishery – a cheap source of protein especially for Roman Catholics, who were obliged to observe 153 meatless days a year – eclipsed all other economic activities in the Americas in value and the number of people employed. The French were leaders in the industry, producing both a "wet" (or "green") cure, in which the fish was taken into the ship's hold and heavily salted or packed in brine, and a "dry" cure, in which the fish was split, lightly salted, and then dried on shore. Although French palates preferred green fish, dry-cured fish kept better in the warmer climates of countries around the Mediterranean, which were major consumers of dried cod. The English, sailing from West Country ports, produced only a dry cure, ignoring the domestic market to exchange their product for bullion, fruits, wines, and other Mediterranean goods. By the 1580s, more than four hundred boats carrying ten thousand men fished off the coast of Newfoundland and others ranged further south along the Atlantic coast and into the Gulf of St. Lawrence (Image 2.1).

Two sidelines of the fisheries emerged as industries in their own right. Beginning in the 1530s, the Basques conducted ambitious whaling expeditions – whale oil was a premium source of light in early modern Europe – on the south coast of Labrador, centred on Red Bay. At its height in the 1560s, as many as thirty Basque ships annually hunted bowhead and right whales, with a workforce that including local Innu, who were skilled in the hunt. By the end of the century, the industry was abandoned, perhaps a result of the general decline of the Iberian fisheries but more likely because of the depletion of the whale stocks. Some scholars have suggested that a Little Ice Age at the end of the sixteenth century brought colder temperatures to the Labrador region that contributed to the disappearance of both the whales and those who pursued them.

Over the course of the sixteenth century, a fur trade with indigenous populations became an increasingly lucrative enterprise. The fashion industry encouraged a market for furs, especially for beaver pelts with the outer guard hairs removed, a process that produced a silky felt for which discriminating hatters in Paris

Image 2.1. The cod fisheries in Newfoundland. This depiction of a Newfoundland fishing station in 1772 is believed to portray Basque methods of piling fish. (From M. Duhamel du Monceau, *Traité générale des pêches* [Paris: Saillant et Nyons, 1772], by permission of Library and Archives Canada/MIKAN no. 2926914)

paid premium prices. Initially, the fur trade was carried on by fishermen, but by the second half of the sixteenth century a few French merchants began equipping vessels solely for the purpose of buying furs from Aboriginal peoples living along the coast from Labrador to present-day Maine. The lure of finding more and better furs drew traders into the St. Lawrence, which tapped regions further west than was possible from bases along the Atlantic coast.

The lingering dream of finding a Northwest Passage also encouraged successive efforts by European explorers, most of them English, to undertake heroic ventures into Arctic regions. One of the most ambitious was Martin Frobisher. With encouragement from Elizabeth I and backing from English merchants involved in trade with Russia, he undertook three expeditions between 1576 and 1578 that took him to what the queen called *Meta Incognita*. Frobisher claimed the land he visited for the English Crown and brought captives back to London for display. When he became convinced that he had discovered valuable ore, his quest for a northern passage turned into a failed mining venture in what is now known as Frobisher Bay on Baffin Island.

During his last voyage, Frobisher unwittingly sailed into a strait that carries the name of Henry Hudson, as does the river that flows into the Atlantic at New York. Hudson's 1609 exploration of the eastern seaboard on behalf of the Dutch East India Company led to the establishment of a trading post at Albany in 1614 and the proclamation in 1624 of the province of New Netherland, with its capital – New Amsterdam – located on Manhattan Island. Hudson, meanwhile, undertook a voyage sponsored by the Virginia Company and the British East India Company, which took him to Hudson Bay in 1610. After a winter on James Bay, his mutinous crew was reluctant to spend a second year seeking the elusive passage to Asia. They placed Hudson, his teenage son John, and six crewmen in a small boat, set them adrift, and returned home.

Although their presence was episodic and seasonal, Europeans had an immediate impact on the peoples they encountered. Diseases eventually took a toll, and indigenous populations declined, though we have no way of determining exactly when and by how much. What is clear is that, for those who survived the contact period, the fur trade modified earlier subsistence patterns and created a growing demand for European commodities, which moved quickly through established Aboriginal trading networks into the central regions of the continent.

Aboriginal responses to the newcomers varied. In Labrador, the Inuit were consistently hostile to the Europeans who visited their shores. This reaction may well have been the result of a longer exposure to the intruders, who persisted in their efforts to seize captives for exhibition back home, but it may simply have been a matter of culture. After all, the Inuit were also considered aggressive by their indigenous neighbours. The Beothuk in

Newfoundland are recorded as initially showing some interest in trade but soon avoided contact, the result, it seems, of confrontations with fishermen, who often reacted violently when the locals pilfered their shore facilities for metal objects. Relations with other Aboriginal peoples on the east coast were more cordial. The Mi'kmaq proved to be especially enthusiastic traders and took advantage of the European presence to extend their geographical range.

As in Europe, there was a shift in the centre of gravity among Aboriginal groups as a result of intercontinental contact. After Cartier's voyages, the Iroquois in the St. Lawrence region disappeared. It is not clear why, but it may be that they were so weakened by diseases that it was easy for Algonquin peoples, who were adept at supplying the furs that Europeans were seeking, to occupy the region. Here, too, the Little Ice Age may have been a factor in undermining the stability of agricultural populations.

TENTATIVE APPROACHES

Neither the fisheries nor the fur trade required permanent settlement, and once they had lived through a North American winter, most would-be settlers had little enthusiasm for experiencing another. Yet European ambitions for overseas expansion remained alive. As the fur trade developed, monarchs, hoping to avoid the risks but reap the rewards of any successes, began offering trade monopolies to private companies in the territories that they cavalierly claimed in return for establishing settlements. Merchants had the most to gain if they could corral all the profits for themselves by securing a monopoly of the trade in fish and fur. Fuelled by the zeal of the Counter-Reformation, the Roman Catholic Church supported new-world ventures, which afforded an opportunity to convert Aboriginal peoples to their brand of Christianity. The nobility in European courts often envisioned recouping their failing fortunes and enhancing their reputations through a colonization project. For those roaming the streets and country roads, housed in orphanages, prisons, and poorhouses, or enslaved and indentured to their masters, ambition had little to do with their involuntary participation in overseas expeditions.

Many of the early colonizing attempts took place on the often barren shores of northern North America because it was the territory closest to the countries from which the colonizers came. Without a lifeline to the metropole, isolated colonies, which all of them initially were, proved vulnerable in the extreme – to Aboriginal hostility, to enemy attacks and pirate raids, and, above all, to the lack of food and supplies. Even those sponsors most determined to sustain their colonizing enterprises often lost their supply vessels in storms, on dangerous reefs, or to enemy attacks, leaving their colonists stranded. And everything worked in slow motion by today's standards. It took three or four weeks, under ideal conditions, to sail from England to Newfoundland and almost as long again to reach the Bay of Fundy.

France was the first off the mark in the competition to establish colonies in northern North America. In 1598 Henri IV, who had temporarily brought an end to the civil war between Roman Catholics and Protestants (Huguenots) in France, appointed the Marquis de la Roche as lieutenant general of the territories named Canada, Newfoundland, Labrador, and Norumbega, with a monopoly of the fur trade. He established a preliminary settlement on Sable Island, admittedly closer to ocean traffic than most areas of North America but essentially little more than a sand dune. Of the forty settlers, all vagabonds and beggars from Rouen, and ten soldiers dumped there, only eleven were left in 1603, when the colony was finally abandoned. That year, the king appointed Huguenot Pierre Du Gua, Sieur de Monts, as viceroy of "la Cadie," "Canada," and "autres terres de la Nouvelle France." In return for a ten-year fur trade monopoly, de Monts agreed to sponsor sixty settlers annually and to support missionary efforts among the local population. The French now had a mission statement and names for two proposed colonies in what they called New France.

ACADIA

Taking his obligations seriously, the Sieur de Monts recruited two Roman Catholic priests, a Protestant minister, masons, carpenters, a miner, a surgeon, and an apothecary for his first expedition in

1604. After exploring the Bay of Fundy region, seventy-nine colonists wintered in their "habitation" on an island at the mouth of the St. Croix River on the present border between Maine and New Brunswick. The site seems to have been chosen because it could easily be defended, but attacks from pirates or the local inhabitants proved to be the least of their worries: thirty-five of the men died of scurvy.

In the spring, de Monts decided to move across the Bay of Fundy to the shore of the Annapolis Basin, where the winters were warmer, the potential for agriculture much better, and the Mi'kmaq, under the leadership of the aging Membertou, accommodating. Only three of the surviving St. Croix settlers were prepared to spend another winter in Acadia, among them Samuel de Champlain, who had become an enthusiastic advocate of colonization. The new location was named Port-Royal, and a fresh crop of settlers was delivered to the site, but the result was the same: nearly one-third of the forty-five colonists succumbed to scurvy.

Despite all odds, the colony survived. In the spring of 1606, Jean de Biencourt de Poutrincourt et de Saint-Just, appointed governor of Port-Royal, brought skilled workmen and several aristocratic relatives and friends to the colony. These included his son, Charles de Biencourt; a cousin from Paris, Louis Hébert, who was an apothecary and horticulturalist; a cousin from Champagne, Claude de Saint-Étienne de La Tour, and his son Charles; and Marc Lescarbot, a lawyer from Paris who recorded his adventures in *Histoire de la Nouvelle France* (1618). As these French aristocrats recreated the old world in the new, the results were impressive. They planted wheat, built a gristmill, raised cattle, and grew fruit and vegetables. In an effort to improve the winter survival rate, Champlain founded l'Ordre de Bon Temps, in which each man took turns providing fish and game for the table. Under Lescarbot's direction, the colonists, accompanied by their Mi'kmaq friends – no strangers to elaborate rituals – performed a seaborne spectacle, Le Théâtre de Neptune, to greet Poutrincourt, Champlain, and their crew when they returned in November 1606 from two months exploration along the Atlantic coast. These were Renaissance men at their best.

Port-Royal proved that Europeans could survive in northern North America, but the colony was not well situated to pursue the fur trade. After 1607, de Monts and Champlain concentrated their efforts on the St. Lawrence. Poutrincourt, meanwhile, worked to expand Port-Royal, but it was wiped out in 1613 by an English expedition under Samuel Argall, dispatched by the governor of the English colony of Virginia, established in 1607. Only Biencourt, his cousin Charles de Saint-Étienne de La Tour, and a few others stayed on, extending their trade with the Mi'kmaq and Maliseet. Following the death of Biencourt in 1623, the direction of the colony passed to Charles de La Tour, who had married a Mi'kmaq, likely the daughter of a local chief. Later blessed by a Récollet priest, the union produced three daughters, all of whom were baptized; one eventually entered the convent of Val-de Grâce in Paris.

Ignoring French claims, the English also set their sights on Acadia. In 1621 James I of England, who also held the Crown of Scotland, issued a grant of New Scotland, defined as the territory extending from the St. Croix to the St. Lawrence, to his fellow countryman Sir William Alexander. After his first attempt to found a colony failed, Alexander tried to raise more capital by selling titles (knights-baronet) and land (thirty-thousand-acre grants) in New Scotland. The initiative met with little enthusiasm, but two more colonization projects were mobilized, one in Cape Breton, led by Lord Ochiltree, and another at Port-Royal under the direction of Sir William Alexander's son. Both ultimately failed but left the legacy of a name and a coat of arms still used by the province of Nova Scotia.

NEWFOUNDLAND

Newfoundland also drew the attention of English colonizers. In 1610 the London and Bristol Company was granted the island of Newfoundland with the view to establishing settlements and developing a fur trade with the Beothuk. John Guy, a prominent Bristol merchant, led an expedition that established a base at what is now Cupid's Cove in Conception Bay. The first winter was mild and only four of the thirty-nine settlers died. In 1612 sixteen women arrived, a sure sign that a new-world community was in the making.

As in Acadia, problems soon arose. The settlement was harassed by the pirate Peter Easton; friction erupted with the migratory fishermen; and eight of the sixty-two settlers died of scurvy during the difficult winter of 1612–13. Finding the land resistant to agriculture and the Beothuk reluctant traders, the company tried to recoup its investment by selling tracts of land to other potential colonizers. One of these was Sir William Vaughan, a Welsh lawyer who saw overseas settlement as a solution to social and economic problems at home. Although his efforts at colonization soon collapsed, in 1626 he published *The Golden Fleece*, a fanciful effort to promote North American real estate.

Vaughan sold off a section of his claims to Sir George Calvert, who in 1621 founded a settlement at Ferryland in a colony he called Avalon. A well-capitalized venture, Ferryland emerged as an impressive community with stone houses, cobbled streets, and walled defences. Calvert, named Lord Baltimore in 1625, was a convert to Roman Catholicism, and allowed both Protestant and Catholic clergy to serve the three hundred colonists. Like other colonizers, Baltimore soon lost heart, complaining to King Charles I that during "the sad face of winter … the ayre is so intolerable cold as it is hardly to be endured."[8] In 1632 Calvert turned his colonizing energies to Maryland.

CANADA

Colonization on the St. Lawrence was initially the result of commercial enterprise. By the beginning of the seventeenth century, more than a thousand Algonquin, Innu, and Maliseet arrived each year at Tadoussac, where the Saguenay River flows south into the St. Lawrence. Trade on this scale was lucrative and had advantages over agricultural plantations further south where labour was always in short supply. Aboriginal peoples willingly engaged in the fur trade, and each nation competed to corner the market in furs, so they could profit as middlemen in the trade with their neighbours. This competition guaranteed a relatively stable supply without the need to import European workers.

With the fur trade in mind, de Monts and Champlain chose the former site of Stadacona, which they named Quebec, as their new base of operations in 1608. Located at the narrows of the St. Lawrence, it had spectacular natural defences and good potential for preempting the interlopers at Tadoussac. Still, the bruising climate conquered them. Of the twenty-five men who spent the winter of 1608–9 in Quebec, only nine managed to escape a scurvy-ridden death.

Quebec might have been yet another failed colonial venture had it not been for Champlain's stubborn determination to make it work. As a result of Champlain's efforts in Paris, de Monts was awarded a new commercial monopoly and Quebec was given a reprieve. The colony remained subject to shifting political whims, but it managed to survive as a year-round fur trade outpost. Until his death in 1635, fur trade monopolists would come and go, but Champlain remained the steady constant, well earning his reputation as "The Father of New France."

Little is known about Champlain's early life other than that he was a devout Roman Catholic and a skilled navigator and map-maker. A dreamer, he imagined building an empire in alliance with Aboriginal peoples and endeavoured to understand their ways. He sent young men to live with France's North American allies, the first being Étienne Brûlé, who in 1610–11 wintered among the Algonquin in the Ottawa River valley. To accommodate a party of Montagnais in 1628, Champlain accepted three girls, aged eleven, twelve, and fifteen, to cement the relationship – he named them Faith, Hope, and Charity – and later he became the godfather of a Montagnais boy whom he christened Bonaventure.[9] Champlain personally invested a substantial sum in the colony, using the proceeds from his own inheritance and a dowry he received when he married, against her will, a twelve-year-old French girl, Hélène Boullé, in 1610. His wife joined him in the colony in 1620 but remained for only four years and eventually entered a convent in France.

Champlain was obliged to be more accommodating to the Algonquin peoples, who controlled the territory in what the French called Canada, and their allies, the Huron (Wandat), who lived around Georgian Bay. In 1609 he became involved in their ongoing war with the Five Nations Confederacy while exploring what is now the Richelieu River. Champlain's firearm scattered the attackers, but a planned military expedition against the Confederacy in 1615 failed. With the Dutch now established on the Hudson River, the Confederacy found its own European allies and access to guns. If the Five Nations became too powerful, they could divert the flow of furs from the interior of the continent to France's hated Protestant rival.

At Champlain's request, Roman Catholic missionaries turned their attentions to Canada. The Récollets, who arrived in 1615, conducted missions among the migratory Algonquin peoples, but they saw the sedentary agricultural villages in Huronia as a more promising base for their missionary efforts. Located at the junction of the commercial crossroads between the southern agricultural nations and the northern nomadic hunters, Huronia was the pivotal point to the interior of the continent, an unknown space that continued to spark the imaginations and cupidity of explorers, traders, and missionaries. Huronia also appealed as a base of operations to the Jesuit missionaries who began arriving in Quebec in 1625.

At this point, Quebec was still only a fur trade outpost with a year-round population of little more than a hundred people, few of them bona fide settlers. Cardinal Richelieu, Louis XIII's chief minister, had larger ambitions for the colony. In 1627 he established yet another commercial enterprise, the Compagnie de la Nouvelle France, also known as the Compagnie des Cents Associés (Company of One Hundred Associates). Granted the territory from Florida to the Arctic, a perpetual monopoly of the fur trade, and a monopoly of all other commerce except the fisheries for fifteen years, the associates, most of them prominent French citizens, were obliged to settle at least two hundred Catholic colonists a year and fund missionary activities.

As this initiative was getting off the ground, war was declared between England and France. David Kirke and his four brothers, financed by London merchants and commissioned by Charles I to displace the French from "Canida," seized Tadoussac and captured the ships of the One Hundred Associates carrying supplies and four hundred colonists to Canada. Blockaded by the English, Quebec surrendered in July 1629. With Port-Royal also in the hands of the English and Scots, New France seemed to be doomed, but European diplomacy dictated otherwise. In 1632 Canada and Acadia were restored to France by the Treaty of Saint-Germain-en-Laye.

The patterns of European imperialism in North America were now set. With colonies serving as pawns in the competition for ascendancy among European powers, they inevitably became engulfed in nation-building strategies. It was still the case that, except on the island of Newfoundland, Europeans lived in northern North America at the sufferance of the local inhabitants, but there would be no wholesale effort to expel the newcomers whose trade goods carried with them the burden of desire. The Roman Catholic Church had also set its sights on North America, operating on the assumption that it was their God-given mission to convert the Aboriginal peoples to their own values and practices. In this, they would have their work cut out for them, but they added an important new element to colonial enterprises.

By this time, too, the European ecological legacy was established.[10] Seeds of cultivated plants and weeds (the dandelion was a hardy immigrant) had taken root, as had European diseases. The Jesuit Pierre Biard noted in 1612 that the Mi'kmaq "are astonished and often complain that since the French mingle with and carry on trade with them, they are dying fast and the population is thinning out.... One by one the different coasts, according as they have begun to traffic with us, have been more reduced by disease."[11] Although the comments of priests sometimes must be taken with a grain of salt, there would be no reason for Biard to lie about this calamity.

The practical tools of imperialism were also in place. Champlain's extraordinary map of New France, attached to his 1632 memoir, documented an eastern North America that we can easily recognize today, including French names that are still used for important landmarks (Image 2.2). In memoirs of their experiences, Champlain, Lescarbot, Biard, and other literate explorers and missionaries described northern North America in terms that their countrymen could grasp. The environment might be formidable, but it could be understood and tamed. With North America now imagined as European space, land surveyors would not be far behind.

TAKING ROOT IN THE ATLANTIC REGION

Following the Treaty of Saint-Germain-en-Laye, the French quickly reestablished their presence in Acadia and Canada and aggressively pursued their interests in the fisheries and fur trade. The English, now ensconced in Massachusetts as well as Virginia, kept a close watch on developments in northeastern North America.

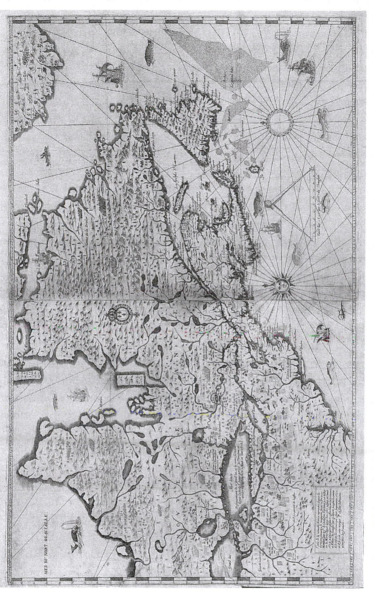

Image 2.2. Samuel Champlain's map of New France, 1632. (By permission of Library and Archives Canada/NMC-051970)

By the 1630s, the West Country fishermen were well established on the "English Shore" of the Avalon Peninsula. Settlement was primarily seasonal, but control over the shore-based fishery was deemed essential to the successful pursuit of the industry. In 1634 Parliament issued a Western Charter outlining the processes for claiming fishing bases and empowering the master of the first vessel to reach a given harbour to settle disputes. Three years later, Charles I granted Sir David Kirke and his associates trading privileges in Newfoundland with the power to tax French and Dutch vessels. Kirke established himself as a merchant in Ferryland, developed a profitable transatlantic trade in fish and wine, and set himself up as a local magistrate. His colonizing career ended in 1651 with the victory of Parliament in the English Civil War. Since Kirke was a royalist, he was arrested and died in a London prison in 1654. The Ferryland plantation survived under the management of his enterprising widow, Lady Sara Kirke, and her equally enterprising sons.[12]

The West Country merchants were less concerned about entrepreneurs such as the Kirkes than they were about competition from independent fishermen. Recognizing the potential of the fisheries, they bought passage from England each year, leased "rooms" (shore bases) to conduct their activities, and eventually entrenched themselves on the English Shore as "planters." After the Restoration of the monarchy in 1660, a West Country lobby convinced London to issue new regulations forbidding independent operators, but their numbers continued to grow because it was difficult to police such distant coasts.

In his efforts to reestablish Acadia, Richelieu turned to Isaac de Razilly, a distinguished naval officer and the author of a report that led to the founding of the One Hundred Associates. He arrived in the colony in 1632 with three hundred soldiers, artisans, and labourers; several Capuchin priests; and a few settlers. Along with his lieutenants Charles de Menou d'Aulnay and Nicholas Denys, de Razilly laid the groundwork for a new Acadia, with an economy based on fishing, lumbering, and fur trading. The exact origin of most of the early settlers is uncertain, but some of them were expert dike builders, probably from Poitou. Dikeland agriculture soon became an identifying feature of the industrious Acadians – fifty families by

Image 2.3. These ink drawings of missionaries teaching Christianity to the Mi'kmaq were used to illustrate Christien LeClercq's *New Rélations of Gaspésia*, published in Paris in 1691. (By permission of Library and Archives Canada/NL22323)

1650 – most of whom settled along the marshlands created by the mighty tides of the Bay of Fundy.[13]

In the first half of the seventeenth century, Acadia was an open field for competing clerical orders, with Capuchin, Jesuit, and Récollet priests doggedly pursuing their missions among the Mi'kmaq and Maliseet. The Capuchins were particularly active, sending at least forty priests and twenty lay brothers to Acadia between 1632 and 1656. Although most priests spent only a few years in the region, they achieved their goals: the Mi'kmaq and Maliseet, deriving benefits from trade and personal relationships, gradually reconciled their beliefs with those of the persistent Christians in their midst (Image 2.3).[14]

Following de Razilly's death early in 1636, his successor, Charles de Menou d'Aulnay, became embroiled in a power struggle with Charles La Tour, who remained on the scene. The jockeying for position, which entangled interests in Boston and Quebec as well as in England and France, lasted until d'Aulnay drowned in 1650. By this time La Tour was a widower, his second wife, Françoise-Marie Jaquelin, having died defending her husband's fort at the mouth of the St. John River from an attack by d'Aulnay in 1645. To consolidate his interests, La Tour married d'Aulnay's widow, Jeanne Motin. The intrigues did not end there. In 1654 an English force led by Massachusetts-based Robert Sedgwick plundered Port-Royal and other French bases in Acadia and took La Tour as a prisoner to London. The English government offered to return his posts in Acadia if La Tour agreed to swear allegiance to England and pay his debts to his Boston and English creditors. To raise the required finances, he sold most of his rights in Acadia to Thomas Temple and William Crowne, who remained officially in control of Acadia until 1667; then, by the Treaty of Breda, the colony was returned to France.

LAURENTIAN INITIATIVES

Champlain, French fur traders, the Jesuits (who insisted on exclusive access to missions), and a few intrepid settlers returned to Quebec in 1633. After the disaster of 1627–28, the One Hundred Associates lost much of its enthusiasm for colonization and gradually devolved its supervisory powers over the colony to local inhabitants. In 1635 an effort was made to advance the fur trade by building a post further up the river at Trois-Rivières. Growing tensions with the Five Nations Confederacy threatened to cripple the fur trade, and after Champlain's death, the colony entered nearly three decades of nail-biting uncertainty.

In this administrative vacuum, missionary efforts flourished. The Jesuits ministered to the local inhabitants, but their major objective was conversion of Aboriginal peoples to Roman Catholicism. Wasting no time, they made an initial foray into Huron country in 1634 and five years later began construction of their headquarters at Sainte-Marie, south of Georgian Bay. Within a decade Sainte-Marie was staffed by eighteen priests and forty-six lay assistants. The Jesuits also established a reserve in 1638 at Sillery, near Quebec, as a refuge for Aboriginal converts, who were increasingly harassed in their own communities.

It is difficult to know exactly what the Huron thought of the "blackrobes" who worked so hard to convert them. In reports to their superiors, the Jesuits claimed that their hosts were impressed by the ability of missionaries to predict eclipses, to make thoughts travel great distances through signs on paper, and to demonstrate stoic courage in the face of death. Christian rosaries, crucifixes, medals, and rings were popular, but it seems that conversion was often accepted as the best way of improving relations with French traders rather than from deep conviction. Different worldviews complicated matters. As Father Jean de Brébeuf, destined to become one of the Church's most celebrated martyrs, reported in a letter to his superiors in France in 1637: "leaving a highly civilized community, you fall into the hands of barbarous people who care little for your Philosophy or your Theology.... If you could go naked, and carry the load of a horse upon your back, as they do, then you would be wise according to their doctrine, and would be recognized as a great man, otherwise not."[15] In 1636 the Jesuits established a school at Quebec to train Aboriginal boys, but it attracted little interest and catered mostly to sons of settlers.

European gender norms dictated that female religious orders minister to women and girls in Aboriginal and colonial communities. In 1639 the Ursulines, a teaching order, and the Hospitalières de Saint-Augustin arrived in Quebec. Marie de l'Incarnation, the head of the Ursulines, was an exceptional administrator, but even her best efforts could not stop Aboriginal girls recruited to her school from trying to escape sisterly discipline. Notions of male superiority that were central to Roman Catholic doctrines also had limited appeal. Nevertheless, a few Aboriginal women were attracted to the ascetic practices – whipping, wearing hair shirts, and standing naked in snowstorms – that were performed by devout Roman Catholics in the colony. One early Christian convert, Kateri Tekakwitha, dubbed the "Lily of the Mohawks" following her death in 1680, continues to inspire people from all over the world who make pilgrimages to her shrine at Kahnawake, near Montreal.

While it had much to recommend it as a fur trade outpost, Ville-Marie (now Montreal), founded in 1642, was the product of missionary zeal. Sponsored by the Compagnie du Saint-Sacrement, a secret organization that fought growing secularism in France, Ville-Marie began as a utopian community governed by rigourous religious principles. The Société Notre-Dame de Montréal, established to undertake the mission, recruited Paul de Chomedey de Maisonneuve, a young military officer, to lead the expedition and Jeanne Mance to serve as nurse and bursar for the colony. In moving to the frontiers of territory occupied by the Five Nations, the settlers were courting danger and found themselves subject to ambush when they ventured outside Ville-Marie's boundaries. They soon heard tales of a tragedy that was unfolding around the missions in Huronia.

TROUBLE IN THE INTERIOR

Following the reestablishment of Quebec, the fur trade frontier on the lower Great Lakes became highly unstable. Smallpox and measles ravaged Aboriginal communities in the 1630s and were particularly devastating for the Huron, whose numbers declined by as much as two-thirds. In addition to bringing disease, the Jesuits divided the community, thus contributing to the disaster. Opponents of the missionaries, many of them women, accused the Jesuits of deliberately unleashing their black magic on them, and Christian converts, some five hundred souls out of a population reduced to about eight thousand by 1646, increasingly stood aside in Huron battles against their enemies.[16] Only threats of cutting off trade saved the Jesuits from being expelled by the increasingly embattled Huron.

Expulsion might have been the happiest fate. In the early 1640s, the Five Nations intensified their attacks, disrupting the annual fur trade flotillas from the interior to the St. Lawrence and taking many captives in raids on enemy communities, seemingly in an effort to restore the loss of numbers owing to disease.[17] In the fall of 1648, they launched a full-scale attack on Huron villages. The campaign produced several Jesuit martyrs, who suffered agonizing deaths, and destroyed the Huron as a people. A few hundred Huron captives were absorbed by the Five Nations, but the majority fled to an island in

Georgian Bay, where most of them died over the winter of 1649–50. The remnants of this once proud trading nation moved to Sillery or migrated westward. Huron allies, including the Petun, Neutral, Erie, and Nipissing, were also dispersed by the triumphant Confederacy.

Although they succeeded in destroying Huronia and improving their numbers, the Five Nations were unable to monopolize the fur trade. With arms supplied by the French, the Ojibwa formed an alliance with the Ottawa and Nipissing to challenge the Confederacy's control over former Huron territory and to establish trade networks with Aboriginal nations north and west. The French, meanwhile, extended their practice of sending young men to live among their Aboriginal allies, and these men, the first of a long line of legendary voyageurs, gradually took charge of flotillas bringing furs from the interior. With the Confederacy still hoping to replace the Huron as middlemen, voyageurs faced constant danger. In 1660 a contingent of seventeen French men under the leadership of Adam Dollard des Ormeaux, along with Aboriginal allies, was besieged in a makeshift fort on the Ottawa River by several hundred warriors of the Confederacy – primarily Onondaga, Mohawk, and Oneida. All the French were killed, as were many of their allies.

The same year, two ambitious fur traders, Pierre-Esprit Radisson and Médard Chouart, Sieur des Groseilliers, returned from an expedition north of Lake Superior with a plan to ship furs to Europe through Hudson Bay. French officials accused the pair of illegal trading. Undaunted, Radisson and Groseilliers floated their idea in London, where a group of merchants agreed to finance an expedition to investigate the prospects. After successfully wintering on James Bay, the expedition returned in 1669 with a cargo of high-quality furs. With proof of concept established, English investors applied to Charles II for a fur trade monopoly in the massive territory drained by rivers flowing into Hudson Bay. The area was called Rupert's Land in honour of Prince Rupert, a cousin of the king and the Hudson's Bay Company's first governor.

CONCLUSION

The lines were now drawn for the next chapter in the story of New France. In 1664 the English captured New Netherland from the

Dutch and were well positioned from their bases on the Hudson River and Hudson Bay to restrict the French to a narrow strip along the St. Lawrence. The English colonies had numbers on their side, with seventy thousand settlers in 1660, compared to scarcely four thousand in Canada and Acadia. Warned by the horror stories disseminated by the Jesuits, few people in France were willing to try their luck in Canada. It was much wiser to brave the fevers of the Caribbean, where France seized control of Guadeloupe and Martinique from Spain in 1635. Although the French government appointed a governor with ultimate military and civil authority in 1637 and established a council in 1647 to assist him, Canada's administrative apparatus remained weak. If the colony was to survive, it needed more help from France.

3

New France, 1661–1763

Between 1661 and 1763, France built a great empire in North America and then lost most of it to the British. Louis XIV laid the foundations for the growth of New France and also sowed the seeds of its decline. In extending its grasp, France laid claim to Newfoundland, Acadia, Canada, Louisiana, and several islands in the West Indies, along with vast areas of the interior of the North American continent occupied by Aboriginal allies and loosely held together by a network of fortified trading posts. New France was many things, but above all, it represented a remarkable case of a colonial jurisdiction punching above its weight.[1]

FOUNDATIONS OF AN EMPIRE

Louis XIV's decision in 1661 to assume personal charge of state affairs was a significant event, not only for France and its colonies, but also for Europe and the world. By creating bureaucratic structures, legal regimes, military might, and symbolic gestures to sustain monarchical powers against the claims of the nobility, the papacy, and other nations, the so-called Sun King emerged as the most powerful force in European affairs. His efforts to dominate Europe during his long reign, which ended in 1715, sparked a series of wars that echoed around the world and ultimately led to the fall of New France (Image 3.1).

The genius behind many of Louis XIV's early successes was Jean-Baptiste Colbert, appointed controller-general of finances in

Image 3.1. Louis XIV by Hyacinthe Rigaud. (http://en.chateauversailles.fr/
history)

1665, with the ministries of marine and commerce added in 1669. To enhance the glory of the monarch, Colbert introduced policies to reform national finances, promote economic self-sufficiency, and build a colonial empire defended by a massive navy. According to the theory of mercantilism that governed economic thinking at the time, colonies were valuable only to the extent that they provided raw materials and markets to advance the imperial goal of building up budgetary surpluses. As European rivalries intensified in the late seventeenth century, Colbert's successors would come to judge colonies not only for their economic contribution to empire but also for their ability to advance French territorial claims.

With overseas colonies firmly at the centre of Louis XIV's power-building exercise, New France became the focus of intense attention. The first initiative involved establishing a colony at Plaisance, on Newfoundland's southeast coast, in 1662. Well positioned to serve as a base for the French fishing fleet, Plaisance was also designed to keep an eye on the English Shore and to protect the approaches to the Gulf of St. Lawrence. Following what was developing as the template for overseas colonies, Plaisance became home to administrators, soldiers, Roman Catholic priests, and, on its beach properties, settlers whose numbers reached about four hundred by the 1680s.

Entangled in French-English relations until 1667, Acadia missed the first decade of Louis XIV's enthusiasm for colonies. A governor and a handful of troops finally reestablished royal authority in the colony in 1670. With a population of about six hundred in 1686, Port-Royal was the heart of French settlement, which was scattered along the region's ample coastline. In the 1670s young families at Port-Royal began on their own initiative to move up the Bay of Fundy to settle around the Chignecto and Minas basins, which soon supported thriving communities based on dikeland agriculture, fishing, fur trading, and clandestine trade with New England. Bureaucratic control of such a dispersed settlement would elude even the most determined administrators.

Most of Louis XIV's attention was focused on Canada, where little could be achieved until the threat of the Iroquois Confederacy was lifted. After attending to matters in the West Indies, Alexandre de Prouville, Marquis de Tracy, and twelve hundred troops, most of them members of the Carignan-Salières regiment, arrived in the colony in 1665. In its campaign against the Mohawk in the winter of 1666, the European-trained army suffered more casualties than it inflicted, but the show of force had the desired effect of keeping the Iroquois at bay and of opening some of their communities to missionaries.

Uppermost on the imperial agenda was increasing the size of the colonial population. Between 1663 and 1673, nearly 2,000 immigrants arrived in Canada, 770 of them single women, who were shipped to the colony to help redress the gender imbalance. More than a third of them came from the Hôpital général de Paris, the state-sponsored institution that housed the disadvantaged in French society. Endowed with a dowry from the state of about fifty livres, higher if they married an army officer, most of the *filles du roi* ("king's daughters") quickly found husbands in a colony where bachelors outnumbered European women six to one.[2] With more women on the scene, soldiers and *engagés* (indentured servants) thought twice about returning to France, where opportunities were more restricted than in the colonies.

The settler population grew impressively.[3] In the entire period before the British conquest in 1760, only fourteen thousand immigrants settled in Canada, and of these only 10,000 married and raised families. From the relatively small number of immigrants, the population increased from roughly fifteen thousand in 1700 to seventy thousand in 1760. Lower mortality rates, a higher standard of nutrition, easier access to land, and less exposure to epidemic diseases help to explain the rapid growth of the population in the colony, but the relatively early age of marriage for women was also significant. In eighteenth-century France, women married on the average at the age of twenty-five, while in Canada it was twenty-two. In Acadia it was even lower. As in France, a married woman in the colonies produced a child on average every two years.[4]

Immigrants to Canada were by no means a typical slice of French society. Four times as many men as women and as many urban as rural migrants chose Canada as their home. Nearly all immigrants were young and single. Although immigrants came from all regions of France, the majority came from Paris and the areas around

La Rochelle, Rouen, St. Malo, and Dieppe, the primary ports for embarkation to New France. Most settlers were French citizens, but 525 came from other areas of mainland Europe, as did 650 British subjects, almost all of them captives of raids on English colonies or vessels. Canada also became home to 900 slaves, both Aboriginal and African, and to 1,800 refugee Acadians following the initial deportation order in 1755. By the 1750s about 4,000 Aboriginal people – mostly Innu, Ottawa, Huron, Abenaki, Mohawk, and Oneida – lived on reserves near Quebec and Montreal.

COLONIAL ADMINISTRATION

In 1663 the charter of the One Hundred Associates was revoked and Canada became a Crown colony. Under royal government, it was administered in much the same way as a province in France. The chief administrative officer was the governor general based in Quebec. Always a military man, and usually a member of the old aristocracy (*noblesse d'épée*), he controlled the military forces in the colony and was responsible for Aboriginal relations. Local governors in Montreal and Trois-Rivières reported to him, as did, in theory, governors located in Port-Royal and Plaisance. With the arrival, beginning in 1683, of Troupes de la Marine, recruited to serve in the French navy, the governor had a substantial military force – twenty-eight companies totalling two thousand men by the beginning of the eighteenth century – to protect the colony from external attack and to quell any civilian unrest.[5] In 1669 the king mandated that every able-bodied man in the colony between the ages of sixteen and sixty serve in the militia, a policy that had no equivalent in France, where arming the general populace was unthinkable.

As in France, the intendant in Canada was the chief provincial administrator, responsible for finance, economic development, justice, and civil administration. Intendants were usually members of the new aristocracy (*noblesse de robe*) and represented the efforts of the king to bring bureaucratic efficiency and centralized control to bear on distant provinces. By the eighteenth century, the intendant was assisted by delegates in the main districts and a number of minor officials such as royal notaries, road surveyors, and customs officials.

Both the governor general and the intendant sat on the Sovereign Council, an appointed body modelled upon the provincial *parlements* in France. Its main functions were to serve as the court of appeal from the lower courts, to issue decrees for the governance of the colony in accordance with royal instructions, and to register the royal edicts that served as the constitutional framework for the colony. In 1703 the name was changed from Sovereign to Superior Council, reflecting the subordinate role it was expected to play. By that time, twelve men sat on the council along with the bishop of the Roman Catholic Church and an attorney general who was trained in law. Civil law in the colony was based on the Custom of Paris – the legal code of the Paris region of France. Although reforms introduced in the colony made the courts more accessible than in France, justice was neither free nor always expeditiously rendered, and access to the legal system was always easier for the elite. French criminal law carried harsh penalties, including beheading, burning at the stake, and breaking on the wheel.

Claiming to be ruler by divine right, Louis XIV insisted on control over the Roman Catholic Church both at home and in his colonies. In defiance of the papacy, the king nominated all Church officials in his realm. Protestants were barred from Canada and Acadia, a policy that prevailed in France following the revocation of the Edict of Nantes in 1685, which had hitherto granted Protestants limited toleration. As an essential arm of the state, the Church operated the schools, hospitals, and charitable institutions; sustained the social order by preaching obedience and submission; and helped to cement Aboriginal alliances through missionary endeavours. New religious communities, especially those reporting directly to Rome, were discouraged from locating in the colony, but Colbert made an exception for the Récollets, who were sent back to Canada in 1670 to balance the power of the Jesuits. The latter were notorious for their political intrigues and had been instrumental in the appointment of François de Laval-Montigny as Bishop of New France, a choice that did not sit well in Paris.

Following his arrival in 1659, Bishop Laval began the process of carving out parishes, and in 1663 he established a seminary in Quebec to train priests. Laval's seminary catered to local boys, but nearly half of the clergy were still immigrants from France in 1760.

In contrast, fully 20 percent of the girls in elite families entered convents, a reflection, it seems, of the few opportunities in public life available to women, and parental strategies designed to pass as much of the family estate as possible to sons.

The parochial system developed slowly, and secular authorities clipped the bishop's powers on the council. When Laval asked that the tithe be set at the customary one-thirteenth of the produce of the land, parishioners objected and it was set at one-twenty-sixth and on grains alone, not the entire agricultural output. Despite the loss of its political power under Louis XIV, the Roman Catholic Church nonetheless had a profound influence on colonial society, where priests presided over ceremonies that marked every stage of an individual's life and offered the only formal education that most colonists received.

SEIGNEURIALISM

Seigneurialism was the typical landholding system in France and the structure around which rural society took shape in Canada. According to seigneurial theory, all the land belonged to the Crown, which made grants of estates (*seigneuries*) to the church and the nobility. The seigneur was required to maintain a home on his (few women were seigneurs) estate and develop it with the help of peasant farmers, called *censitaires*, a term derived from the annual fees known as *cens et rentes* that the peasants paid to their seigneur for their lot concessions (*rotures*). In New France, notaries called the concessions *habitations*, and thus the people who lived on them became known as *habitants*. Under seigneurial regulations, the seigneur could require his censitaires to work a certain number of days on his seigneury, grind their wheat in his mill for a price, and pay a fee if the concession changed hands. In these ways, the wealth of peasant labour was accumulated by the seigneur in the time-honoured feudal tradition.

By 1760, 185 seigneuries had been granted in Canada. Apart from the religious communities that ultimately accounted for about one-quarter of the grants, few seigneurs were successful immigration agents. They simply waited until population growth worked in their favour. Instead of a three-field system encircling a village, as was typical in many feudal jurisdictions in Europe, seigneurial grants became long, narrow trapezoids fronting along the St. Lawrence and other rivers. This type of survey allowed farmers to live near their own fields and gave them access to the best transportation routes, but it also meant that rural areas were difficult to defend in times of war and that villages (and therefore local services) were slow to develop.

Seigneurialism reflected the hierarchical class structure typical of France, but neither the seigneurs not the peasantry replicated the status of their metropolitan counterparts, who were themselves experiencing dramatic changes. In the colonies, most seigneurs owed their status to the king, not to hereditary rights, and they had no official military role, as they did under the most feudal regimes of Europe. The bulk of the seigneur's income in New France came from trade, military service, and government positions, not from the rents extracted from tenants. So significant was commercial activity to the social structure of the colony that a special ordinance, issued in 1685, made it possible for the colonial nobility to engage in trade, a privilege denied to the nobility in France. More than half of the seigneurs in Canada forsook their rural estates for urban dwellings, a good indication of where their interests lay.[6]

Peasants, too, were different in the colonies. Carving a farm out of the North American wilderness was a backbreaking task, but after three generations of hard work, subsistence could be relatively secure. Living on the margins of the North American agricultural frontier, habitants often experienced crop failure owing to the short growing season and also battled the hazards of smut, rust, droughts, and pest infestations. Still, they were fortunate in that they rarely encountered famine, a fate common among the peasantry in many regions of France. In wartime the state requisitioned peasant produce and labour, but habitants were subject to lower levels of taxation than their French counterparts and, by all accounts, were much less deferential to authority, a trait common among the lower classes throughout North America, where land was plentiful and labour scarce.[7]

THE COLONIAL ECONOMY

Convinced that the fur trade had a detrimental influence on stable colonial development, Colbert envisioned Canada as a compact colony on the St. Lawrence, sustained by a diversified economy. The fur trade was placed under the direction of a state-controlled company, while the settlers were expected to focus their energies on agriculture, the fisheries, and other essential industries. Intendant Jean Talon, who arrived in Canada in 1665, energetically pursued Colbert's agenda by encouraging the cultivation of hemp and flax, distributing imported livestock, and constructing a brewery and a shipyard. He urged settlers to convert the colony's vast timber resources into barrels, casks, potash, soap, and tar, and made plans to develop the deposits of iron near Trois-Rivières and coal in Cape Breton.

Despite these efforts, the economy remained anemic. Some scholars have blamed mercantile restrictions for the slow economic development of the colony, but they were too often defied to be the culprit. The reality is that Canada was isolated in winter and produced few commodities that could not be procured more easily elsewhere. Throughout its history, the colony's major economic mainstays were state investment and the fur trade.

When the Iroquois threat was reduced in 1666, furs again began moving through Montreal. Dreams of great wealth and stiff competition drove young men to make the hazardous journey into the *pays d'en haut*, the area around the Great Lakes, to reach new trading partners. Hard on their heels came the intrepid missionaries, determined to win new souls for Christ. Curiosity about what lay beyond the next horizon also drove western expansion. In 1671 Talon dispatched two expeditions to seek a route leading to the Pacific, and the following year he commissioned fur trader Louis Jolliet to follow up earlier efforts by Sulpician priests, whose order had become the seigneurs of Montreal in 1663, to find the rumoured river that flowed into the Gulf of Mexico.

After Talon returned to France in 1672, the initiative for territorial expansion was seized by Governor General Louis de Buade, Comte de Frontenac. A man of high ambition, Frontenac had a fortified trading post built at Cataraqui (present-day Kingston, Ontario) and obtained rights for his friend René-Robert, Cavelier de La Salle, to trade in the Mississippi Valley. La Salle finally reached the Gulf of Mexico in 1682, but his irascible behaviour and aggressive trading practices invoked the ire of Aboriginal and

European fur traders alike. In 1687 La Salle was murdered, apparently by his own men.

With the fur trade frontier in chaos, the Iroquois, some of them closely allied with traders based in Albany, New York, once more became a threat to New France. Taking the offensive, the French sent two military expeditions to subdue the Seneca, who had attacked French posts, and, for good measure, dispatched a small force to Hudson Bay in 1686, where it succeeded in capturing three of the four Bay Company posts. In August 1689, fifteen hundred Mohawk descended on Lachine, just outside Montreal, putting fifty-six homes to the torch and killing their captives, sometimes after torturing them. More raids in the Montreal region followed, including one in 1692, when fourteen-year-old Madeleine de Verchères took the initiative in driving back the Mohawk attackers. The French replied in kind, sending captured warriors to France to serve as slaves for the Mediterranean fleet, and offering their Aboriginal allies bounties on scalps and prisoners taken from the enemy.

In addition to the pressure to push ever westward, the fur trade created two social problems that troubled French authorities: the use of alcohol as an item of exchange and the loss to the colony of so many young men who entered the trade, often in defiance of the law. Colbert introduced regulations both to control the sale of alcohol to Aboriginal allies and to limit the role of the *coureurs de bois*, as the unlicensed fur traders were called, but his efforts proved futile. The fur trade frontier had become a law unto itself, a dangerous space that the historian Richard White describes as a "middle ground," where the worlds of the Aboriginal peoples and the Europeans overlapped and where issues relating to trade, sex, violence, and spiritual beliefs were negotiated on a case-by-case basis with the outcome of the negotiations never predictable.[8]

TWO DECADES OF WAR

Louis XIV's decision to end religious toleration in 1685 – and the flight of nearly two hundred thousand Huguenots to sympathetic countries – stiffened the resolve in Protestant nations to stand up to French aggression. In 1688–89 the so-called Glorious Revolution, which put the Dutch stadtholder William of Orange and his wife,

Mary, on the English throne, spelled disaster for Louis XIV's ambitions to expand French borders into the Netherlands. William brought England into a defensive alliance known as the League of Augsburg and the fighting began.

North Americans were immediately drawn into the European conflict. As soon as war was declared, Frontenac launched raids against New England and New York in an effort to disrupt the English alliance with the Iroquois. This strategy had the desired effect of putting the Albany traders temporarily out of business, but they also brought direct attacks on New France. In the spring of 1690, an expedition from New England under the command of Sir William Phips looted Port-Royal and then sailed up the St. Lawrence to Quebec. With winter approaching and smallpox ravaging his troops, Phips was forced to withdraw without achieving his objective, but the capacity of the English colonies to mount seaborne expeditions meant trouble for French colonies.

On the Newfoundland front, in 1690 English privateers took Plaisance, which was then looted by residents of Ferryland. After several failed attempts, the French captured Ferryland in 1696 with the help of privateers from St. Malo. In the fall and winter of 1696–97, Jacques-François Momberton de Brouillon, the governor of Plaisance, and the Canadian-born naval captain Pierre Le Moyne d'Iberville led a force of Canadians, Acadians, and Aboriginal allies, supported by French troops, which destroyed most of the English fishing bases on the Avalon Peninsula. The local planter gentry was badly mauled, including David and Sara Kirke's three sons, all of whom died as a result of the campaign. D'Iberville then led an expedition to Hudson Bay, which succeeded in capturing Fort York. In 1697 the Treaty of Ryswick ended the war without territorial losses to the French Empire in North America, but this was only the first round in a long fight (Image 3.2).

The near century of warfare between and among Aboriginal peoples and Europeans in North America prompted a general desire on all sides for peaceful relations. In July of 1701 more than thirteen hundred representatives of Aboriginal peoples from Acadia to the Mississippi Valley assembled near Montreal to negotiate peace among themselves and renew their alliances with the French. The Montreal agreement, along with negotiations in Albany between

the English and the Iroquois, helped to reduce the violence on the fur trade frontier – at least for a time.

While people in North America were sorting out their relations, France became embroiled in another war. This time, Louis XIV planned to establish his grandson on the throne of Spain, thus uniting two of Europe's great empires. His long-standing enemies, including the English and the Dutch, were determined to blunt these imperial ambitions. Again North America was integral to military strategy. As a preemptive move, French authorities dispatched d'Iberville to the mouth of the Mississippi in 1698 to lay claim to what became known as Louisiana. His younger brother John Baptiste Le Moyne de Bienville was named its governor in 1701. In the same year, France moved its western base from Michilimackinac to Detroit in an effort to intimidate the Iroquois and contain the English.

As soon as war between England and France was officially declared in 1702, Governor Phillippe de Rigaud, Marquis de Vaudreuil (1703–25), instructed the Canadian militia and their Aboriginal allies to harass communities on the New England frontier. Canada was soon flooded with prisoners – more than a hundred hostages were taken in the 1704 Deerfield raid alone. In Newfoundland, English fishing communities, which had been reestablished following the devastation of the previous war, were again the objects of brutal raids. The New Englanders fought back, attacking the out-lying settlements in Acadia and taking hostages of their own, but they achieved no strategic objective. Finally, in the autumn of 1710, General Francis Nicholson led a force of 1,500 colonial troops and Iroquois allies, supported by British marines and grenadiers, against Port-Royal. The garrison of 258 soldiers held out for only a week before surrendering. In 1711 the English launched an attack led by Sir Hovenden Walker on Quebec, but their expedition came to grief on the treacherous shoals of the lower St. Lawrence River.

Image 3.2. A Canadien militiaman going into battle on snowshoes during the 1697 Newfoundland campaign. Since the Canadians and their Aboriginal allies often scored the most success against their English enemies in winter hit-and-run campaigns, snowshoes were an essential piece of military equipment. (From [Claude-Charles] Bacqueville de La Potherie, *Histoire de l'Amérique septentrionale* (Paris 1722) Library and Archives Canada/C-113193)

European considerations dictated the terms of the peace that was negotiated at Utrecht in 1713. To secure the Bourbon dynasty on the Spanish throne, Louis XIV agreed to abandon Hudson Bay, Acadia, and Newfoundland to Great Britain (the name applied to the political union of the kingdoms of England and Scotland in 1707) and to recognize British authority over the Iroquois Confederacy (soon to be expanded to include the Tuscarora). France retained possession of two islands protecting the entrance to the Gulf of St. Lawrence – Île Saint-Jean and Île du Cap-Breton (rechristened Île Royale) – and was granted fishing rights on the north coast of Newfoundland, the so-called Treaty Shore, running from Cape Bonavista to Pointe Riche (see Map 3.1).

CONSOLIDATING NEW FRANCE

The death of Louis XIV in 1715 brought a five-year-old child, Louis XV, to the throne of France. Between 1715 and 1723, Philippe, Duc d'Orléans, acted as regent for the young king. The Regency ushered in three decades of peace in which France moved to consolidate its North American empire.

The Fortress of Louisbourg on Île Royale was the most ambitious initiative undertaken in this period. Named in honour of the king, Louisbourg was designed to protect the St. Lawrence entrance to France's continental empire and provide a North American base for the lucrative fisheries. Construction of the fortified town began in 1719 and cost the French treasury an enormous sum, absorbing 10 to 20 percent of France's budget in the first two decades of its existence. Although it fell both times it was attacked and was never very effective in protecting the St. Lawrence, Louisbourg soon emerged as a major trading entrepôt, the number of ships calling at the port exceeded in North America only by Boston, New York, and Philadelphia. By the 1740s Louisbourg was home to a cosmopolitan population of nearly three thousand people – administrators, fishermen, merchants, and soldiers, along with the indentured servants and black slaves that catered to their needs.

France also turned its attention to Louisiana, which became the object of a disastrous scheme put to the Duc d'Orléans by the Scottish financier John Law to encourage investment in colonial enterprises.

Map 3.1. North America, 1713. (Adapted from W. J. Eccles, *France in America*, rev. ed. [East Lansing: Michigan State University Press, 1990], 122)

When the "Mississippi bubble" burst in 1720, investors vanished. Louisiana survived, but only because the French state willed it so, importing six thousand African slaves to do the backbreaking work required to produce the tobacco, silk, indigo, cotton, and rice that eventually became the colony's main exports. In 1717 the Illinois country was attached administratively to Louisiana. Sporadic military campaigns against the Fox nation slowed development, but by mid-century, the population had reached more than three thousand and large, slave-worked estates were shipping wheat, flour, corn, cattle, and swine to Louisiana and the French West Indies.

France's determination to outmanoeuvre the Hudson's Bay Company prompted ever-longer journeys along the north shore of Lake Superior and into the Prairies. Between 1732 and 1742, Pierre Gautier de Varennes, Sieur de la Vérendrye, intrigued by the notion of a "western sea" believed to be a gulf that opened to the Pacific, pushed westward, establishing a chain of trading posts stretching from Lake Superior to the western plains. La Vérendrye never reached the Pacific, but one of his sons saw the foothills of the Rockies. Faced with stiff competition from the Montreal traders, the Bay men were obliged to make their own expeditions into the interior to persuade the Aboriginal peoples living there to bring their pelts to company posts on Hudson Bay. In 1754 Anthony Henday embarked on a journey that took him as far as present-day Alberta.

As a strategic necessity, the fur trade and its expensive infrastructure – fortified posts, military garrisons, and administrative personnel – were subsidized by the Crown. Fort Frontenac, Fort Niagara, and Fort Detroit were maintained as king's posts, with goods sold at low prices to undermine competition from the English. Further west, the posts were usually leased to private entrepreneurs, most of them to officers in the Troupes de la Marine.[9] Whole industries developed in France to serve the demands of an ever-expanding number of Aboriginal allies, who were enthusiastic participants in the consumer revolution of the eighteenth century.

The aggressive pursuit of the fur trade inevitably had a detrimental impact on the animal population. As the supply of beaver began to decline from overtrapping in the eighteenth century, traders focused on other fur-bearing animals, such as mink and marten. The slaughter in the wilderness netted the French more than 250,000 pelts in 1728, rising to over 400,000 by the 1750s.[10] Since the trade often produced more furs than the Paris fashion industry could absorb, the surplus was either smuggled to the English or rotted in musty warehouses.

THE ATLANTIC BORDERLANDS

Like the North American interior, the Atlantic frontier remained fluid and unsteady. The Treaty of Utrecht in 1713 settled nothing. Encouraged by colonial officials in Boston and Quebec, Great Britain and France continued to jockey for power in a space that Europeans knew as Acadie or Nova Scotia. The British installed an administration at Port-Royal, renamed Annapolis Royal, but they were outnumbered by Aboriginals and Acadians, who maintained their ties with France.

French intrigues poisoned relations among the peoples living in the region. Eager to assert itself against the British wherever possible, France began to quibble about the boundaries of the colony, arguing that only peninsular Nova Scotia, and not even all of that, was part of the agreement reached at Utrecht. From its base in Louisbourg, France strengthened its alliances with the Mi'kmaq and Maliseet and encouraged Acadian men to serve as members of a potential militia in the heart of British Nova Scotia. Roman Catholic missionaries, permitted by the Treaty of Utrecht to minister to their Aboriginal and Acadian charges, operated as political agents in undermining British control.

The continuing French presence suited Aboriginal interests in the region. After more than a century of relations with the French, they had little enthusiasm for an alliance with the British, whose religion and language were foreign to them. With Anglo-Americans encroaching on their territory, the Abenaki, Penobscot, and Passamaquoddy joined the Maliseet and Mi'kmaq in a loose military alliance, known as the Wabanaki ("Dawnland") Confederacy. During the summer of 1715, Mi'kmaq mariners seized Massachusetts fishing vessels off Cape Sable, declaring that "the Lands are [ours] and [we] can make War and peace when [we] please."[11] Nova Scotia's governor, Richard Philipps, managed to extract a promise of friendship from the Maliseet, but the Mi'kmaq remained hostile, driving New England fishermen out of Canso in 1720 and, two years later, capturing thirty-six trading vessels off Nova Scotia. The New Englanders were quick to retaliate, setting off an "Indian War" along the New England–Nova Scotia frontier. In the summer of 1724, a contingent of Mi'kmaq and Maliseet attacked Annapolis Royal, burning part of the town and killing several British soldiers. A treaty concluded in Boston in December 1725 and ratified at Annapolis Royal in June 1726 finally ended hostilities. The text stated that signatories to the treaty were obliged to recognize British sovereignty, but would not "be molested in their Persons, Hunting [,] Fishing and Shooting & planting ... nor in any other [of] their Lawfull occasions...." Since formal treaties were a British innovation and the meanings of words may have been lost in translation, it was unlikely that the agreement would hold.

Most Acadians would have preferred to live under a French Catholic sovereign, but they were unwilling to jeopardize their security by challenging the new regime. Since the area had passed between the rival empires several times before, the Acadians understandably interpreted the settlement reached at Utrecht as similarly provisional. Most of them passed up their right under the treaty to move within a year to French-controlled territory, but they repeatedly refused British requests to take an unqualified oath of allegiance, demanding that they be exempted from fighting against the French and their Aboriginal allies. For three decades, the Acadian strategy of neutrality was allowed to stand. During that time family life flourished and the population grew impressively. The expansion of North Atlantic trade, much of it focused on Île Royale, offered unprecedented illicit opportunities for the Acadians to increase their wealth and well-being.[12]

CANADIAN SOCIETY

Three decades of relative peace also benefitted the settler society that was emerging on the banks of the St. Lawrence. As the population grew and communications across the Atlantic improved, the values of European society became more firmly rooted in Canada. Class distinctions were jealously guarded by the tight little knot of military officers, administrators, and Church officials holding letters patent of nobility. Although avenues for upward mobility narrowed in the eighteenth century, ambitious artisans, traders, and habitants aspired to the trappings of the noble lifestyle. By 1760, nearly 50 percent of the seigneurs in the colony were commoners, who also sought, but only rarely received, coveted positions in the Troupes de la Marine for their sons. Definitely French in tone and structure, Canada was increasingly defined by its colonial-born citizens, who identified themselves as *Canadiens*.

The towns of Quebec and Montreal, with populations of about five thousand and four thousand respectively by the mid-eighteenth century, supported a wide range of artisans who produced most of the colony's goods and services and trained others in the skills of their trade. In the absence of guilds, which the Crown forbade in Canada, the state regulated the activities of bakers, butchers, midwives, notaries, and surgeons, while the Church was authorized to supervise the activities of itinerant schoolmasters and private tutors. Many of the furnishings that graced the elegant homes and public buildings of the towns came from France, but local artisans produced ex-votos, portraits of notable citizens, carved pine furniture, and exquisitely crafted silver plate for those who could afford them.

Colonial society was not immune to the Enlightenment that was beginning to transform European societies. When Peter Kalm, a Scandinavian scientist and university professor, toured the English and French colonies in 1749–50, he concluded that "the common man in Canada is more civilized and clever than in any other place in the world that I have visited." He was also impressed by Governor Roland-Michel, Barrin de la Galissonière, who held forth on "ways of employing natural history to the purposes of politics, the science of government."[13] For the most part, colonials relied on their mother country for intellectual stimulation. They neither produced their own newspaper nor imported a printing press. Other than travel accounts and a few plays in verse for special occasions, Canadians produced little formal literature.

As in France, urbanites engaged in activities proscribed by the Church, including gambling, prostitution, and maintaining mistresses. In Montreal the care of foundlings became one of the prime concerns of the Soeurs Grises, or Grey Nuns, a religious community

founded by Marie-Marguerite d'Youville that received official sanc-
tion from the Crown in 1753. A death rate among the unfortunate foundlings of 80 percent – typical of similar institutions in
Europe – underscored the fragility of life in institutional settings in
the preindustrial world. Nor was it only in orphanages that death
was an ever-present reality for the young. Yvon Desloges estimates
that two out of three children in the town of Quebec died before
they reached the age of fifteen.[14]

Life expectancy was also short for the Aboriginal and African
peoples employed as slaves in Canada. African slaves were more
common in Louisbourg, Louisiana, Illinois, and the French West
Indies than in Canada, where indigenous captives formed more than
half of the enslaved population. Throughout the French Empire,
black slaves were governed by the Code Noir, which obliged slave
owners to house, feed, and clothe their chattels properly, but their
lives were almost universally tragic. Few records have survived
of slave resistance to exploitation. An exception is Marie-Joseph
Angélique, who was convicted of setting fire to her owner's house
in April 1734 and hanged for her crime after being tortured to exact
a confession.[15]

By the mid-eighteenth century, the Canadian economy was beginning to mature. More than fifty sawmills were kept busy producing
squared timber and lumber primarily for local use. In the 1730s a
bog-iron industry began operating on the banks of the St. Maurice
River to provide the colony with forged iron for stoves, cauldrons,
pots, axeheads, and other tools. With the inducement of a royal
bounty, Canadians built 150- and 200-ton vessels to carry flour,
wood products, and stoves to Louisbourg and the West Indies and
also constructed several ships-of-the-line for the French navy at the
royal shipyards on the St. Charles River near Quebec. The most
successful merchants by the 1730s were François Havy and Jean
Lefebvre, representing the firm of Dugard in Rouen. Retailing goods
in both Quebec and Montreal, they also invested in sealing expeditions along the Labrador coast and exported wheat to Louisbourg.

State-supported trade and expenses associated with the military establishment invited corruption at many levels, but it was
developed to a high art by Intendant François Bigot. In the
1750s he organized a ring of Bordeaux merchants and Canadian

collaborators to monopolize the lucrative supply trade. Twenty-two scoundrels amassed huge fortunes from their illicit activities. When the Seven Years' War ended and the bills of exchange were discounted, their wealth evaporated, and several of the ringleaders, Bigot among them, faced prosecution when they returned to France.

WAR OF THE AUSTRIAN SUCCESSION, 1744–1748

Military expenses moved sharply upwards when the lack of a male heir in the Hapsburg line provoked another war in Europe over the succession to the Austrian throne. While Britain and Holland supported the claims of the Archduchess Maria Theresa, France and Prussia opposed her right to rule. Three weeks before the news reached Annapolis Royal and Boston in 1744, Governor Le Prévost Duquesnel at Louisbourg, having received word that war had been officially declared, authorized privateers to prey on New England shipping, dispatched a force to capture Canso, and made plans to attack Annapolis Royal.

Alarmed by these developments, the New Englanders organized an expedition to capture Louisbourg. A volunteer colonial militia of forty-three hundred men led by William Pepperell, supported by a squadron from the West Indies under the command of Commodore Peter Warren, reduced the mighty fortress after a grueling seven-week siege in the spring of 1745. The following year, France assembled a massive force of fifty-four ships carrying seven thousand men, commanded by the Duc d'Anville, to recapture its much-prized military base. Dogged by storms, disease, and bad luck, the expedition retreated without even reaching its objective.

With communications between France and its North American colonies at the mercy of the British fleet, French colonials were left to pursue their own wartime strategies. Authorities in Quebec took steps to secure their frontiers by launching raids against New York and Massachusetts and increased the volume of trade and gift-giving among their Aboriginal allies. On their eastern front, three hundred militiamen under Captain Louis Coulon de Villiers embarked on a winter campaign against Annapolis Royal. En route they learned that five hundred New England militia were quartered in Acadian homes in Grand Pré. Acting on Acadian intelligence, they made a surprise attack, killing seventy New Englanders, including their leader, Colonel Arthur Noble, and forcing the rest to surrender. Further reprisals were temporarily averted when the two sides agreed to a negotiated peace. By the Treaty of Aix-la-Chapelle in 1748, France gave up its conquests in the Netherlands and India in return for Louisbourg. The New Englanders were appalled by Britain's apparent lack of concern for their safety and insisted that their northeastern frontier be properly defended.

THE UNEASY PEACE, 1749–1755

This time London listened. In the spring of 1749, Edward Cornwallis led an expedition of twenty-five hundred soldiers, settlers, and workers to found Halifax on the south shore of Nova Scotia. As the first serious attempt to colonize the territories ceded by France in 1713, Halifax marked an important turning point in British colonial policy in North America (Image 3.3).

Cornwallis, who served as governor of Nova Scotia from 1749 to 1751, was a determined administrator. When the Mi'kmaq refused to reconfirm the Treaty of 1726, he responded by offering a reward of ten guineas for every "savage taken or his scalp." The Mi'kmaq in turn, with the help of French missionaries Pierre-Antoine-Simon Maillard and Jean-Louis Le Loutre, issued a declaration of war against the British for having settled their lands without permission and for undertaking to exterminate them. Soon the British found themselves under attack on the outskirts of Halifax. Cornwallis's successor, Peregrine Hopson, managed to persuade a few Mi'kmaq to sign a treaty of peace and friendship in 1752, but it had little impact. Meanwhile, the French built Fort Beauséjour on the Isthmus of Chignecto in 1750. Cornwallis reacted quickly to this audacious land grab, dispatching Lieutenant Colonel Charles Lawrence and two regiments to construct a fort within sight of Beauséjour. It was only a matter of time before this standoff would be resolved.

Authorities in Quebec strengthened the approaches to Canada and were determined to forestall the efforts of the Ohio Company of Virginia, established in 1748, to sell half a million acres to land-hungry settlers. In 1752 the governor of New France, the Marquis

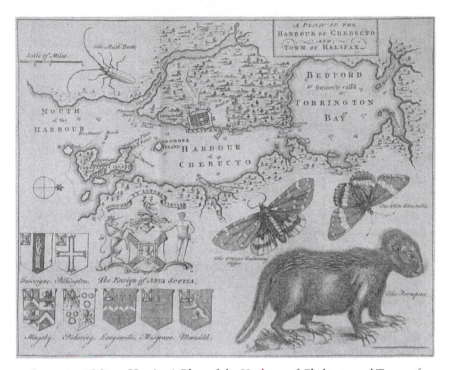

Image 3.3. Moses Harris, *A Plan of the Harbour of Chebucto and Town of Halifax*, 1750. This early map of Halifax, embellished with coats of arms of various Nova Scotia baronetcies, several insects, and a highly fanciful porcupine, reflects the mapmaker's and the general European interest in natural history in the mid-eighteenth century. (From *Gentleman's Magazine*, London, July 1950, by permission of Nova Scotia Archives and Records Management/N-9893)

Du Quesne, sent an expedition into the Ohio region to establish forts at strategic locations. George Washington led a small detachment of militia to expel the intruders in 1754 but was trounced in a bruising nine-hour encounter. By the terms of the capitulation agreement, the Virginians promised to abandon all claims to the disputed Ohio territory. Meanwhile, Fort Duquesne loomed out of the swampy ground that is the site of present-day Pittsburgh.

With a formal declaration of war almost a certainty, France dispatched Jean-Armand, Baron de Dieskau, with three thousand Troupes de Terre to Canada. Like the Troupes de la Marine, they were placed under the governor, who by 1755 was Pierre de Rigaud de Vaudreuil. The son of an earlier governor of the colony, he was the first Canadian-born appointee to the highest position in the colonial administration. Vaudreuil's strategy was to launch surprise attacks at various points along the American frontier to keep the colonists terrorized, unnerve the British soldiers, and take advantage of one of France's major military assets: its Aboriginal alliances.

The success of the French on all frontiers forced the Anglo-American colonies into cooperation. In 1755 the British launched a formal attack against the outer defences of New France: Fort Beauséjour in Acadia, Fort Frédéric on Lake Champlain, Fort Niagara on the lower Great Lakes, and Fort Duquesne. British authorities sent two regiments of regulars, under the command of Major General Edward Braddock, to assist the colonial effort. Unused to frontier conditions, Braddock failed miserably in his campaign against Fort Duquesne and lost his own life in an encounter with the French. Only on the northeastern front did the campaign proceed as planned. A colonial militia of nearly 2,500 men under the command of Lieutenant Colonel Robert Monckton captured Fort Beauséjour on 12 June 1755 after a brief siege. With only 160 regular soldiers and 300 Canadian militia and hastily conscripted Acadians, the French position was hopeless.

THE ACADIAN DEPORTATION

Even before the fall of Beauséjour, British authorities in Halifax had decided to expel the Acadians who had moved north of the Isthmus of Chignecto in support of the French cause. The capture of Fort Beauséjour sealed the fate of all Acadians. With news of Braddock's defeat fresh in his mind, Lieutenant Governor Charles Lawrence acted immediately to force the Acadians to do his bidding or face the consequences. Delegates from Acadian communities were summoned to Halifax and ordered to take an unqualified oath of allegiance. When they stubbornly refused to do so, Lawrence and his council agreed, on 28 July, to the deportation order.

Events moved quickly. Instructions were sent to the military commanders to seize the men, boys, and boats in Acadian communities, so that the women and children would not try to escape. Within weeks, transports from Boston arrived to distribute the Acadians, along with what possessions they could carry, to other British colonies on the Atlantic seaboard. Acadian houses and outbuildings were put to the torch and all land and livestock became the property of the Crown. Once war between Britain and France was officially declared in 1756, more deportations followed. At least eleven thousand Acadians were removed from the region between 1755 and 1762.

For those who survived the shipwrecks and appalling refugee conditions, the deportation marked the beginning of a lifetime of wandering. It took some Acadians the length of North America and others to the West Indies, to Britain, to France, and even to the Falkland Islands. Some of the refugees made their way to Louisiana, where their descendants, called *Cajuns*, still live. Others managed to escape to Canada, before it, too, was conquered. A few managed to hide out in the woods, assisted by Mi'kmaq and Maliseet, who were also hounded by British and colonial forces. Some escapees were captured and used as forced labour in the colony during the war; others were brutally murdered. The historian John Mack Faragher has argued that the Acadian expulsion, while not technically an act of genocide (a word first used to describe Hitler's atrocities), fits the United Nations definition of "ethnic cleansing," a term coined in the early 1990s to describe violent conflict in the Balkans.[16]

THE SEVEN YEARS' WAR, 1756–1763

In 1756 ongoing warfare on the frontiers of New France finally merged into the Seven Years' War. It was essentially a continuation of the War of the Austrian Succession, this time with France and Austria pitted against Britain and Prussia. Fought both in Europe and in its colonies around the world, this war profoundly altered the balance of power in North America.

After war was declared, French and Aboriginal raiding parties made life intolerable for the English colonists living in frontier communities. Meanwhile, Dieskau's successor, Louis-Joseph, the Marquis de Montcalm, led a successful expedition against Oswego, thus blocking British entry to the Great Lakes, and in 1757 conducted another campaign down the Lake Champlain route that resulted in the capture of Fort William Henry. While these were important victories for Montcalm, they brought criticism from Vaudreuil, who felt that the European style of warfare was too formal for frontier conditions. The tensions between the two titans made it difficult to coordinate military strategy and only became worse when Montcalm was promoted in 1758 to lieutenant general, a rank that put him in command of all French forces in North America, including those who reported to Vaudreuil.

William Pitt's accession as prime minister in 1757 brought new energy to the British war effort. Focusing military strategy on the colonies, he directed British troops and naval resources to the conquest of New France. Jeffery Amherst led a force of more than thirteen thousand men who took the fortress of Louisbourg, defended by four thousand soldiers, on 26 July 1758 after a seven-week siege. In July 1758 Montcalm won another major victory at Carillon (Ticonderoga) against a massive British army, but he made no effort to follow up his success and instead retreated to the St. Lawrence heartland. Lieutenant Colonel John Bradstreet, the son of a British officer and Acadian mother living in Annapolis Royal, took Fort Frontenac in August, effectively cutting the French supply line into the interior.

The defenders of Louisbourg had kept the British engaged long enough to prevent a campaign against Quebec in the summer of 1758, but the heart of New France now lay exposed. In June 1759 the Royal Navy under the command of Vice Admiral Charles Saunders made its way up the St. Lawrence, equipped with new surveys of the river by James Cook, who accompanied the expedition. The mighty armada carried 13,500 sailors and more than 8,600 seasoned troops under the command of General James Wolfe.[17]

Even before British ships appeared on the horizon, conditions in Quebec had become desperate. The presence of a combined force of four thousand regular French troops, up to ten thousand militiamen, and one thousand Aboriginal auxiliaries created congestion and added pressure to the limited supplies of food available in the colony. Nearly everyone was subject to rationing and some faced starvation. Only the arrival of twenty-two supply ships from France in May made it possible to feed the soldiers and civilians in the town during the siege. An outbreak of typhus added to the misery.

Then the bombardment started. From their base on Pointe Lévis, across the river from Quebec, Wolfe's forces launched artillery shells

Image 3.4. *The Death of General Wolfe*, by Benjamin West. In taking Quebec and dying in the attempt, Major General James Wolfe earned a prominent place in the pantheon of British heroes. He is less revered in Canada, where descendants of the conquered Canadians figure prominently in how historical memory is constructed. (By permission of National Gallery of Canada/8007)

into the walled town, but repeated landing attempts were driven back. With fall rapidly approaching, it looked as if the Canadian winter would trap the British fleet in a sea of ice. Determined to succeed, Wolfe managed to land nearly forty-five hundred soldiers at Anse-au-Foulon, a cove about three kilometres above Quebec, on the night of 12 September. They scrambled up a steep cliff to the Plains of Abraham, where they stood in battle array on the morning of 13 September. Montcalm lined up his troops outside the town walls and ordered them to charge in three columns. It was over in less than fifteen minutes. As the French retreated in disarray under a withering British volley, Montcalm was mortally wounded and Wolfe died on the battlefield. Casualties were heavy on both sides – 658 for the British and 644 for the French (Image 3.4).

The British carried the day, but they still held only the Plains of Abraham. Having had enough, the shell-shocked inhabitants of the walled capital formally surrendered on 18 September. After a difficult winter, which included an outbreak of scurvy, the occupying army under Brigadier James Murray faced an attack by a force from Montreal, seven thousand strong, led by the Chevalier de Lévis. Murray suffered defeat in the encounter, but Lévis was obliged to retreat with the arrival of British reinforcements in the spring. British forces converged on Montreal, where Governor Vaudreuil surrendered to General Amherst on 8 September 1760.

Amherst refused to grant the honours of war to the French troops, but he responded to Vaudreuil's pleas for leniency in dealing with the conquered Canadians. Under the Articles of Capitulation, all who wished to do so could leave the colony and take their possessions with them. Those who remained were promised security of property and person. Canadians were granted freedom to practise their religion, but the status of enforced tithing remained in doubt and the request to permit the king of France to name the Roman Catholic bishop of the colony was denied. Amherst reserved for future consideration the rights of the Jesuits, Récollets, and Sulpicians to continue their ministries, but the female religious orders, which had played a crucial role in the care of sick and wounded soldiers on both sides, were granted their customary privileges. The continuance of slavery and the right of owners to bring up their slaves "in the Roman Religion" were also guaranteed. Although France's Aboriginal allies had no place at the negotiating table, Vaudreuil was instrumental in securing agreement that they were to be "maintained in the lands they inhabit" and were not to be "molested" for having fought against the British. The Acadians who had sought refuge in Canada were not so generously treated. Permitted to go to France, they were specifically excluded from the guarantees against deportation granted to the Canadians and their Aboriginal allies.

The last battle in the war in North America was fought in Newfoundland, where a French expedition took St. John's in June 1762. On 15 September, a force led by Amherst's brother, Lieutenant Colonel William Amherst, attacked the French at their base on Signal Hill, forcing them to surrender three days later.

Until the peace treaty was signed in Paris on 10 February 1763, New France was ruled by martial law. The British gave some thought to exchanging their conquered territory for Guadaloupe, but the Treaty of Paris confirmed British possession of all of New France, except for Saint-Pierre and Miquelon. The French also retained the right granted in 1713 to fish on the Treaty Shore of Newfoundland. Louisiana, which had not been a theatre of war, was divided along the Mississippi, with Britain receiving the eastern section and navigational rights to the river. In a separate treaty, France ceded the area west of the Mississippi to its ally Spain.

In the aftermath of the conquest, between two and three thousand people – primarily administrators, merchants, and military leaders – moved to France. Most of the seventy thousand people living in Canada had been born in the colony and had little choice but to accept the fact that they were now British subjects.

CONCLUSION

The Seven Years' War marked the end of the French Empire in continental North America. During the negotiations, France showed surprisingly little interest in retaining Canada, which the philosopher Voltaire dismissed as "a few acres of snow." Fishing bases on the eastern Atlantic and islands in the West Indies were what really mattered. For Great Britain, the war only added to the burdens of empire. Its colonies, old and new, posed real administrative challenges, and Aboriginal populations allied with the French remained hostile. Rather than putting an end to imperial rivalries in North America, the Seven Years' War opened the door to new and potentially even more unsettling power struggles.

4

A Revolutionary Age,
1763–1821

Great Britain emerged from the Seven Years' War as the dominant imperial power in North America, but its ascendancy was soon challenged. In 1776 an alliance of British colonies along the Atlantic seaboard declared independence and fought a successful war, supported by France and Spain, to establish their claim to nationhood as the United States of America. By 1793 Great Britain was again at war with France, which was experiencing a bloody revolution of its own. The French and Napoleonic wars dragged on for more than two decades, engulfing most European countries, and, in 1812, the United States was sucked into the fray against its former mother county. The American and French revolutions signaled the difficult birth of the "modern" age characterized by liberal political regimes, industrial capitalism, and bourgeois values. When the fighting finally stopped in 1815, Great Britain reigned supreme over the emerging new world order. The territory remaining under British control in North America was redefined in the crucible of this revolutionary age.

MAKING ADJUSTMENTS

Great Britain had incorporated conquered peoples into its empire before, but swallowing New France offered unprecedented challenges. In the spring of 1763 the fur trade frontier erupted in bloody chaos, and when military occupation gave way to civilian rule, major difficulties arose in efforts to integrate the *Canadiens* into British political and legal institutions. The feisty mood in the older British colonies on the Atlantic seaboard further complicated decisions on how to manage this most recent addition to the empire.

For the Aboriginal peoples on the western frontier, the British conquest brought unprecedented hardship. No longer able to play one side against the other to their advantage, they faced plummeting prices for their furs, reduced access to trade goods, and aggression from land-hungry settlers. With their very survival at stake, they attacked and captured most of the British-occupied fur trading posts in the Upper Mississippi and Ohio regions and killed more than two thousand settlers. It took the British nearly two years to regain control, despite the fact that their attackers no longer had easy access to guns and ammunition. In desperation, Commander in Chief Jeffery Amherst even suggested that blankets infected with smallpox be used "to extirpate this execrable race."[1]

Aboriginal fury was informed by a clear understanding of the consequences of the accommodations made in North America's middle ground. According to accounts of the stirring rhetoric of Pontiac, the Ottawa chief who initiated the uprising, the European presence had brought disaster in the form of disease, economic dependence, incessant warfare, and addiction to alcohol. The first step in reversing these trends, Pontiac proclaimed, was annihilating the "dogs dressed in red," who were the harbingers of further ruin. Unfortunately for Pontiac and the people who followed his lead, this insight came too late. Aboriginal peoples in the interior were no more willing to give up European commodities than were the Europeans themselves. This reality was underscored in the Atlantic region, where the Mi'kmaq, Maliseet, and Passamaquoddy included government-sponsored trading posts among their principal demands when they made their peace with the British in 1760 and 1761.[2]

The Royal Proclamation of October 1763 reflected the first attempt by the British to establish policies for governing their newly acquired territories and for managing relations with Aboriginal peoples in North America. In what seemed like a better administrative arrangement, Canada was reduced in size to a small colony along the St. Lawrence and renamed Quebec; Labrador was attached to Newfoundland and the fur trade country declared "Indian territory" (see Map 4.1). Aboriginal peoples could sell their land

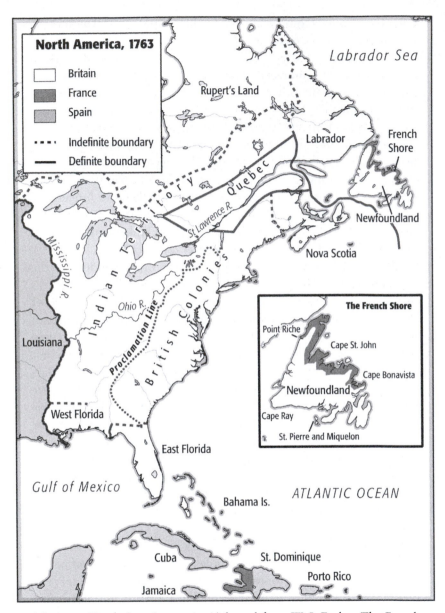

Map 4.1. North America, 1763. (Adapted from W. J. Eccles, *The French in North America, 1500–1783* [Markham, ON: Fitzhenry and Whiteside, 1998], 236)

only through arrangements approved by the British Crown, and would-be fur traders required a licence from the governor. When the 1763 boundary drawn between settlements and indigenous territory along the Allegheny Mountains proved impossible to sustain, a new one further west was negotiated at Fort Stanwix in 1768. Since neither the Aboriginal delegates – mostly Iroquois – nor the British could control the people they claimed to bargain for, the boundary was widely ignored.

In 1764 James Murray, the commander of the occupying forces, became the civilian governor of Quebec. By the terms of his appointment, Quebec was to become a colony like most of the others in North America, ruled by a governor advised by an appointed council and an elected assembly. Since Roman Catholics were denied political rights under British law, only the few Protestant immigrants to the colony – no more than a thousand in the first decade after the conquest – were eligible to vote and hold public office.

Murray quickly came to the conclusion that British institutions were unsuited to Quebec. To prevent the English minority from using its power to exploit the Canadiens, he postponed calling an assembly and governed much as the French had done, with an appointed council and subordinates in Trois-Rivières and Montreal. Murray also granted commissions to former militia captains and eased the tension in the legal system by permitting Roman Catholics to practise law and serve on juries. Believing that the Church played a central role in maintaining social order, he paved the way for Abbé Jean-Olivier Briand to be consecrated by French bishops in 1766 so that the institutional structure of the Church remained intact.

Despite these concessions, the Canadien elite remained unhappy under British rule. Seigneurs felt keenly the loss of status and income associated with their administrative and military commissions under the French regime, and Canadien merchants, saddled with heavily discounted French currency, faced predictable difficulties competing with British and New England merchants who followed in the wake of Wolfe's army. Only the habitants continued to live much as they had before the conquest. Without war to disrupt their seasonal round, agricultural production increased and the population grew rapidly.

Image 4.1. This cartoon appeared in *London Magazine* in July 1774. With the devil looking on, British politicians and Anglican bishops support the Quebec Act, which lifts restrictions on the Roman Catholic Church in the colony. (By permission of Library and Archives Canada/C-38989)

Murray's bias toward the Canadiens outraged the English-speaking merchants in the colony and led to his recall in 1765. His successor, Sir Guy Carleton, was initially prepared to accommodate the Protestant minority, but he soon adopted Murray's position on colonial governance. As military men, they were conscious of the larger political developments on the continent. With France no longer a threat to their security, Anglo-American colonists were becoming more aggressive in their resistance to imperial policies designed to protect Aboriginal peoples and to recover the costs of colonial administration. The conquered Canadiens, Murray and Carleton reasoned, still subscribed to conservative political values that would better serve British imperial interests than the republican notions that inspired their rebellious southern neighbours.

Carleton's views were reflected in the Quebec Act (1774) (Image 4.1). Designed to strengthen the elites in the colony, the act was based on the misguided perception that Church leaders and seigneurs would ensure the loyalty of the habitants in time of war. To that end, the tithes of the Church were guaranteed, the seigneurial system was legally recognized, and appointments to governing councils were opened to Roman Catholics. English criminal law remained in force, but French civil law was reintroduced in the colony. No reference was made to an elected assembly. The act also extended Quebec's boundaries into the Ohio territory, north to the borders of Rupert's Land, and eastward to include Labrador. By making concessions to Roman Catholics, denying a representative assembly, and bringing the western frontier under Quebec's jurisdiction, the British signaled that imperial interests would override those of their seaboard colonies.

THE ATLANTIC COLONIES IN TRANSITION

In Nova Scotia, British control depended on attracting loyal settlers. Shortly after Halifax was founded, nearly twenty-five hundred Protestants from continental Europe were recruited to the colony, many of them settling in the community of Lunenburg in 1753. The expulsion of the Acadians and the capture of Louisbourg opened the way for a more comprehensive settlement plan. In 1758 Governor Lawrence was instructed to call an elected assembly and to issue proclamations offering free land to bona fide settlers. Designed to appeal to New Englanders, who had long cast envious eyes on their northeastern frontier, the proclamations assured them that their concerns about governance and religious freedom would be addressed. There would be two elected assembly members for each settled township, freedom of religion for Protestant dissenters, and exemption from quitrents (land taxes) for ten years.

Their westward migration blocked by the war in the interior, eight thousand New Englanders took advantage of this extraordinary opportunity. Known as "Planters," the old English term for settlers, they brought a distinctly "Yankee" culture to the colony, reflected in their Congregational churches, penchant for trading, and stubborn individualism. Above all, they embodied the modern view that the historian John Weaver argues increasingly characterized Anglo-American imperialism: that land was "an article to be measured, allocated, traded, and improved."[3]

The New Englanders were only the largest of several immigrant groups that planted themselves firmly in Nova Scotia soil in this period. Among them were Acadians, granted permission in 1764 to return to their beloved homeland providing that they took the oath of allegiance, which many were now prepared to do. Since their original communities were now occupied by new immigrants, they were allocated land in other regions of the colony. Nova Scotia also became home to fish merchants and their employees from the Channel Islands, Irish (both Protestant and Roman Catholic), Yorkshire English, German Protestants from Pennsylvania, and, with the arrival of the *Hector* in Pictou harbour in 1773, the first of successive waves of immigrants from Scotland.

John Reid has argued that British control over Nova Scotia remained uncertain in the context of the countervailing power of the Mi'kmaq and Maliseet, who remained unhappy with the British regime.[4] Yet numbers were shifting dramatically in favour of immigrants – at least twenty thousand settlers in 1775 compared to an indigenous population of no more than four thousand. The opposite occurred in Cape Breton (the former Île Royale), where the Acadian and French residents were shipped away and Louisbourg razed to the ground to eliminate any temptation for its recapture.

Another drama unfolded on St. John's Island (renamed Prince Edward Island in 1798). Of great interest to land speculators once it was confirmed as a British possession, it was surveyed into sixty-seven townships by Samuel Holland in 1764. Three years later, in one of the most spectacular "lotteries" in Canadian history, the British government granted most of the lots to favourites of the court in London. According to the conditions of the grants, the proprietors were required to settle and improve their estates and sustain colonial administration through the payment of quitrents, or forfeit their holdings. Unfortunately, the escheat process never worked well in practice. The proprietors used their influence to secure a separate administration for the Island in 1769 with a capital at Charlottetown, named in honour of the queen. Since proprietorial interests had strong supporters both on the Island and in Great Britain, the "land question" would bedevil Island society until legislation was passed to abolish the system in the 1870s.

The Island's class-based approach to land granting compared unfavourably with the system of freehold tenure prevailing in

Nova Scotia, but immigrant communities nevertheless struggled into existence. In their initial flush of enthusiasm, several proprietors made serious efforts to fulfill their obligations, among them John MacDonald, who spearheaded a settlement scheme designed to bring Roman Catholic tenants, fleeing political oppression in Scotland, to his new-world estate. By 1775, the roughly three hundred Acadians and Mi'kmaq living on the Island in 1775 were outnumbered by twelve hundred colonists.

Despite official policy discouraging settlement, Newfoundland drew a steady stream of immigrants from the home ports of the British fleet and the south coast of Ireland, where crews were recruited for the fishing season. More than twelve thousand year-round settlers called themselves "Newfoundlanders" by 1775. As the population increased, the local economy expanded. New Englanders competed with British merchants in supplying Newfoundland residents with manufactured goods, provisions, and rum in return for fish, which they sold in the West Indies in defiance of the British navigation acts that restricted colonial trade to British vessels.

After the Seven Years' War, British authorities took steps to establish tighter control over the Newfoundland fishery. This initiative was undertaken on the long-held assumption that the fisheries were a nursery for British seamen pressed into service in time of war and therefore essential for national security. The new imperial thrust was put into effect by Captain Hugh Palliser, who was appointed governor of Newfoundland in 1764, a position that required his presence only in the summer months. During his four-year tenure, he challenged the rights of "owners" of shoreline property and, in his efforts to protect the Innu and Inuit living in Labrador, seized the bases of seal fishermen. He also welcomed a proposal from the Moravians to establish a mission in Labrador, which got under way in 1771 with the founding of Nain (Image 4.2).

In 1775 the British government reaffirmed its opposition to settlement in Newfoundland in the so-called Palliser's Act. Like many of Britain's imperial policies in this period, the clearly labeled "Act for the encouragement of the fisheries carried on from Great Britain and for securing the return of the fishermen ... at the end of the fishing season" flew in the face of colonial reality.

Image 4.2. An idealized depiction of a Moravian missionary meeting with the Inuit in Nain, Labrador, ca. 1800. (By permission of Library and Archives Canada/C-124432)

THE AMERICAN REVOLUTIONARY WAR

The Quebec Act and Palliser's Act were included among the "intolerable acts" that raised the ire of Anglo-American colonists. After 1763, legislation passed by the British Parliament, including taxes on paper, sugar, and tea, without the approval of the elected colonial legislatures, had galvanized resentment. Tensions reached a point of no return early in 1774 when, in response to riotous indignation in Massachusetts over mercantile restrictions on their trade, British authorities closed the port of Boston, suspended the Massachusetts assembly, and dispatched more troops.

In September 1774 the First Continental Congress, which included delegates from twelve British colonies – all except Newfoundland, St. John's Island, Nova Scotia, Quebec, and Georgia – met in Philadelphia to demand that the coercive acts against Massachusetts be repealed. When Britain refused to back down, the colonial militia was placed on alert and clashed with British troops at Lexington and Concord in April 1775. At a Second Continental Congress convened in May, "Patriot" delegates voted to raise an army under George Washington to defend "American liberty." In addition to driving British troops out of Boston, they planned to march on Quebec, which was easier to attack without supporting naval power than the British stronghold of Halifax. Ice-bound Quebec might succumb during a winter siege, especially if the habitant population proved susceptible to throwing off the British yoke.

In September 1775 an army of two thousand militia led by Richard Montgomery moved down the Lake Champlain–Richelieu River route toward Montreal, while another force under Benedict Arnold struggled overland to Quebec along the Kennebec and Chaudière rivers. Carleton, who had sent half of his garrison to assist General Thomas Gage in Boston, was left with only six hundred regulars for the defence of the colony. In effect, the fate of Quebec hung on the reaction of the colonists to the invading forces. The seigneurs and Church officials remained loyal, but most of the Canadiens were in no mood to engage in another war. Montgomery's troops received support from some of the habitants living on the Richelieu River; Montreal, where disgruntled English merchants were more likely than their Canadien counterparts to support the Patriot cause, capitulated without a fight. In the vicinity of Quebec, people were more disposed to repel the invading forces, especially after the Protestant invaders desecrated some of their churches. A bumbling attack on the fortified town, on the evening of 31 December, failed, and in May 1776 the American siege was hastily lifted when British ships arrived bearing ten thousand troops. The presence of a large military force kept the civilian population in line.

Like the Canadiens, the Iroquois were caught in what was essentially a civil war and divided about what to do. The Mohawk, led by Mary (Molly) Brant and her brother Joseph, and some Seneca fought with the British from the outset. Most of the Oneida and Tuscarora, perhaps influenced by their ties with Congregational ministers, leaned toward the Americans. Onondaga and Cayuga remained neutral until American troops invaded their territory in 1779. With their homelands at stake, the Iroquois proved to be among Britain's most effective allies. This was not the case for many Mi'kmaq and Maliseet, who in July 1776 sent delegates to a meeting in Watertown, Massachusetts, at which they agreed to support the Patriot cause.

By that time, the Thirteen Colonies had declared independence from Great Britain, and the war quickly escalated. The defeat of Britain's forces in the battle of Saratoga in 1777 brought France and Spain into the fray against their long-time enemy. With France onside, the Americans planned another invasion of Quebec, but this strategy was abandoned when the two allies failed to agree on who should rule the colony if it were captured.

Protected by the British navy, the Atlantic region remained free from invading armies, but not from raids by New England privateers. Nearly every outport settlement from Nova Scotia to Labrador was raided by one of the estimated four thousand schooners licensed by the Continental Congress to plunder, burn, or sell British vessels at auction. In November 1775, privateers landed in Charlottetown, destroying homes, seizing provisions, and carrying away the colony's leading officials, including the acting governor, Phillips Callbeck. Most raids were similarly selective, but they did little to endear pioneer settlers to the revolutionary cause.

There were a few enthusiasts for independence. In the fall of 1776, two members of the Nova Scotia assembly, Massachusetts-born Jonathan Eddy and Scottish-born John Allan, led an attack against the British garrison at Fort Cumberland (formerly Fort Beauséjour). The fewer than two hundred volunteers involved in the skirmish – mostly New England–born along with a few Acadians, Mi'kmaq, and Maliseet – were easily scattered by soldiers from Halifax. As the fighting moved to the middle and southern American colonies, Nova Scotians turned their attention to profiting from the increased British military presence. New Englander Planters, who were especially troubled by the developments in their former homeland, found escape from worldly realities in an evangelical movement led by itinerant preacher Henry Alline.

In 1781 a British force led by Charles Cornwallis suffered a crushing defeat at Yorktown, Virginia, and the war gradually wound down. Two years later, in another treaty negotiated in Paris, the British agreed to recognize the independence of the United States, a decision that would have profound implications for what was left of "British" North America. A flood of immigrants, a reorganized colonial administration, and a new – though poorly surveyed – boundary line followed in the wake of the war, laying the foundations for a second transcontinental nation in North America.

Under the terms of the peace treaty, the British agreed to abandon to the Americans all territorial claims south of the Great Lakes, a decision that angered their Aboriginal allies, whose interests had not been addressed in the negotiations. The British kept the news of this betrayal of the Treaty of Fort Stanwix from the Iroquois as long as possible and then attempted to soften the blow by issuing eighteen hundred gallons of rum.[5] Pressured not only by their desperate Iroquoian allies but also by Montreal merchants, who had lost a lucrative fur trade frontier, the British continued to occupy the western posts south of the Great Lakes until Aboriginal policy in the region could be determined.

THE LOYALISTS

When the American Revolutionary War ended, at least sixty thousand self-styled "Loyalists," along with their fifteen thousand slaves, left the United States to start their lives over again. Nearly half of the Loyalists moved to Nova Scotia, more than doubling the population there, and another fifteen thousand found sanctuary in Quebec.[6] More fortunate than most refugee peoples, they were the beneficiaries of British largess in the form of land, provisions, temporary shelter, and, in a few cases, financial compensation for their losses. Nevertheless, many Loyalists experienced unbearable hardship in their efforts to get reestablished on the northern frontiers of European settlement, where the climate and lack of amenities often came as unhappy shocks.

The Loyalists were as diverse as the society from which they came. While many were soldiers disbanded from colonial and regular regiments, others were refugees hounded by their Patriot neighbours; still others were opportunists attracted by the promise of free land and provisions. Nearly 90 percent had been born in North America, and most were drawn from the lower and middling classes. More than half of the Loyalists were women, children, and

Image 4.3. This painting by William Booth shows a black woodcutter in Shelburne, Nova Scotia, in 1788. (W. H. Cloverdale Collection of Canadiana/ By permission of Library and Archives Canada/C-40162)

slaves, whose fortunes were dictated by family decisions to support the British cause. Some three thousand black Loyalists, who were granted their freedom in return for deserting their Patriot owners, also joined the exodus to British North America. Treated shabbily, they were offered smaller grants of land in less desirable areas than their white counterparts, and their petitions for justice were often ignored. In 1792 nearly twelve hundred black Loyalists left the Maritime region when offered passage by abolitionists in London to the new colony of Sierra Leone in Africa (Image 4.3).[7]

A disproportionate number of the Loyalists who settled in Nova Scotia came from urban centres such as Boston, New York, and Charleston, where British armies had been stationed at various times during the war. Unsuited to the hardships of pioneer life, they were tempted to sell their land and ship out. As many as 25 percent of the Loyalist migrants eventually abandoned "Nova Scarcity." In contrast, most of the refugees who flooded into Quebec were farmers from upstate New York and the back country of Pennsylvania and New England. They were better prepared for the conditions that awaited them.

Getting the Loyalists established in their new homes posed huge administrative challenges. In Nova Scotia, Governor John Parr moved quickly to escheat unsettled land grants, ignoring the claims of Mi'kmaq, Maliseet, and Passamaquoddy, who were now required to petition for land in the same way as the Loyalist refugees. Surveyors laid out townships throughout the colony, and instant cities sprang up at Port Roseway (Shelburne) and Parrtown (Saint John). When Loyalists on the St. John River complained that Halifax was too remote for a timely response to their concerns, the British government created two new colonies in 1784: New Brunswick and Cape Breton, with capitals at Fredericton and Sydney, respectively. Since efforts to escheat unsettled land on St. John's Island failed, only five hundred Loyalists, most of them disbanded soldiers, made their home there.

On the St. Lawrence, the Loyalists settled in Montreal, Quebec, and smaller communities from the Gaspé to the Richelieu River, but Governor Frederick Haldimand diverted most of the immigrants to the north shore of Lake Ontario. Before he could establish townships in this region, he was obliged under the terms of the Proclamation of 1763 to secure the agreement of the Anishnabe living in what became the province of Ontario. When approached by Haldimand, they relinquished control over some of the best agricultural land in British North America, often for seemingly little in return. By 1788, much of the rest of the land north of Lake Ontario had been ceded in return for guns, ammunition, clothing, and other commodities, and the process of displacement continued well into the nineteenth century.

Several reasons have been advanced for the willingness of the Anishnabe to accommodate the Loyalists. Their lack of unity made it difficult to negotiate from strength, and the dependence on European trade goods was also a factor. Even more relevant were the worldviews that the two sides brought to the negotiations. Indigenous peoples willingly gave up the *use* of land that they held in common – but not exclusively and not forever. As they would discover to their regret, land once used for hunting and fishing quickly gave way to agricultural communities and exclusive ownership. More regrettably, a growing body of evidence confirms that the settlers and those who negotiated on their behalf bargained in bad faith. Treaties were couched in terms so vague that they could be interpreted in various ways, and both authorities and settlers pushed their advantage when they felt they could get away with it. Thus, as the historian Peter Baskerville notes, Aboriginals, "rather than the British, paid the costs of rewarding the Loyalists."[8]

In 1784 surveyors began laying out townships in the St. Lawrence–Bay of Quinte region, which became home to disbanded regiments. Great Britain's Iroquoian allies, among them Joseph Brant, were offered land along the Grand River. Like her brother, Molly Brant, who settled near what is now Kingston, Ontario, was awarded a pension and compensation for her losses by the British government. Loyalists arriving from the frontier districts of New York and Pennsylvania settled around Fort Niagara and at Sandwich (present-day Windsor), where they mingled with French settlers living near Fort Detroit. When the British finally agreed to evacuate the posts in the southwest by Jay's Treaty in 1794, settlers moved from Detroit to British-controlled territory. By that time, the colony was attracting significant numbers of "late Loyalists," residents of the United States who had second thoughts about staying in the new republic and who were eager to take advantage of the generous terms for land grants in British territory.

In the past, historians have argued that the Loyalists were the founding families of the English fragment in Canada and the bulwark of an enlightened conservatism.[9] This claim is too simplistic and even wrongheaded, given earlier settlement patterns in the Maritimes and Newfoundland and the ideological diversity that characterized the Loyalists. What is clear is that the Loyalists hastened the Anglicization of northern North America and advanced the broad North Atlantic culture that was transforming Western societies. In urban centres, they raised the level of political debate and contributed to the growth of civil society by establishing private clubs, service organizations, and debating salons. The Loyalist legacy in both Quebec and the Maritimes included churches, schools, newspapers, and literary expression, along with stately homes and public buildings constructed in the latest Georgian style.

Fed up with republican excesses, Loyalist elites did their best to enhance the conservative side of the British North American political ledger. Those aspiring to gentility secured larger grants of land for themselves and tried by methods fair and foul to dominate colonial assemblies. In an effort to shore up the traditional power structures, two Church of England bishops were appointed: John Inglis as Bishop of Nova Scotia in 1787 and Jacob Mountain as Bishop of Quebec in 1793. The 1789 founding of Kings College in Windsor, Nova Scotia, as an exclusive academy for the sons of the Church of England elite, underscored the hierarchical thinking that inspired the Loyalist leadership.

Significantly, there was criticism of these policies from other Loyalists, whose commitment to the Crown did not involve giving up their "rights as Englishmen." In Saint John pitched battles ensued when elites tried to control elections in 1785. Many Loyalists were influenced by Enlightenment thinkers and openly expressed egalitarian sentiments. A young Rebecca Byles, writing in 1785 to her aunts in Boston from her exile in Halifax, predicted that, given the military preoccupations of men, women would soon be taking up "the most important offices of church and state." "I feel a rebellious spirit arise," Byles crowed, "and congratulate myself that I was born in a land where the rights of the subjects are more on an equality."[10]

WARS AND RUMOURS OF WARS

The Loyalists were the advance guard of a massive Anglo-American migration to what became Canada, but before the floodgates could be opened, two decades of warfare intervened. In 1789 a popular revolution broke out in France, and three years later the triumphant republicans set out to export their revolutionary ideals across Europe. When Napoleon seized control of his war-ravaged country in 1799, he, too, took on his European neighbours.

Developments in Europe and demands from Loyalists for an elected assembly, common law, and freehold tenure led Great Britain to make a third attempt to create workable political institutions in Quebec. In 1791 the Constitutional Act divided Quebec into two colonies: Upper and Lower Canada. In Upper Canada, where the Loyalists made up the majority of the settler population, British laws, including freehold land tenure, prevailed. Lower Canada, with its overwhelmingly French-speaking population, retained the seigneurial system and French civil law. To encourage immigration to Lower Canada, provision was made for freehold tenure outside of seigneurial tracts, including what became known as the Eastern Townships, south of Montreal.

The democratic tide was sufficiently strong to ensure that each colony received an elected assembly, but it was constrained by the veto powers of the appointed legislative council, of the governor, and, ultimately, of authorities in Great Britain. Because the members of the council held office for life, were granted huge tracts of land, and were even eligible for titles, they were clearly meant to become the nucleus of a colonial aristocracy. In Upper Canada, one-seventh of the land in every township was designated as Crown Reserves to ensure that colonial authorities had a source of revenue independent of grants from the assembly. Another one-seventh of the land was reserved for "the Support and Maintenance of a Protestant Clergy," presumably the "established" Church of England, to add strength to the monarchical principle and make the clergy less reliant on their own congregations.

Loyalty became a significant issue in the frontier colony of Upper Canada, where immigration from the United States helped to boost the population to nearly eighty thousand by 1812. Part of the general westward movement of settlers, it was encouraged by John Graves Simcoe, the colony's first lieutenant governor, who believed that Americans would become loyal subjects once they experienced the superiority of British political institutions. Simcoe offered "late Loyalists" the same generous terms that Loyalists received, and the great land rush was on. An enlightened administrator, Simcoe introduced legislation designed to abolish slavery gradually in Upper Canada, but his ambitious plans for schools and a university failed to materialize. He also inaugurated a network of military roads that were intended to move troops expeditiously in wartime but proved their value as convenient highways for immigrants. Opposition to the governor and his land-rich clique was voiced in the assembly, relocated in 1793 from Newark to York (renamed Toronto in 1834), but most settlers were too busy getting established to mount a coherent movement for reform (Image 4.4).

Image 4.4. York, 1804, by Elizabeth Francis Hale. (Courtesy of Library and Archives Canada/C-40134)

Conditions were different in Lower Canada. When governors used patronage to sustain the power of the English-speaking elite, they were soon confronted with an organized Canadien opposition in the assembly. One of the most significant developments in this period was the emergence of a francophone middle class that included lawyers, journalists, and clerks educated in new classical colleges, staffed by priests fleeing the excesses of the French Revolution. Frustrated by their lack of power, leaders of this new middle class became more nationalistic in their rhetoric, and exerted their rights as British subjects to pursue their goals. Through the Parti canadien, established in 1805, they focused on the assembly as a forum for protecting their language, religion, and laws, and they voiced their opinions in *Le Canadien*, the first newspaper to express francophone political interests. In 1810 Governor James Craig responded to popular opposition by dissolving the assembly for the second time in as many years and imprisoning the editors of *Le Canadien*. Since war with the United States seemed a certainty, British authorities moved quickly to replace him with a more conciliatory administrator.

THE WAR OF 1812

In 1812 demands for political reform in Lower Canada were temporarily suspended when war was declared between Great Britain and the United States.[11] The issues leading to war – Aboriginal policy on the frontier and the rights of neutral shipping on the high seas – directly affected the British North American colonies, and they were the easiest target for an American attack on the former mother country. Since so many people living in Upper Canada had recently emigrated from the United States, some American military leaders agreed with their former president, Thomas Jefferson, that capturing the colony would be a "mere matter of marching." Many Upper Canadians also held this view and tried to avoid militia duty in what seemed like a lost cause.

To demonstrate that Britain could win a war with the United States, Major General Isaac Brock, who commanded British troops in Upper Canada, authorized an assault on Michilimackinac soon after war was declared. Success in this engagement on the western frontier brought the Aboriginal peoples in the Ohio Valley, led by the Shawnee chief Tecumseh, into an alliance with the British. Their primary goal was to secure the land lost in the decades-long struggle against the Americans invading their territory. With the help of his Aboriginal allies, Brock seized Detroit and then confronted an American army crossing the Niagara River. Brock was killed in the battle of Queenston Heights on 13 October 1812, but his army carried the day, taking nine hundred Americans prisoners.

The Americans regrouped. In the spring of 1813 they occupied York and torched its legislative buildings, but they failed to capture Kingston and thereby gain control of Lake Ontario. Later in the year, Commodore Oliver Perry defeated the British fleet on Lake Erie at the Battle of Put-in-Bay, forcing the British to abandon Detroit. In October 1813 an American army defeated British forces under Brock's successor, Colonel Henry Proctor, at Moraviantown near present-day Chatham, Ontario. Tecumseh died in the battle and his forces were scattered. Later that fall, an American army en route to Montreal was defeated in battles at Châteauguay and Chrysler's Farm, and forced to retreat. The Americans continued to range freely in the Niagara peninsula, setting fire to Newark (Niagara-on-the-Lake) before departing in December 1813.

As in the American Revolutionary War, the Atlantic colonies were spared invading armies during the War of 1812, but they profited greatly from the general wartime demand for timber, fish, and food-stuffs. Conditions had improved enormously when Jefferson, in his efforts to prevent involvement in the Napoleonic Wars, placed an embargo on trade with belligerents in 1807. Outraged, New England merchants openly flouted the regulations by trading with Halifax, Shelburne, Saint John, and St. Andrews, which the British designated as free ports. This clever policy served its purpose of keeping the British army and navy supplied and brought unprecedented opportunities to the Maritime region. Privateering flourished, making fortunes for merchants in Halifax and St. John's who bought captured vessels at prize courts and sold them at a profit.

The war took a dramatic turn in 1814. With Emperor Napoleon exiled to Elba, Great Britain focused its attention on North America. In August British troops attacked Washington, burning the White House and other public buildings. A month later a British army occupied part of the coast of present-day Maine. These developments and Napoleon's escape from Elba brought the war to an abrupt end. By the Treaty of Ghent, signed 24 December 1814, both parties agreed to peace and the return of any captured territory. The news was slow to reach New Orleans, where a prolonged battle continued into the winter of 1815.

Two agreements signed after the war helped to establish peaceful relations between the United States and Great Britain. In 1817 the Rush-Bagot agreement limited the number of armed vessels on the Great Lakes and Lake Champlain to those required to control smuggling. In the same year agreement was reached over the disputed islands in Passamaquoddy Bay. Boundaries were further clarified by the Anglo-American Convention of 1818, in which the forty-ninth parallel was recognized as the boundary between the Lake of the Woods and the Rockies. American rights to the inshore fisheries of the Atlantic region were also restricted. Although the United States and Britain never again declared war on each other, they continued to build roads, canals, railroads, and defensive structures with military considerations in mind.

The War of 1812 is largely a footnote in British and American history books, but it left a powerful legacy in British North America. In the immediate aftermath of the war, the American invasion became the justification, especially in Upper Canada, for anti-republicanism and a rationale for treating all dissent against British institutions as treason. If there ever had been any prospect of American manifest destiny rolling across northern North America, the War of 1812 put paid to such a notion. The seeds of anti-American sentiment planted during the American Revolutionary War were nurtured by the War of 1812 to the point where the government in Upper Canada actively discouraged American immigration and even called into question the political and property rights of American-born settlers.

Following Confederation, the War of 1812 became a popular vehicle for shoring up Canadian nationalism. The brave colonial militia emerged as the hero of the piece – though evidence suggests that at least half of the Upper Canadian men called out for militia duty during the war failed to appear – and two individuals became cultural icons: Major General Isaac Brock, who died defending the British connection, and Laura Secord, who claimed to have overcome great obstacles in delivering valuable intelligence to the British commanders in June 1813. More than any war before or since, the War of 1812 was useful for highlighting Canada's multicultural accommodation, with English and French Canadians – and eventually First Nations – represented as working together to turn back the tide of American aggression.

The War of 1812 ended the effective resistance of Aboriginal peoples living in the Ohio Valley against the tide of white settlement. During negotiations leading to the Treaty of Ghent, the British tried to secure territory south of the Great Lakes exclusively for their Aboriginal allies, but the United States refused to consider such an idea. The treaty restored the boundaries that had existed before the outbreak of the hostilities, a policy that included the restoration of the land possessed by Britain's Aboriginal allies, but as the historian J. R. Miller argues, this moral obligation was "unenforceable and unenforced."[12]

FUR TRADE RIVALRIES IN THE WEST

The 1818 decision to draw a boundary along the forty-ninth parallel in the middle of North America reflected growing encroachment from all sides. South of the border settlers moved steadily westward, while north of it the fur trade created a new middle ground.

After the conquest of New France, the fur trade rivalry between the St. Lawrence and Hudson Bay intensified. British traders based in Montreal occupied French posts in the interior, and Aboriginal peoples on the Plains entered trading partnerships with whoever offered the best deals. The Blackfoot, Cree, and Assiniboine, who had acquired horses through trade with their neighbours to the south earlier in the century, were particularly eager to purchase guns to enhance their roles as hunters and warriors. In competition with each other for dominance in the fur trade, they also encouraged the competition among companies to get better prices and more conveniently located posts.

To outdistance rivals from Montreal, the Hudson's Bay Company opened its first interior post at Cumberland House in 1774. The American Revolution served as a catalyst for the Montreal traders to organize into a single company to compete more effectively. By 1804 the North West Company had absorbed other Montreal-based competitors and was going toe to toe with the Hudson's Bay Company in its efforts to gain supremacy. Competition led to the proliferation of trading posts, which by 1804 numbered more than four hundred, up from seventeen only three decades earlier.[13] The Montrealers initially had an advantage with their experienced French-Canadian voyageurs, birchbark canoes, and wintering partners, but the Baymen soon proved worthy competitors with their flat-bottomed York boats, their Scottish personnel (many of them from the Orkneys), and their own interior posts.

As the traders pushed further into the interior, they explored and mapped what to them was new territory. Hudson's Bay Company employee Samuel Hearne, travelling in 1771–72 as the only European in the company of Chipewyan guides, reached the Arctic Ocean by way of the Coppermine River. En route they met and murdered a group of Inuit, who were long-standing enemies of the Chipewyan. In 1789 Alexander Mackenzie, exploring on behalf of the North West Company, reached the Arctic Ocean along the river that bears his name, and in 1793 he reached the Pacific by an overland route. He just missed George Vancouver, who was following up the work of Captain James Cook in exploring and mapping the Pacific coast (Image 4.5).

Image 4.5. This sketch of a Nootka house with salmon hanging from the ceiling for drying was drawn by John Webster, a member of James Cook's 1778 expedition. (By permission of Dixson Library, State Library of NSW, DL PXX2)

In 1778 Cook had reached the Bering Sea in his search for the elusive Northwest Passage, but he was not the first European in the region. The Russians Vitus Bering and Aleskei Chirikov explored what is now the Alaska coast in the 1740s, leading to a brisk trade in sea-otter pelts, which were greatly treasured by Aboriginal peoples and elites in China and Europe. A growing Russian presence on the Pacific coast, in turn, prompted the Spanish to extend their influence further north. In 1774 Juan Pérez reached Haida Gwaii (renamed the Queen Charlotte Islands by the British), prompting Spain to formally claim the region. War between Great Britain and Spain was averted in 1790 with the Nootka Sound Convention, which permitted joint occupation of the Pacific coast north of San Francisco. Five years later, the Spanish withdrew from the region.

By that time, a brisk sea-otter trade, increasingly dominated by New Englanders and the British, was under way. As in other areas of North America, Aboriginal traders usually had the upper hand in transactions with Europeans, but negotiations were often accompanied by violence. In 1785 a ship's captain unleashed a cannon attack on the people living at Nootka Sound, leaving twenty people dead. Not surprisingly, Aboriginal people sought vengeance for their mistreatment. In one encounter in 1803, disarmed traders under their leader Muquinna used equipment on board the ship *Boston* to murder all but two of the twenty-seven crew members.

As beaver on the plains became scarce, the Nor'Westers began to pursue trade in the British Columbia interior. Alexander Mackenzie's exploration in the mountainous area was followed by those of David Thompson and Simon Fraser, who provided the North West Company with critical knowledge of the area's river systems. Fraser established posts across the Rockies in Carrier and Sekani territories during a journey from 1806 to 1808, and Thompson descended the Columbia River in 1811, proving that it connected to the coast.

Diseases accompanied the fur traders, but at least one pandemic arrived by a circuitous route. An outbreak of smallpox in Mexico in 1779 was carried indirectly by horses through the Plains, cutting a swath through the Assiniboine, Ojibwa, Cree, and Blackfoot, and reaching the Pacific coast in 1782. The scourge took its usual toll of more than half the population, with disastrous consequences for Aboriginal communities. During his explorations around the Strait of Juan de Fuca, Vancouver found deserted villages with human skeletons "promiscuously scattered about the beach in great numbers." It seemed, Vancouver reported, that "the environs of Port Discovery was a general cemetery for the whole surrounding country."[14]

The expanding fur trade and its consequences created havoc in the interior of the continent. As the Ojibwa of what is now northwestern Ontario gradually depleted the fur-bearing animals in the region, they were obliged to range more widely in their annual hunt. They bumped into Aboriginal peoples living on the Plains, who were also on the move. Equipped with guns and horses, the Blackfoot expanded south and west from their base in northern Saskatchewan. Initially indifferent to the fur trade, the Blackfoot nonetheless became integral to the trading networks by supplying pemmican, a mixture of dried buffalo, fat, and berries, which became the staple of diets in fur trade country.

As a result of these developments, the scale of warfare increased dramatically, taking the lives primarily of young men. The growing gender imbalance encouraged polygamy. So, too, did the fur trade itself. The work of Aboriginal women was essential to the preparation of the pelts, and more wives meant more furs for trade. Although there is little direct evidence of how the wives felt about their situation, it may well be the case, as Elizabeth Vibert has argued, that polygamy had the potential to spread the burdens of child care, the production of food and clothing, and the processing of furs.[15] In fur trade country, many Aboriginal men counted their wealth by the number of wives and horses they possessed, rather than other material possessions, and like European men, they found others to do their work if they could do so.

It is in this context that the practice of European traders taking "country wives," common since the earliest days of contact, became a singular feature of society in the Northwest. Alexander Ross, a North West Company employee, claimed to have known a voyageur who had twelve wives, fifty horses, and six running dogs, and who asserted that there was "no place where a man enjoys so much variety and freedom as in Indian Country."[16] Not all fur traders were willing to take on so many wives, but the value of such relationships included not only sex, companionship, domestic labour, children, and local knowledge, but also closer alliances with Aboriginal trading partners. From the perspective of Aboriginal women, relationships with white fur traders often promised improved material well-being, enhanced status among their own people, and in some cases partners for life.

THE MÉTIS

"Country marriages," forbidden by the Hudson's Bay Company hierarchy and by Roman Catholic missionaries who began arriving in the region in 1818, created a new people, known as "Métis" by the French and "half-breeds" by the English. They established their own communities and developed a sense of identity separate from Aboriginal and Euro-Canadian cultures. While the offspring of French fathers spoke Michif, a combination of French and Cree, those with British fathers combined Cree with the Scots dialect of the Orkneys to speak Bungi. Métis music and dance steps combined Aboriginal, French, and Scottish traditions. In the Red River area,

Métis developed their own means of transportation, carts made entirely of wood with saucer-shaped wheels to avoid getting stuck in the Prairie mud. People of mixed heritage played a central role in the fur trade economy: the sons of British employees tended to be hired as labourers at the posts; Métis men were valued as boatmen and guides. Their communities also became the major producers and distributors of pemmican.

The arrival of settlers changed everything. In 1808 Lord Selkirk, a Scottish landowner, philanthropist, and peer in the British House of Lords, purchased shares in the Hudson's Bay Company with the goal of promoting agricultural settlement in the Red River valley. Selkirk had earlier sponsored settlements in Prince Edward Island and Upper Canada in his effort to provide a new lease on life for Scottish tenants being pushed off their land. His settlement at Red River had an additional goal: to supply the Hudson's Bay Company with food that would otherwise be imported at great expense.

In 1812 thirty-five immigrants arrived in the colony, but their numbers were reduced by scurvy, and the Prairie climate defeated their attempts to grow wheat. Even more problematic was the hostility of the Nor'Westers, who viewed the settlement as a means of disrupting the company's links between Montreal and the interior. The Métis were particularly concerned about a colony established in an area where many of them made their homes. Their fears were confirmed when the colony's governor, Miles Macdonnell, issued a proclamation in January 1814 against the export of pemmican from the region, threatening both the North West Company's supplies and the income of the Métis.

Encouraged by Nor'Wester Duncan Cameron, the Métis organized into a militia under Cuthbert Grant. Violence escalated, and in June 1816 Grant's forces killed twenty colonists in a confrontation at Seven Oaks. Selkirk hired Swiss mercenaries to improve the colony's defences and charged Grant and other Métis leaders with murder, but the courts and a British-appointed commission concluded that Seven Oaks was not a premeditated Métis massacre of Selkirk settlers.

The confrontation added another reason for the Nor'Westers and the Hudson's Bay Company to abandon their ruinous competition. Pressured by the British government, the two companies merged in

1821 under the name of the Hudson's Bay Company, and its administrators immediately began consolidating operations. The Red River settlement, which had languished for nearly a decade, became home to discharged employees and, in the following decades, to retirees, who were reluctant to reintegrate into British or Canadian society.

CONCLUSION

Between 1763 and 1815 the ties linking northern North America to Great Britain were strengthened and consolidated. British and American immigrants served to Anglicize areas that were once dominated by France, while two invasions by the United States and the expansion of wartime trade bound the eastern colonies more tightly to Great Britain politically and economically. On the western frontier, the fur trade served the same purpose, bringing Aboriginal populations in Hudson's Bay Company territory more fully into the British orbit of commerce and culture. These trends would continue until the 1840s, when the British Empire experienced yet another dramatic transformation that would have major repercussions for British North America.

5

Transatlantic Communities, 1815–1849

It was an *annus horribilis* in Montreal. On 25 April 1849, an angry mob descended on the legislature, forcing politicians to flee and burning the building to the ground. The rioting continued for a week before being quelled by British troops stationed in the city. Over the summer, prominent Montreal merchants, despairing of their well-being in the era of British free trade, discussed various remedies for their plight. In October they issued a manifesto calling for annexation to the United States. While many European nations had experienced uprisings the previous year and were no strangers to manifestos – 1848 was, after all, the year of the *Communist Manifesto* – the Canadian version of public protest was distinctly odd. The perpetrators were mostly conservatives ("Tories" in the vocabulary of the day), rather than liberals and radicals. Clearly, much had changed since the War of 1812.[1]

POSTWAR IMMIGRATION

Between 1815 and 1850 nearly a million people emigrated from Great Britain to British North America. Phillip Buckner has argued that the Anglicization of the northern half of North America in this period, owing largely to immigration from Great Britain, is one of the most significant developments in the history of the British Empire.[2] It is, without question, a major chapter in the history of Canada. The tide of immigration receded for a time in the 1850s, but by then the British character of much of settler society had been set. The Irish, who had been incorporated into Great Britain by the Act of Union in 1801, made up 25 percent of a British North American population approaching 2.5 million, while those identified as English and Welsh accounted for about 20 percent, and the Scottish nearly 16 percent.

Pushed out of their homeland by political oppression and periodic famines, at least 450,000 Irish emigrants landed in British North American ports between 1825 and 1845. About one-third of them moved to the United States, but 300,000 more arrived in the wake of the Great Famine that descended on Ireland in 1845. In Newfoundland Catholics predominated among the nearly half of the population that claimed Irish origins. Unlike the Maritime colonies, where Irish Protestants and Catholics were represented in nearly equal numbers, Upper Canada/Canada West attracted a majority of Irish Protestants. Irish Catholics were a significant component of the 50,000 immigrants who settled in Lower Canada/Canada East, where, by the mid-nineteenth century, more than half the people living in Montreal and one-third in Quebec City claimed British heritage.

The Scots also took root throughout British North America. At 45 and 33 percent, respectively, Prince Edward Island and Nova Scotia had the highest proportions of people claiming Scottish origins, and Scots were the overwhelming majority of the immigrants in the territories occupied by the Hudson's Bay Company. Like the Irish, they brought their religious values with them, including the Roman Catholic traditions of the Highlanders and the Presbyterian beliefs that prevailed in the Lowlands. Protestant Scots were represented in the merchant class in numbers well above their proportion of the population, and they were often found in the ranks of those founding educational institutions.

Following the War of 1812, the British colonies no longer attracted many immigrants from the United States, which had its own frontier to conquer. African Americans were an exception. As was the case during the American Revolutionary War, the British offered freedom to slaves who deserted their masters to support the British cause in the War of 1812, and about two thousand black refugees settled in Nova Scotia and New Brunswick in 1815. Upper Canada, where Simcoe had introduced an act for the gradual abolition of slavery in 1793, was the most popular destination for free blacks and refugee slaves, but all the British colonies became safe havens after the British Parliament passed legislation in 1833 formally abolishing slavery throughout the empire. The passage in 1850 of the Fugitive Slave Act, which required states where slavery had been abolished to return runaway slaves, increased the flow of African American immigration. Canada West served as the principal terminus for the "underground railroad," the term used to describe the network of sympathizers who provided assistance to those seeking to escape the long arm of slavery.[3]

By the mid-nineteenth century, fewer than twenty-five thousand Aboriginal people could be found in the eastern colonies. Most of them lived a precarious existence on reserves near immigrant communities or in remote locations. For Newfoundland's Beothuk, who had retreated into the interior in response to European settlement, survival proved impossible. The last Beothuk, a young woman named Shanawdithit, died in 1829 (Image 5.1). The more than one hundred thousand Aboriginal people living in the west fared better, but settler society was edging ever closer, especially on the Pacific coast, where American, British, and Russian interests competed for ascendancy.

The United States continued to eye British North America as a potential area for expansion. In this context it became important to settle boundary disputes, which might serve as a pretext for annexation. The Webster-Ashburton Treaty fixed the border between New Brunswick and Maine and in the Great Lakes area in 1842. Two years later, a noisy election in which presidential candidate James Polk threatened to push the American boundary to Alaska – his slogan was "Fifty-four forty or fight" – prompted the British government to return to the negotiating table. In 1846 the Oregon Treaty drew a boundary to the Pacific coast, and in 1849 Vancouver Island was declared a Crown colony with its capital at Victoria. A gold rush erupted in California the same year, drawing immigrants from all over the world. Within a decade, gold was also discovered on the Fraser and Thompson rivers. Prospectors rushed in. Again British authorities moved quickly to assert control, establishing in 1858 a colony clearly demarcated as "British Columbia" with its capital located at New Westminster. The message could not have been clearer.

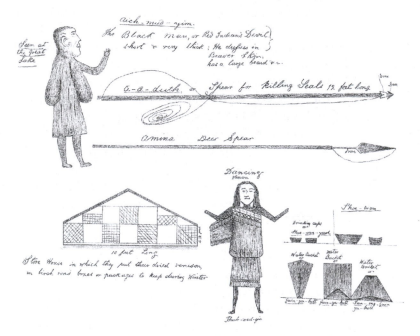

Image 5.1. In the last year of her life Shanawdithit lived in the home of philanthropist William Epps Cormack, where she drew sketches depicting Beothuk culture. This drawing shows a devil clad in beaver skin, spears for killing seals and deer, a dancing woman, and a variety of containers. (By permission of Library and Archives Canada/C-028544)

Although the far north of the continent remained beyond regular contact with the wider world, it continued to lure explorers seeking the elusive Northwest Passage. The most determined was Sir John Franklin, who led three expeditions (1819, 1825, and 1845) into Arctic regions and, when he went missing, inspired thirty rescue missions between 1847 and 1859. In the course of searching for Franklin, a team led by Robert McClure actually crossed the Arctic on foot. It was not until the 1980s that researchers from the University of Alberta found the remains of several of Franklin's unfortunate crew members, who had died of scurvy, lead poisoning, and exposure, and who probably resorted to cannibalism in a desperate effort to survive.[4]

While land, waged labour, fortune, and adventure beckoned immigrants to British North America, their experiences were often tragic. Many of them never reached their destination, dying en route in what were sometimes little more than coffin ships. For those who made it across the ocean with enough capital to buy land, the struggle had just begun. Establishing a functional farm on the frontier was a daunting challenge even for those who were accustomed to an agrarian way of life, which was not always the case. Many immigrants were soldiers discharged from military service and urban labourers down on their luck. They might have liked the idea of becoming members of the rural gentry or yeoman farmers, but the reality often broke their backs and their spirits.[5]

Social tension accompanied the immigrants, who were rivals for land, jobs, and status. As the destination of the majority of immigrants in this period, Canada West was riddled with tensions between earlier settlers, many of them originally from the United States, and newcomers from Great Britain. In the Ottawa River valley, gangs of Irish and Canadien labourers battled for forestry jobs in the so-called Shiners' War in the 1830s and 1840s. The Irish hired to build canals in Upper Canada/Canada West not only engaged in strikes when their employers tried to take advantage of them but also competed with each other, often violently, for poorly paid construction work. In Lower Canada, where the St. Lawrence served as a conduit for most immigrants, Canadiens accused the British of trying to extinguish them through diseases brought by the newcomers. More than five thousand people in Lower Canada died in a cholera epidemic that arrived with the ships in the spring of 1832. An immigrant station was established that year at Grosse Île, an island in the St. Lawrence near Quebec City, but it did little to prevent another outbreak of cholera, which claimed 2,358 Lower Canadians in 1834.

THE COMMERCIAL ECONOMY

With the arrival of so many people, colonial economies grew dramatically. The Industrial Revolution, which restructured the British economy and helped to account for massive outmigration after 1815, increased the demand for colonial staples – fish, fur, minerals, timber, and wheat – which were given preference in British markets under the mercantile system. Britain's decision to adopt a policy of free trade in 1846 caused anxiety among colonial producers, but they managed to weather the crisis and benefitted from the expansion of global trade in the 1850s and 1860s.

No other British North American jurisdiction was as dependent on a single staple as Newfoundland. From 1815 to 1914 the colony produced on average a million hundredweight of salt cod a year, most of it exported to markets in southern Europe, Brazil, and the British West Indies. To this was added a profitable trade in sealskins and seal oil – the latter used for lighting and lubricants. Sealing was a dangerous occupation, but at its height in the 1850s, it employed fourteen thousand "ice hunters" and accounted for nearly a quarter of the colony's exports by value.

The demand for timber locally and in the British market stimulated a robust forest industry throughout eastern British North America. During the winter months, men worked in the woods cutting logs, which they drove each spring down swollen rivers to waiting sawmills. Farmers supplemented their income by producing staves, hoops, and barrels, but shipbuilding, financed by British and colonial capitalists, emerged as the most important value-added component of the forest industry. Saint John was the largest shipbuilding centre in the Maritimes, where almost every harbour worthy of the name produced vessels. Quebec City, which had seven shipyards employing 1,338 people in 1851, was the major shipbuilding port in the Canadas. In addition to building and selling vessels, colonials participated in the rapid expansion of the carrying trade, sailing the seven seas with whatever cargoes were on offer.

More than half of the people in the eastern colonies at midcentury lived on mixed farms, producing meat, grains, and vegetables for their own and local consumption. Surpluses found a ready market in nearby towns and beyond. In the Maritimes, potatoes, along with dried fish, filled the holds of ships bound for the West Indies. Upper Canada emerged as the breadbasket of British North America, with wheat exports accounting for nearly half of the cash income on many farms by 1850. In Lower Canada soil exhaustion and the reduced size of seigneurial holdings forced farmers to switch from wheat to mixed crops and livestock. In rural areas of Canada East, there were almost as many agricultural labourers as farmers in 1851, testimony to the fact that the seigneurial system could no longer sustain the growing rural population.

After 1821, the Hudson's Bay Company held a virtual monopoly in the British North American fur trade. Company officials streamlined operations in the old Northwest and expanded their trading activities on the Pacific coast and in Labrador. While trade thinned the ranks of fur-bearing animals, no species was as endangered as the plains buffalo. A growing demand in the United States for buffalo hides, used to make sturdy leather belts for power transmission in factory machinery, increased the income of Aboriginal peoples involved in the trade, but the mass slaughter of these giants of the plains would lead to their near extinction by the 1870s, precipitating a major crisis in food supply.

The exploitation of British North America's mineral wealth got off to a promising start with efforts to provide the coal resources necessary to meet the growing industrial demand. In 1826 the London-based General Mining Association began developing Nova Scotia's coal resources, over which it had a monopoly. The company brought skilled British miners to the coalfields of Cape Breton and Pictou County and introduced modern technology, including steam-driven machinery, vessels, and even an early railway. On the Pacific coast, the Hudson's Bay Company began exploiting coal resources near Nanaimo in 1852, employing both Scottish and Aboriginal labourers.

In the first half of the nineteenth century, commercial activity expanded to serve the growing population. Fortunes were made in such consumer industries as brewing, distilling, and milling, and shopkeepers in communities large and small sold local and imported commodities. Artisans made shoes, clothing, carriages, saddles, and other consumer products, while the services of blacksmiths, carters, and household servants were much in demand everywhere. The founding of banking institutions testifies to the wealth that was gradually accumulating in the colonies. In the wake of the War of 1812, the Bank of Montreal (1817), the Bank of New Brunswick (1820), the Bank of Upper Canada (1821), and the Halifax Banking Company (1825) began operations.

Although commerce in staples and other commodities shaped colonial economies, the seasonal rhythms of household production determined most people's general well-being. Preindustrial rural families produced most of their own food, clothing, and shelter,

Image 5.2. Clearing the town plot: Stanley, New Brunswick, 1834, by W. P. McKay. Scenes such as this one were common on the British North American settlement frontier. In their haste to establish themselves, immigrants cut down trees and burned the stumps, a process that often led to runaway fires. One of the most destructive forest fires occurred in 1825 along the Miramichi River in New Brunswick, where flames consumed more than 2 million hectares of land and took the lives of 160 people and countless animals. (By permission of Library and Archives Canada/ C-000017)

selling any surpluses of their labour to purchase imports such as tea, spices, and metal products. What was most important was that everyone, including young children, work together to support the family economy (Image 5.2). Families in which both parents lived for the mother's entire childbearing years were large, averaging seven or eight children. Infant mortality was high, with one in five children dying in the first year of life; one in twenty births resulted in the death of the mother. As a result of these realities and the likelihood of death from infections, diseases, malnutrition, and accidents, men and women in colonial British North America had an average life expectancy of about fifty years, ten years longer if they managed to survive to the age of twenty.

In the first half of the nineteenth century, fewer than one in five British North Americans lived in communities of a thousand people or more. The largest urban centres at midcentury were Montreal (fifty-seven thousand) and Quebec City (forty-two thousand).

Toronto, Saint John, and Halifax each boasted about thirty thousand people. Benefitting from a ready supply of power from the Lachine Canal and cheap labour from hard-pressed rural seigneuries, Montreal emerged as a major industrial and processing centre and served as a nexus of the trade in wheat and timber from Upper Canada/Canada West, which by 1850 was the most populous and, arguably, the most dynamic of all the British colonies.

Town and country in British North America were bound together by commercial exchange, which extended to the frontiers of settlement. In the Canadas, Montreal and Toronto were emerging as the focus for road, water, and eventually rail transportation networks to their economic hinterlands. In the Atlantic region, year-round ocean communication forced Halifax, Saint John, Charlottetown, and St. John's to compete with Boston, New York, Liverpool, and London for economic control over the regional economy. Victoria's closest links were by sea with San Francisco, which grew rapidly following the California gold rush. As the American frontier of settlement moved steadily westward, inhabitants of the Red River colony also felt the influence of their southern neighbour.

SMALL WORLDS

While the colonies were developing their own unique identities in their diverse North American settings, they all quickly replicated the class, ethnic, gender, and racial hierarchies that prevailed throughout the North Atlantic world. They also proved ingenious in adapting the pecking order to local conditions.

British North America never developed the hereditary aristocracy that the framers of the Constitutional Act of 1791 had envisioned, but tight little cliques of merchants, professionals, and politicians dominated every aspect of colonial life. As in most of the North Atlantic world, elite women, through marriage, helped to consolidate and perpetuate power within their narrow circles and played central roles in charitable institutions that ministered to the poor. Individual members of the colonial elite might experience failure, but as a group they were becoming more powerful. In his research on Hamilton, Canada West, in the mid-nineteenth century, Michael Katz calculated that 10 percent of the adult men dominated the economic, political, and social life of the city in the 1850s.[6]

A class of labourers survived by performing manual work, often on a seasonal basis. For some British North Americans, wage labour was only a stage in their life cycle, a chance to earn a little money before returning to the family farm or setting up in business, but for a growing number it was a lifetime condition. Most skilled labourers, such as printers and ship pilots, earned a living wage; unskilled labourers were poorly paid and more vulnerable to cycles of boom and bust, the rhythms of the seasons, and payment in kind rather than cash. Both the fisheries and the timber trade nurtured the "truck system" in which merchants provided men with the equipment and provisions they needed for the season's work in return for the product of their labour. Many workers never saw their wages and were perpetually bound to their merchant-supplier by a web of debt. The same system often prevailed in farming communities, where merchants held mortgages on indebted farms. In Lower Canada and Prince Edward Island, rents to seigneurs and proprietors were notoriously in arrears, and tenants could be – though they rarely were – forcibly ejected from their lands.

In this period, poverty and the problems associated with it – malnutrition, disease, and early death – seemed to be everywhere. Poverty arrived on immigrant ships, was rampant on most Aboriginal reserves, and produced a growing number of beggars, who trudged from door to door seeking assistance. Crop failures could reduce a farm family to near starvation even when they had the support of neighbours and kin. Without such support, the situation could be fatal. Cases of death from hunger and exposure were reported in colonial newspapers, but the daily grind of poverty often escaped public attention and invariably strained the capacity of mutual aid societies, charitable organizations, and the limited government assistance available to deal with it.

Class differences were compounded by gender norms that undermined the agency of women. Under British common law, which prevailed outside of Lower Canada, men were recognized as the heads of their households, with wives and children under their control. The husband's right to dispose of the family property was limited only by a widow's legal claim to one-third of it, and most men willed their property to a son or other male relative. After marriage in Lower Canada, where the Custom of Paris prevailed, all wealth became the couple's joint property but was administered by the husband. The surviving widow had a dower right to half of the estate, while the other half was divided equally among the children.

In both legal regimes a woman could insist on a contract that allowed her to control the property that she brought to the marriage, and for women who ran their own businesses, *sole femme* status was an option, but few asserted their independence in these ways. Love and mutual respect often restrained men's powers over their wives, but relationships were only as companionate as the husbands allowed.[7] Since a husband had the right to discipline his wife and children, domestic violence was difficult to control. Divorces were almost impossible to obtain, frowned upon by the church and state as a threat to social stability. If a woman left her husband, she received no property settlement, and custody of the children invariably went to the father.

As in most patriarchal systems, women's sexuality and reproductive powers were carefully controlled. Girls and women were supervised within families, while pressure from church, state, and community encouraged strict conformity to acceptable sexual behaviour. In both Canadien and British cultures, a socially questionable marriage – a widow who married too soon after her husband's death, a couple too unequal in age or of different religious persuasions – might result in a *charivari*, a noisy gathering that sometimes resulted in a violent assault against the offending couple. Young women who became pregnant outside marriage, especially those without family to share the burden of their shame or to help them raise a child, sometimes resorted to infanticide. Although anyone convicted of infanticide, abortion, rape, or homosexuality was subject to the death penalty, lighter sentences for these crimes were usually imposed. Domestic service and prostitution were often the only options for poor women, and both careers flourished in port cities, especially those with a substantial military presence.

By the mid-nineteenth century, humanitarian sentiment was sweeping across the North Atlantic world, but it failed to check the everyday racism that prevailed in the colonies. A Select Committee on Aboriginals reporting to the British House of Commons in 1837 condemned "the vast load of crime" inflicted on indigenous peoples in the colonies and urged the "the due observation of justice and the protection of their Rights," but something got lost in the execution of this worthy goal.[8] Following the committee's report, responsibility for Aboriginal policy was gradually transferred from British to colonial governments, which were even more reluctant than the British Parliament to spend public money on those in need. In Canada West treaties arranged by W. B. Robinson with the Ojibwa in the upper Great Lakes region in 1850 included several new provisions, among them the rights to royalties on any minerals found on their reserves, but little was done to enforce such provisions.

Racialized differences became a defining feature of the Red River colony, which by 1850 had an estimated population of five thousand, a majority of them of mixed ethnic heritage. Identified by their language and religion, the French-speaking Métis tended to keep to themselves, while the children of English-speaking traders and Aboriginal women saw themselves as superior to their French-speaking equivalents and sought respectability on European terms. Marriage practices reflected the careful calibration of race that infected Red River society. By the 1820s, most fur traders preferred women who had white fathers over Aboriginal women when taking country wives. George Simpson, the highest-ranking official in the Hudson's Bay Company, had relationships with several country wives until he married his Scottish cousin in 1829. Margaret Taylor, his country wife at the time, learned that she and their two children would be "turned off" only when Frances Simpson arrived in Red River along with her pianoforte.[9]

Notwithstanding strong antislavery sentiment in the colonies, people with black skin faced discrimination wherever they went. Black men who owned land could vote in British North America, but they complained in Nova Scotia that they could not do so without being intimidated. Segregated schools were officially sanctioned in Canada West in 1850, and operated unofficially elsewhere. In Chatham four hundred people gathered in August 1849 to protest against a proposed black settlement in the area. The protesters then passed a resolution stating: "That in the opinion of this meeting, it would be unconstitutional, impolitic and unjust government to sell large portions of the public domain in SETTLED PARTS of this province, to foreigners, the more so, when such persons belong to a different branch of the human family, and are BLACK."¹⁰

Like racism, religious prejudice hung like a dark cloud over all relationships in British North America. The laws preventing Roman Catholics from voting, acquiring land, and worshiping in public had been abolished in the colonies before Great Britain removed restrictions on the civil rights of Roman Catholics throughout the empire in 1829, but religious hatreds intensified with the arrival of Irish immigrants. In the 1830s the Orange Order, devoted to looking after its own members and maintaining Protestant ascendancy over Roman Catholics, took root in all of the colonies. Orangemen favoured Protestants over Catholics for jobs and political office and escalated the violence that punctuated elections and annual celebrations designed to keep religious antagonism alive.

Roman Catholics, meanwhile, took advantage of official toleration to advance their own power in a society controlled by Protestants. The new authority of the Roman Catholic Church was most obvious in Lower Canada/Canada East, where the return of the Jesuit Order in the 1840s led to the expansion of clerical influence and an assertion of papal power, a doctrine known as ultramontanism. Under Ignace Bourget, Bishop of Montreal from 1840 to 1876, the Roman Catholic hierarchy insinuated itself into colonial politics to blunt the forces of liberalism and to restrict the role of the secular state in matters relating to law, education, and social welfare. Religious feeling ran so high in Montreal that troops were called out in 1853 to deal with a primarily Irish Catholic mob that descended on the hall where a celebrated anti-papal Italian patriot, Alessandro Gavazzi, was giving a lecture. Ten people were killed in the confrontation and many more injured.

In every colony, Church of England clergy tried to claim exclusive rights to grants for higher education, to the conducting of marriages, and, in Upper Canada, to revenues from the sale of clergy reserves. Numbers, however, were not on their side. As elsewhere in North America, British North Americans were increasingly attracted to evangelical faiths, which emphasized individual piety, personal "conversion," and separation of church and state. Such views defied conservative values advanced by those of Roman Catholic and Church of England persuasion, and paralleled the

Image 5.3. Methodist camp meeting, 1859, Grimsby, Canada East. Itinerant Methodist preachers held outdoor meetings in rustic settings such as this one in an effort to attract new converts. (Courtesy of Archives of the United Church of Canada, Toronto/90.162P/2019N)

secular demand for greater personal freedom and democratic consent. The Methodist and Baptist churches grew more rapidly than other evangelical denominations in the colonies, but Quakers, Lutherans, Congregationalists, and a host of smaller sects all had their followings. Whatever their practices, Christian churches competed with each other for adherents and played a central role in shaping the intellectual, social, and political life of British North Americans (Image 5.3).

EVOLVING POLITICAL CULTURES

Political institutions became a major focus for reform in British North America. It could hardly be otherwise. When the United States and France turned the world upside down by investing power in "the people" rather than in divinely sanctioned, hereditary monarchs, they unleashed a political genie that could not be put back in the bottle. British North Americans had a wide range of reform options to draw upon, including an evolving parliamentary democracy in Great Britain, a full-fledged republican system in the United States and France, and demands for a socialist alternative that informed some of the protests that rocked European capitals in 1848. For those who lamented the erosion of traditional political institutions, Europe also offered models. Conservatism, as represented in monarchical and aristocratic power, was still a force to be reckoned with in Great Britain, and the papacy, emerging from a century of retreat, threatened Roman Catholics who dared to embraced liberalism or socialism with excommunication.[11]

With plenty of grievances to fuel political unrest, all of the eastern colonies of British North America moved along the continuum from imperial dependency to responsible government between 1815 and 1855. Responsible government refers to a political system in which the executive council (cabinet) is drawn from the majority party in the elected assembly and requires support of the assembly to remain in office. It is the political apparatus that, with some modification, exists in Canada today. Although it was a genuine reversal of the hierarchy of power that had previously prevailed, responsible government was not entirely a democratic triumph. Only a relatively small number of privileged men emerged as the power brokers under responsible government, which was also a half measure in another sense. The British Parliament continued to legislate on defence, foreign policy, and constitutional amendment, and could reject colonial legislation that contravened imperial policy.

In retrospect, there is an air of inevitability about how colonial political systems evolved, but other options, most notably annexation to the United States, were not out of the question. Few imagined that the colonies, singly or together, could go it alone. Self-government within the British Empire prevailed because so many colonial citizens came from the old country and Great Britain was a global power with much to offer in economic and military terms. Such a governing system was not bestowed on just any colony. At the same time democratic procedures were being strengthened in northern North America, the British West Indies lost their elected assemblies, to be governed much as Quebec had been in the three decades after the conquest. Only settler societies comprised of white British stock could be trusted to govern themselves.

Because Upper and Lower Canada erupted in rebellion in 1837–38, they receive the most attention from historians, but each colony produced its own variation on the theme of political reform. Everywhere, opposition became a struggle between disaffected elements in the elected assembly and the appointed governor and his councils, who in turn were often backed by the Colonial Office in London. The major issue was always access to power, but the debates usually revolved around the control of the public purse and the right to dispense patronage – political appointments, Crown land grants, and government contracts – which was monopolized by a small group of government officials and wealthy merchants. Inevitably, class, ethnic, and religious identities complicated what were often muddled processes at the best of times, and a roller coaster of economic upheavals – agricultural crises, failures in the fisheries, and the adoption of free trade – added to the tensions.

For the disenfranchised, political agency in this period was difficult but not impossible. Aboriginal leaders repeatedly petitioned legislatures for land and redress and travelled to London to present their demands at the seat of empire. Excluded from voting and holding political office, women signed petitions on their own behalf and for reforms of various kinds, and a few were inspired to make larger claims for women's rights as defined by the Declaration of Sentiments adopted by reformers in Seneca Falls, New York, in 1848. Believing themselves to be victims of a less democratic age, tenant farmers sometimes resorted to violence in their efforts to shake off the shackles of aristocratic land regimes. Indeed, most politicians both before and after the introduction of responsible government had their hands full keeping a lid on the noisy reform impulse that swept across the North Atlantic world in the nineteenth century.

REBELLIONS IN THE CANADAS

Political tensions ran deepest in Lower Canada, where the exclusion of the Canadien middle class from power and lingering resentment from the conquest were compounded by the agricultural crisis on the seigneuries. Historians debate whether the rebellion in Lower Canada was democratic or nationalist in its thrust, but the rhetoric suggests that it was a little of both.[12] In Upper Canada, which absorbed the majority of the immigrants in this period, the ideological lines were more clearly drawn. Social tensions ran high between old and new settlers, but most reformers agreed that fundamental political rights enjoyed in Great Britain were being denied in the colonies. The only question was whether radical or moderate reformers would shape the outcome.

In Lower Canada, the Parti canadien, led by lawyer and seigneur Louis-Joseph Papineau, spearheaded the demand for reducing the power of the Château Clique that hovered around the governor at his residence, the Château St.-Louis, in Quebec City. Ethnic and class tensions smoldered as the Parti canadien balked at mercantile proposals for state-funded canal construction on the St. Lawrence and demanded grants of new seigneuries before they would approve road-building expenditures for immigrant communities in the Eastern Townships. In 1822 Montreal merchants and their imperial allies attempted to reduce the influence of the Canadien-dominated assembly by uniting Upper and Lower Canada, but the Parti canadien allied with the Roman Catholic Church managed to scuttle the scheme.

The Parti canadien won elections handily, but the refusal of governors to respond to the assembly's demands prompted a radical turn. In 1826 the Parti canadien changed its name to Parti patriote and began promoting policies that had inspired revolutionaries in France and the United States. The list of grievances grew steadily. Early in 1834 the Patriotes introduced in the assembly ninety-two resolutions that demanded, among other things, an executive council chosen by the assembly, an elected legislative council, and the assembly's approval of government appointments and salaries. The resolutions carried a veiled threat that a declaration of independence might result if Britain did not accept the proposals. While moderates retreated from the Parti patriote, anglophone radicals, such as Dr. Edmund O'Callaghan and Dr. Wolfred Nelson, won assembly seats in the 1834 election under the Patriote banner. The legislative deadlock only intensified. In an effort to bring the assembly to heel, Colonial Secretary Lord John Russell issued ten resolutions in March 1837, which rejected the call for elected councils and authorized the new governor, Lord Gosford, to appropriate provincial revenue without the approval of the assembly. Backed into a corner, the Parti patriote resolved to overthrow British rule through a campaign of civil disobedience and, if necessary, by force.

Over the summer of 1837 paramilitary groups from both sides – the loyalist Doric Club and the Fils de la liberté – came to blows, and the situation worsened when Lord Gosford dismissed the assembly for refusing to support long-term funding for the salaries of government appointees. The Patriote central committee responded with a call for a constitutional convention in December 1837, to be preceded by an economic boycott, rallies, and petitions. On 6 November, a clash between rival factions became Gosford's pretext to arrest Patriote leaders and call in troops from the other British American colonies to suppress the protest movement. Papineau fled to the United States; other Patriote leaders took up arms.

On 23 November, a mainly habitant Patriote army under Wolfred Nelson defeated British troops at St. Denis on the Richelieu River, but two days later government forces overwhelmed the Patriotes, who had regrouped at St. Charles. Over the next few weeks British troops and their supporters plundered and burned St. Denis and the Patriote strongholds of St. Eustache and St. Benoît, resulting in scores of deaths. Martial law was declared and more Patriote leaders fled across the border, where they regrouped with the support of sympathetic Americans. In November 1838 they invaded Lower Canada, gathering about four thousand supporters as they advanced toward Montreal. No match for the British troops, they were easily defeated. The government arrested 850 Patriotes: 12 of them were hanged, 58 deported to Australian penal colonies, and 2 banished (Image 5.4).

In Upper Canada the Reform Party was less cohesive, but it confronted an equally stubborn clique, popularly known as the Family Compact. Issues relating to land became a central focus of the reform movement in Upper Canada. As major beneficiaries of their control over settlement, the Family Compact resisted demands for land reforms, secularization of clergy reserves (or at least their distribution among all religious denominations), and greater power

Image 5.4. *The Insurgents at Beauharnois, Lower Canada,* 1838, by Katherine Jane Ellis. The artist and her family were held hostage by the rebels in November 1838 until British troops arrived to free them. (Courtesy of Library and Archives Canada/C-013392)

for the elected assembly. Reformers also united around the defence of the civil rights of Upper Canada's American-born population, for whom ownership of land and voting qualifications were called into question until the matter was finally settled in their favour by the British government in 1828. In assembly elections, the oligarchy could count on significant support from British immigrants against the allegedly pro-American Reformers and also found allies in the Orange Order and the Roman Catholic hierarchy.

Upper Canadian reformers were deeply divided. The moderates found their voice in the persons of Dr. William Baldwin, a scion of the Irish Protestant gentry, and his son Robert, who were prepared to accept an appointed executive council as long as the members had the support of a majority in the elected assembly. The radicals, led by Scottish-born newspaperman William Lyon Mackenzie, went further, demanding that the elective principle be followed for all government positions including the executive council. In contrast to Lower Canada, the reformers in Upper Canada periodically lost control of the assembly, which meant that elections were hotly contested, and none more so than the election of 1836. Claiming that Reformers supported annexation to the United States, Governor Francis Bond Head manipulated voting procedures and condoned intimidation at the polls by gangs of Orangemen. The Reformers cried foul but were virtually shut out, winning only seventeen seats in the sixty-three-member assembly. With the moderates eclipsed by Head's actions, Mackenzie created a constitution for Upper Canada modelled on that of the United States and rallied men who were convinced that a militant uprising was their only option.

Their rebellion was a fiasco. Developments in Lower Canada prompted Mackenzie's followers in Toronto to push the date for the assault on the capital ahead to 4 December. Since news of the change of date failed to reach all the rebels, their ranks were thin and thinned even more when they learned that Governor Head had quickly assembled fifteen hundred volunteers. Mackenzie's force of about four hundred men was easily dispersed. When word of rebellion in Toronto reached the London District, Dr. Charles Duncombe hurriedly organized local militants to make a stand, but pro-government volunteers, better armed than their opponents, carried the day, as they did in other areas of the colony where people took up arms.

The Upper Canadian rebellion of 1837 resulted in 885 arrests, nearly half of them in the areas around Toronto and London. Most of those arrested were established farmers or tradesmen, considerably older than the usual age for rebels. They were also more likely to trace their origins to the United States than to Great Britain. Two men were hanged for their part in the rebellion: Samuel Lount, a Pennsylvania-born farmer and blacksmith, and Peter Matthews, also a farmer, who was the son of a Loyalist and veteran on the British side of the War of 1812.

Mackenzie and other rebel leaders fled to the United States, where they regrouped with the help of sympathetic Americans and their Lower Canadian counterparts to conduct raids across the border. A combination of British troops, lack of popular enthusiasm, and the unwillingness of the United States to alienate Great Britain by supporting the rebels doomed their efforts. On 14 January 1838, Mackenzie was forced to withdraw from Navy Island on the Canadian side of the Niagara River, where he had proclaimed the Republic of Upper Canada. Subsequent raids were easily crushed, and harsh penalties were imposed on convicted rebels.

RESPONSIBLE GOVERNMENT

The colonies now had the attention of British authorities. In 1838 John George Lambton, Earl of Durham, was appointed governor general of British North America and charged with preparing a report on the causes of the Canadian rebellions. Heir to coal mines in Newcastle, England, he was liberal in his approach to political reform, but, like many of his countrymen, he was convinced of the superiority of British culture. After spending only a few months in the colonies, he produced a report that carried two main recommendations: the union of Lower Canada and Upper Canada and the granting of responsible government.

Durham adopted the position of Upper Canada's moderate reformers, blaming the Family Compact for the colony's slow development. While Durham felt that political reform would reduce the power of the colonial oligarchy, he was suspicious of the Canadiens, whom he judged as essentially backward in their thinking, condemning them as "a people with no literature and no history." Durham concluded that the rebellion in Lower Canada was a case of "two nations warring in the bosom of a single state," ignoring the evidence of ideological issues that crossed ethnic lines. To ensure harmony and progress, he recommended eclipsing the power of the Canadiens by uniting the Canadas and making English the official language of the new colony.

In 1840 the British Parliament acted on the first of Durham's recommendations, passing the Act of Union to create the United Province of Canada. Responsible government was rejected as too dangerous a departure, and the political structure that prevailed before the rebellions was restored. Not surprisingly, the hybrid colony was unpopular everywhere. With the eighty-four assembly seats divided equally between Canada East and Canada West, Upper Canadians feared French and Catholic domination while the Canadiens in Lower Canada were outraged by the creation of an assembly in which francophone representatives would be a minority.

After the rebellions, republicanism was discredited, but moderate reformers picked up the pieces and continued their struggle for responsible government. They were led in Canada West by Toronto lawyer Robert Baldwin and in Canada East by Louis-Hippolyte LaFontaine, a lawyer and former Patriote. Initially perceived as a traitor by many Canadiens, LaFontaine gradually gained their confidence and made accommodation with the rejuvenated Roman Catholic Church by agreeing not to curb its powers over social institutions. Although the two made strange bedfellows, the alliance garnered votes in Canada East for the Reform Party at this crucial period of its development.[13]

The Reformers battled successive governors until events in Great Britain worked in their favour. Following the adoption of free trade in 1846, imperial authorities softened their attitude toward political reform in settler colonies. When the 1848 election returned a Reform Party majority in both Canada East and Canada West, the recently appointed governor general, Lord Elgin, acting on instructions from the Colonial Office, called upon LaFontaine and Baldwin to form a ministry. Elgin understood that he was obliged to sign legislation passed in the assembly even if he did not personally support it.

Image 5.5. *The Burning of the Parliament Building in Montreal*, c. 1849. Attributed to Joseph Légaré. (© McCord Museum, Montreal, M11588)

The Tories felt betrayed by Great Britain, both politically and economically, but they had nowhere to turn. When the Lafontaine-Baldwin administration passed a bill to compensate Lower Canadians who had suffered losses in the rebellion, many of them confirmed rebels, a Tory-inspired mob in Montreal attacked the governor's carriage and torched the building where the hated legislation had been passed (Image 5.5). So despairing were some of Montreal's prominent merchants about their prospects in the era of free trade and responsible government that some of them, including a future prime minister of Canada, opted for what in some circles was considered treason – annexation to the United States.

VARIATIONS ON A THEME

By the time the united Canadas had achieved responsible government, Nova Scotia had already made history. In 1847 Nova Scotia's lieutenant governor, Sir John Harvey, was instructed by Colonial Secretary Lord Grey to choose his advisers from the party that commanded a majority in the assembly. The Reformers were victorious in an election held later that year, and in February 1848 a Liberal government under the leadership of James Boyle Uniacke became the first "responsible" administration in the British Empire. Newspaper publisher Joseph Howe, who had defended himself against a charge of libel by the ruling elite in a celebrated trial in 1835, was the articulate spokesman for political reform in Nova Scotia, but he had sufficiently offended British authorities to deny him the party leadership.

The land question was the animating force of political life on Prince Edward Island. By the early 1830s, landlords still controlled about 90 percent of the colony's farmland, and 65 percent of the Island's thirty-three thousand inhabitants were either tenants or squatters. In 1831 William Cooper, a former land agent for absentee proprietor Lord James Townsend, won a hard-fought election for a seat in the Island legislature on a platform of "Our country's freedom and farmers' rights." He became leader of the Escheat Movement, which won an overwhelming victory in the 1838 election. When Cooper travelled to London to plead his case for a general escheat of the proprietary grants, he was refused even a hearing from Colonial Secretary Lord John Russell. Thereafter, reform on the Island focused on responsible government, which was granted in 1851.

New Brunswick was the quintessential "timber colony," and revenues from the sale, leasing, and licensing of Crown lands, spent at the lieutenant governor's prerogative, became the object of the assembly's reform efforts. The struggle intensified with the appointment of Thomas Baillie as commissioner of Crown lands in 1824. Charged with bringing bureaucratic efficiency to the administration of Crown lands, Baillie alienated virtually everyone in the colony while chalking up vast surpluses in the colonial treasury. Charles Simonds, a powerful member of New Brunswick's timber aristocracy and president of the Bank of New Brunswick, led the assembly's efforts to gain access to Crown land revenues. Recognizing that the Reformers had the support of some of the most powerful men in New Brunswick, officials in the Colonial Office agreed to turn over the revenues from Crown land to the assembly in return for guaranteeing the salaries of government appointees. When Lieutenant Governor Archibald Campbell, a staunch upholder of the old regime, refused to accept the new political order, he was replaced by Sir John Harvey, who acquiesced to the colonial secretary's injunction to choose councillors who had the confidence of the assembly. Still missing was a full-fledged party system to exercise power and a governor who withdrew from the governing executive, conditions that finally prevailed in 1854.

In 1815 Newfoundland differed from the other settler colonies in being denied the apparatus of colonial government. The population of the colony had expanded to more than twenty thousand during the French and Napoleonic wars, and it was clear to reformers that representative government, security of land tenure, legal institutions, and the full range of English civil rights were long overdue. The reform movement in the colony was led by William Carson, a medical doctor from Scotland, and Irish-born merchant Patrick Morris, who made their case in St. John's newspapers. In 1820 British reluctance to grant full colonial status to Newfoundland was brought into question by two separate court cases in which indebted Irish fishermen, James Landrigan and Philip Butler, were sentenced to receive thirty-six lashes with a cat-o'-nine-tails for contempt of court. Such draconian punishment prompted the introduction of circuit courts, and in 1825 Newfoundland was declared a Crown colony with a civilian governor.

When Great Britain itself began to broaden its electoral base though Catholic Emancipation in 1829 and the Reform Bill of 1832, it became even more difficult to deny similar rights to Britons in Newfoundland who were becoming increasingly insistent that reforms be forthcoming. In 1832 Newfoundland was granted representative government. When class and religious tensions poisoned the political atmosphere, the Colonial Office tried to mute divisions in 1842 by creating an amalgamated legislature, in which a portion of the members were appointed rather than elected, but the fully elected assembly was restored in 1848 and responsible government granted in 1855.

There were no assemblies in the Northwest or the Pacific coast to galvanize opposition to the Hudson's Bay Company, whose officers tried to impose British laws and customs in their vast domain. Employees of the company were expected to attend church, deal with Aboriginal employees according to company regulations, avoid drunkenness and adultery, and submit their letters to responsible officials for censorship before sending them. Company employees often flouted their employer's regulations and occasionally assaulted or murdered a superior, but they had little opportunity for organized resistance. A harbinger of things to come occurred in 1849 when Métis trader Pierre-Guillaume Sayer was charged with infringing the Hudson's Bay Company's monopoly by selling furs to Americans. Aware of the tensions in the community, the jury found Sayer guilty but recommended mercy on the grounds that he genuinely believed that he had the right to sell furs to whomever he wished. The company avoided a likely confrontation by dropping the charges, but the days of monopoly were numbered.

Vancouver Island, established as a Crown colony in 1849, was administered by the Hudson's Bay Company on condition that it recruit settlers and accept a Crown appointee as governor. As elsewhere in the empire, land was the medium for financing colonies on the cheap and the land rights of Aboriginal peoples were given short shrift. In December 1849 Hudson's Bay Company secretary Archibald Barclay informed James Douglas, who assumed the role of governor in 1851, that following the establishment of British sovereignty in 1846, Aboriginal claims extended only to their cultivated fields and building sites. "All other land," he asserted, "is to be regarded as waste, and applicable to the purposes of colonization."[14]

CONCLUSION

If Rip van Winkle had fallen asleep in 1815 and awakened in 1849, he would have been shocked by the transformation of the British colonies nestled along the Atlantic coast and the St. Lawrence–Great Lakes system. Most of the workable agricultural land had been granted to immigrants from Great Britain, and British accents, interests, and values prevailed almost everywhere. Stimulated by British demand and capital, fish, timber, and wheat choked colonial ports, which were extending their reach both locally and internationally. The next thirty-five years would yield even more dramatic changes for a sleepy Rip van Winkle, who would awake in 1885 to find a railway running from the Maritimes to the Pacific coast and the name Canada applied to the whole of northern North America.

6

Coming Together, 1849–1885

Following Great Britain's adoption of free trade and acceptance of colonial self-government, British North Americans were preoccupied with how to position themselves in the new industrial order. Their strategies were conceived in the context of Britain's global empire based on industrial supremacy, financial institutions, and free trade. With British support, business and political leaders in the colonies developed the infrastructure to launch their own industrial revolutions and soon began to imagine a larger stage on which to play out their ambitions. Despite major obstacles in their path, a confederated Canada was proclaimed on 1 July 1867, and four years later its boundaries stretched to the Pacific coast. Pushing aside Aboriginal and Métis populations on the Prairies and taking the Rocky Mountains in their stride, Canadians in 1885 celebrated the completion of the longest railway in the world – the Canadian Pacific – which spanned the continent. These were, by any measure, awesome achievements.

RESPONSIBLE GOVERNMENT IN ACTION

Within a decade of the granting of responsible government, the foundations were put in place to sustain a more liberal and market-oriented society. Aristocratic privilege, monopolies, proprietary land regimes, and inheritance laws encumbering estates for the benefit of women and children were all swept away in the name of progress. Often stoutly resisted, the liberal order was a bundle of contradictions and rarely extended to those without the power to claim it, but for better or for worse, it was the framework in which public policy was structured.

The lay of the land was reflected in the legislation adopted in the early years of responsible government. In Nova Scotia the assembly repealed the law banning trade unions, put an end to the General Mining Association's monopoly over the colony's mineral resources, and experimented briefly with universal manhood suffrage, taking care to exclude Aboriginals, paupers, and women from the franchise. The New Brunswick legislature transformed King's College into the secular University of New Brunswick, introduced the secret ballot in elections, and adopted, albeit briefly, prohibition of the sale of alcohol. In Prince Edward Island, Reform leaders lacked the resources to buy out all of the landlords, but they passed a Land Purchase Act to launch the process on a voluntary basis and adopted a Free Schools Act. After decades of fractious electoral manoeuvring, Newfoundland's political leaders muted sectarian divisions by dispensing patronage with a more even hand so that they could turn their attention to economic development.

In the Canadas, the LaFontaine-Baldwin ministry inaugurated a decade of far-reaching legislative action. They reformed the legal system to make it more amenable to the liberal order, implemented a Municipal Corporations Act to give structure to local government, and pledged the government's credit for the construction of railways. Laws were also enacted to lift the restrictions on French as an official language and to create the University of Toronto as a nondenominational institution. As in other colonial jurisdictions, electoral reforms leading to a broader suffrage excluded women and men without property.

When Baldwin and LaFontaine retired from the political scene in 1851, the old divisions between Tories and Reformers gave way to new alliances. In 1854 conservatives in Canada East, known as the *Bleus*, formed a coalition government with the Tories in Canada West led by Family Compact stalwart Allan MacNab. Two policies of their Liberal-Conservative administration, abolition of seigneurial tenure and the clergy reserves, testify to the convergence of political values in this period. As the ministry found its feet, two inspired leaders emerged: John A. Macdonald, an ambitious young lawyer from Kingston, and George-Étienne Cartier, a rebel in the 1830s but now a successful corporate lawyer in Montreal. In 1857 Cartier introduced the Grand Trunk Railway bill and legislation to reform the legal system in Canada East, leading to a modernized Civil Code that replaced the Custom of Paris in 1866. As in common law jurisdictions, it included major revisions to contract, labour, and family law to meet the needs of the modern age.

The Reform Party in Canada West found a ready following among farmers and artisans whose lives and labours were being dramatically transformed. Trumpeting themselves as "true grit" liberals, they found an articulate spokesman in George Brown, the Scottish-born editor of the Toronto *Globe,* who was elected to the assembly in 1851. Moderate liberals in Canada East, known as the *Rouges,* were led by Antoine-Aimé Dorion. Because of the Catholic Church's intense hostility to liberalism in all its manifestations, Dorion's support came primarily from freethinkers and Prostestant anglophones in the Montreal area. A Brown-Dorion coalition briefly held power in 1858, but they were soon eclipsed by the conservative members in the assembly.

SEIZING THE MOMENT

When free trade was introduced, a few colonial merchants saw annexation to the United States as the only solution to unstable market conditions, but this option was quickly abandoned. There were fortunes to be made within the British imperial framework for those nimble enough to seize the moment. The British economy was entering a boom period that lasted for two decades, while an industrializing United States offered a potential market for primary products, as did the demand stimulated by the Crimean War (1854–56) in Europe and the Civil War in the United States (1861–65). The discovery of gold in California, Australia, British Columbia, and New Zealand added fuel to economies everywhere.

Following the lead of their mother country, the eastern colonies agreed to free trade among themselves in 1851, and three years later, Britain negotiated free trade in natural products between the British North American colonies and the United States. Under the Reciprocity Treaty, which remained in effect until 1866, colonial wheat, timber, fish, coal, and agricultural produce found American markets, while Americans enjoyed access to the inshore fisheries in the Atlantic region and to the Great Lakes–St. Lawrence canal system. Despite the enthusiasm for free trade, New Brunswick and the Canadas increased the tariffs on imported manufactures not only to raise much-needed funds for railway development but also to encourage home-based industries.

Given the vast distances to be conquered, it is not surprising that British North Americans quickly fixed upon railways as the key to economic growth. In 1849 Thomas C. Keefer, an engineer from Canada West, published *Philosophy of Railroads*, in which he waxed lyrical about the potential of "the iron civilizer" to "overcome the prejudices of mental weakness," to eliminate the transportation handicap imposed by colonial winters, and to keep the colonies from falling behind in the "arduous rivalry" with the United States.[1] Railways quickened the pace of life in the communities they served, stimulated heavy industry, and increased the potential for political corruption. In 1854 government leader Francis Hincks made £10,000 as a result of insider knowledge relating to the Great Northern Railway contract, but no laws prevented him from enjoying the windfall.

Railways also created massive deficits for colonial governments, which abandoned all notions of laissez-faire liberalism when it came to rail transportation. Between 1852 and 1867, the British North American colonies sank more than $100 million into railways and built thirty-two hundred kilometers of track. The United Canadas and their British backers were brought to the brink of bankruptcy by their investment in the Grand Trunk Railway, which had an ice-free terminus in Portland, Maine, and stretched from Quebec City to Sarnia and on American lines to Chicago. As a solution to failing railways, colonial politicians and British financial interests argued that more railways were needed – to link the colonies with each other and with American lines, and even with the Pacific coast.

British North America's Industrial Revolution came of age with the railway, but its origins can be found in earlier transportation developments. Beginning in the 1820s, canals were built to overcome obstacles in the St. Lawrence–Great Lakes water system near Montreal (Lachine Canal) and Niagara Falls (Welland Canal) and to provide an alternative military route through the Ottawa River (Rideau Canal). The strategic location of the Lachine Canal and the hydraulic power it created made Montreal an obvious location for industrial investment. By the mid-1850s, the city was home to factories producing everything from sewing machines and steam engines to rubber and cigars. Montreal was also the headquarters of the Grand Trunk Railway, which in the 1860s employed nearly eight hundred people in its sprawling facilities.

Steam-powered vessels, meanwhile, promised to end dependency on wind and sail. In 1809 John Molson, an ambitious Montreal brewer, in partnership with two Englishmen, launched the steamship *Accommodation*, which soon had many successors on the St. Lawrence and the Great Lakes. The Atlantic Ocean was more difficult to conquer, but crossings by steam were achieved by the early 1830s. In 1840 Samuel Cunard, a major figure in the Maritime timber trade, inaugurated regular transatlantic steamship service to carry mail between Great Britain and North America. One of the early passengers was novelist Charles Dickens. He found the cabins cramped and uncomfortable in 1842 during his thirteen-day voyage from Liverpool to Halifax on the sidewheeler *Britannia*, which was a far cry from the luxury liners that Cunard Steamships would build by the end of the century.

Telegraphic communication, the e-mail of the Industrial Age, developed quickly after it was successfully tested by the American inventor Samuel Morse in 1844. Three years later a telegraph line linking the Canadas to the American system was completed, and by 1848 Maritimers could communicate telegraphically with Canadians via Calais, Maine. Underwater cable connected Prince Edward Island to the mainland in 1851 and to Newfoundland in 1856. A decade later, a cable was successfully laid between Valencia, Ireland, and Heart's Content, Newfoundland, inaugurating almost instantaneous communication between Europe and North America.

THE GREAT TRANSFORMATION

Industrial capitalism transformed more than production processes and communications. It created a new class structure based on the relationship to production, introduced a rampant materialism that challenged traditional spiritual values, and encouraged the growth of cities. It also redistributed wealth, drove a wedge between the public world of work and the private realm of the family, and altered the relationship of human beings to their natural environment. Over time, reformers managed to soften some of the rougher edges of what Karl Polanyi described as "the great transformation,"[2] but no one was left untouched by the relentless demands of the industrial juggernaut.

The factory system sounded a death knell for artisans whose skills were rendered obsolete by steam-powered machines. In desperation, craftsmen sometimes tried to destroy the mechanical demons that threatened their livelihood – as was the case among shoemakers in Montreal when the sewing machine was introduced in 1852 – but workers soon began pressing for better working conditions and a fairer distribution of the profits of their labours. Factory owners fired anyone they found trying to organize the shop floor, but colonial wage earners were not deterred, taking their cue from their comrades in Europe and the United States in protesting their exploitation. On 10 June 1867, just three years after the International Workingmen's Association had been founded in London, more than ten thousand workers marched in the streets of Montreal behind the Patriote flag of 1837 in an expression of labour solidarity.

British North America's industrial workforce was overwhelmingly male. Almost all of the captains of industry were men, and men were hired exclusively in the milling, woodworking, and metal industries. In factories producing clothing, footwear, tobacco, and processed foods, work was broken down into easy, repetitive tasks that were often performed by women and children, who also made up the majority of those employed in the "sweated trades," where work was performed by the piece at home. Wherever they laboured, women and children received substantially lower wages than men.

New production processes had a profound influence on the family. In the preindustrial world, home was the centre of work, education, and care, but by the mid-nineteenth century, middle-class families were increasingly making a distinction between their public and private spaces. While women's place was deemed to be in the home, the public world of business and paid labour was the domain of men whose masculinity was defined by their ability to support a family. The lines between the two spheres were always blurred, and working-class families could rarely survive on the wages of a single male breadwinner,[3] but the conceptual framework offered the justification for excluding women from politics, professions, and positions of authority everywhere. The paid work of women was largely confined to domestic service, low-paying factory jobs, schoolteaching, and shopkeeping; eventually nursing, clerical work, and telephone exchanges opened more opportunities for women. In many working-class families, wives earned a marginal income by doing piecework, keeping boarders, or taking in laundry.

The intellectual currents that accompanied industrialization proved especially troubling. Scientific claims had long alarmed traditionalists, but Charles Darwin's *The Origin of Species*, published in 1859, produced a firestorm of controversy. His assertion that all living things had evolved from a single, primitive form of life, and had developed by a process of natural selection, flew in the face of Christianity's human-centred view of creation. While most Christians accepted the discrepancy between Darwin's findings and divine revelation as a mystery that would be explained in God's good time, others became more skeptical about religion. Still others, including Sir William Dawson, the president of McGill University, who was internationally renowned for his study of fossilized plants and animals in the rock formations along the Bay of Fundy, attempted to refute Darwin's theories on a scientific basis. The debate between Creationists and Evolutionists still rumbles on.

THE RAGE FOR REFORM

By the mid-nineteenth century, notions of progress seen in mechanized processes were being applied to society at large. Social reform was sometimes spearheaded by governments, which were eager through institutions such as prisons and asylums to impose social control on people unwilling or unable to conform to desirable behaviour. When governments faltered through lack of money or inclination, voluntary organizations rose to the occasion.

Colonial churches, the most prominent voluntary institutions in colonial society, were in the vanguard of reform. Using Christ's Sermon on the Mount as their inspiration, Protestant churches

formed missionary societies, fought slavery, encouraged education, founded hospitals and shelters, and urged charity, temperance,
and civic reform. A reinvigorated Roman Catholic Church also
expanded its social services to address the needs of its adherents. In
this period, female religious orders, responsible for much of the work
related to education, health, and welfare, expanded dramatically.
Nondenominational organizations also proliferated, championing
everything from literacy to the prevention of cruelty to animals.

The temperance movement eclipsed all others in its reach. From
its beginnings in the late 1820s, the movement to restrict the consumption of alcohol quickly engulfed all of British North America.
It was sustained by a variety of organizations, among them the Sons
of Temperance and the Women's Christian Temperance Union, both
originating in the bastion of voluntarism, the United States. When
efforts to encourage personal restraint failed to work, temperance
advocates demanded that governments prohibit the manufacture,
sale, and use of alcoholic beverages. In the age of progress, it was
difficult to refute the arguments of prohibitionists that drinking
undermined family life and was both a waste of money and a detriment to hard work.

Reformers also demanded that the state play a larger role in
supporting formal education. If every child could be required to
attend state-supported "common schools," it was argued, both individuals and society at large would benefit. Egerton Ryerson, the
Methodist superintendent of education for Canada West from 1844
to 1876, was clear on this point, viewing education as "not the mere
acquisition of certain arts, or of certain branches of knowledge,
but that instruction and discipline which qualify and dispose the
subjects of it for their appropriate duties and employments of life,
as Christians, as persons of business, and also as members of the
civil community in which they live."[4] Common-school legislation
was so controversial that politicians championed it only at their
peril. Nevertheless, most colonies in this period adopted general tax
assessment to finance public schools and found ways to accommodate the opposition of the Roman Catholic Church, whose leaders
insisted that confessional schools be eligible for state support.

In their quest for improvement, Canadians laid the foundations
for seventeen universities by the 1860s. Most institutions of higher

learning were sponsored by churches, and those claiming to be nondenominational, including Dalhousie, the University of New Brunswick, McGill, and the University of Toronto, often had close ties to one of the major churches. Opened only to men, colonial colleges had small enrolments and taught primarily theology, the liberal arts, and a smattering of science. McGill, Queen's, Toronto, and Laval supported training in medicine, but men seeking a medical degree often attended universities in Great Britain, while ambitious young women enrolled in medical colleges open to them in the United States.

The changing times encouraged an intellectual awakening among a broad base of the colonial population. Originating in Scotland to promote education among the artisan class, Mechanics' Institutes appealed to those sold on the idea of self-improvement and could be found in many colonial communities. Newspapers, which were expanding dramatically in this period, kept their readers abreast of what was happening at home and abroad. Most colonial churches and political parties sponsored their own newspapers and tried desperately to expand their readership to ensure their survival.

Although the colonies had yet to produce a body of art, literature, and science identified as uniquely their own, a few tall poppies emerged in almost all branches of knowledge and the creative arts. Romantic notions of Aboriginal and colonial life inspired such sojourning artists as Cornelius Kreighoff and Paul Kane. Joseph Légaré, an ardent Patriote, was more biting in his social commentary, producing works depicting the cholera epidemic of 1832 and the burning of the Parliament buildings in 1849. By midcentury, Thomas Chandler Haliburton and Susannah Moodie had gained an international reputation for humorous sketches of colonial life. While colonials tended to focus on practical inventions, such as processes for producing kerosene oil or making paper out of pulpwood, two men were knighted for their pioneering work in the emerging fields of geology and paleontology: William Logan, the director of the Geological Survey of the United Province of Canada, and William Dawson.

Beginning in the 1840s francophones responded to Durham's unkind comment that French Canadians were a people with no literature and no history by producing a great outpouring of both.

François-Xavier Garneau's *Histoire du Canada*, which appeared in several volumes between 1845 and 1852, had a long shelf life, though its liberal perspective was muted in subsequent editions because of the growing influence of the Roman Catholic Church. In Canada East, branches of the Institut Canadien served as debating societies, libraries, and newsrooms for those who had the courage to become members in the face of growing clerical disapproval. The Church hierarchy was so incensed by the freethinking supported by the Institut that it threatened excommunication of its members and, in one celebrated case, fought a five-year battle (1869–1874) to prevent one Institut member, Joseph Guibord, from being buried in consecrated ground in Montreal.

IMAGINING A TRANSCONTINENTAL NATION

By midcentury, a passion for nationalism had infected the Atlantic world. Movements for German and Italian unification attracted large followings, and most Latin American colonies threw off the yoke of their imperial masters. In 1867 efforts by French emperor Napoleon III to establish control over Mexico ended with the execution of the leader of his puppet government, Archduke Maximilian, by a Mexican firing squad. Everywhere imperial regimes were on the defensive, including in Great Britain, where Irish patriots were determined to dissolve the hated union imposed upon their island in 1801.

The adoption of self-government within a British imperial context and incipient nationalism among francophones in Canada East made it more difficult to imagine a singular national identity for the British North American colonies. Far more compelling was the idea of a transcontinental nation on the model of their neighbour to the south. In 1857 two scientific expeditions to the Prairies, one sponsored by the united Canadas and the other by the Royal Geographical Society in London, advanced the idea of western expansion by reporting that the region was more amenable to agricultural settlement than earlier commentators had suggested. When gold was discovered the same year on the Pacific coast, the expansionist dream floated westward.

The reality on the Pacific coast was less a dream than a nightmare. James Douglas, who added the governorship of British

Image 6.1. The Cariboo Wagon Road opened in the 1860s. (Image A-00350 by permission of Royal BC Museum, BC Archives)

Columbia to his duties when the colony was created in 1858, was keen to maintain law and order in the goldfields, but he had his hands full, despite the support of four Royal Navy vessels packed with marines sent to assist him. First in the Fraser Canyon and then in the Cariboo region, instant shack communities appeared, grew dramatically, and then became ghost towns once the ore was tapped (Image 6.1). The population of Victoria swelled from fewer than four hundred to more than five thousand in the space of a few months in 1858.

The 1861 census recorded fifty thousand people in British Columbia. Most of them were white men, but before the sojourners decamped for opportunities elsewhere, a multiethnic society flourished. On first learning of the gold rush, Mifflin Gibbs led several hundred African Americans to Vancouver Island, where they participated in civic elections and formed the Victoria Pioneer Rifle Corps to protect the colony from potential American aggression. The gold rush also attracted more than six thousand Chinese, who, like black immigrants, experienced blatant discrimination and segregation in residential areas and public places. When the gold rush ended, most Chinese moved on, but those who stayed became the early residents of the "Chinatowns" that became part of the landscapes of Victoria and Vancouver in the 1880s.

Plans for creating permanent, family-based, white settlements in British Columbia came hard on the heels of the gold rush. In April 1862 the first of several "bride ships" arrived, carrying British women recruited under the supervision of the London Female Emigration Society to become wives of the unmarried men in the colony.[5] Thereafter, families such as the one headed by the governor would no longer reign over polite society on the Pacific coast. Born in Demerara (now part of Guyana), James Douglas was the son of a free, coloured Creole who was never officially married to his Scottish Planter father; Douglas's wife, Amelia Connolly, who bore him eleven children, was part Cree.

Aboriginal peoples fared poorly in the freewheeling environment of the gold rush. Although they were no strangers to violence – in 1850 two warships were sent to punish Aboriginals on Vancouver Island who had killed three Hudson's Bay Company employees – the influx of such a large number of immigrants swept away any pretense to the rule of law. A smallpox epidemic in 1862 further weakened their capacity for resistance. Douglas had negotiated treaties on Vancouver Island, but he ignored such practices on the mainland. When the ever-present missionaries tried to help, they only added more weight to collapsing indigenous cultures.

COMING TOGETHER

The future of all British North America colonies soon became bound up with failing political institutions in the Canadas. Since its creation in the aftermath of the rebellions, the United Province of Canadas had never worked well. Canada West, with its largely Protestant Anglo-American population demanding public schools and ambitious economic programs, stood in marked contrast to Canada East, where francophones were determined to protect their language, laws, and Roman Catholic schools. By the late 1850s, the opposing parties in the assembly, where each section held half of the seats, were so equally balanced that it became difficult to form a government. In Canada West, whose population had grown dramatically, it became expedient to argue that seats in the legislature should be apportioned by population rather than by section. This democratic notion had little appeal among the francophone minority.

With the collapse of yet another coalition government in 1864, George Brown suggested the creation of an all-party committee to discuss constitutional reform. He and Dorion favoured a federal union of the two Canadas, but the committee decided that they should first attempt a larger union of the British North American colonies. Brown approached Cartier and Macdonald with the idea of a "Great Coalition" to achieve this goal. Despite deep personal enmity between Brown and Macdonald, they collaborated in creating a new ministry under Macdonald's leadership.

Their timing was good. In the Maritimes, expanding markets and the healthy state of shipping and shipbuilding encouraged politicians to imagine their region, with its ice-free ports, as a gateway to the continent. When Joseph Howe assumed the premiership of Nova Scotia in 1860, one of his priorities was a line linking Halifax to the St. Lawrence, generally referred to as the Intercolonial Railway, but funding proved elusive. The collapse, in 1862, of railway negotiations with the Canadas seemed to close the book on the project, but London deemed otherwise.

Failing British North American railway investments threatened the survival of some of Great Britain's major financial institutions, including Barings Bank and Glyn, Mills, and Company.[6] In January 1862 men with financial interests in the colonies formed the British North American Association to lobby the British government in support of both the Intercolonial Railway and the union of the colonies under one administration, which would make managing development projects less complicated. The colonial secretary, the Duke of Newcastle, warmed to the two-pronged approach. In 1863 British financiers bought the Hudson's Bay Company in the expectation of reaping a profit when the Canadians incorporated the Northwest into their union. The fix was in.

Joseph Howe's Liberals lost the 1863 election to the Conservative Party, which by 1864 was led by Charles Tupper, an Edinburgh-trained medical doctor. Ambitious for his province and himself, Tupper inadvertently sparked the process leading to Confederation by promoting the idea of Maritime union. Early in 1864, the issue was debated in the Nova Scotia assembly, which agreed to send delegates to a conference on the subject. There the matter rested until the Canadians asked to be invited to the discussions. A meeting was set for 1 September in Charlottetown, the closest Maritime capital by seagoing vessel from the Canadas.

British North American union might well have foundered had the context been different. By 1864 British governments, whether Liberal or Conservative, were eager to reduce the costs of colonial administration and military protection. The defence issue loomed large as a result of the American Civil War (1861–65), which pitted the slaveholding South against the industrializing North. As the war dragged on, a number of incidents on the high seas and along the border helped to increase tensions between Great Britain and the North, exposing the vulnerability of the colonies. In 1861 Great Britain was obliged to send fifteen thousand troops to British North America, but despite ongoing tensions with the United States, the Colonial Office served notice in 1864 that troops would soon be withdrawn. To make matters worse, the Americans announced that they would not renew the Reciprocity agreement, which expired in 1866. Colonial politicians had a lot to think about.

THE ROCKY ROAD TO CONFEDERATION, 1864–1867

At the Charlottetown Conference, delegates quickly shelved discussion of Maritime union to focus on Canada's proposal for a British North American union (Image 6.2). A month later, the delegates met in Quebec City to hammer out the details of a merger that could be presented to their respective legislatures.[7]

The agreement reached at Quebec in 1864 was largely the handiwork of the Canadian delegates, who dominated the negotiations. Macdonald preferred a legislative union to reduce the powers of the provinces, but regional and cultural differences dictated a federal arrangement whereby the powers of the state were divided between

Image 6.2. By 1864, when this photograph of the Fathers of Confederation was taken in Charlottetown, photography had begun to replace artistic renderings of significant historical events. (Courtesy of Library and Archives Canada/C-733)

national and provincial administrations. While representation by population would prevail in the House of Commons, the Senate was to be an appointed body with Canada East, Canada West, and the Maritimes each allotted twenty-four seats. French and English were made official languages in the House of Commons and federal courts. The English Protestant minority in Canada East was granted the rights that prevailed for Roman Catholic schools in Canada West.

Under the Quebec proposals, the federal government had control over what seemed to matter most: "peace, order and good government." This phrase covered international and interprovincial trade, criminal law, Indian affairs, currency and banking, and interprovincial transportation. The provinces had responsibility for matters concerning civil rights and property; control over commerce within their borders, natural resources, and public lands; and civil law, municipal administration, education, and social services. Federal and provincial governments would split responsibility for agriculture, the fishery, and immigration. Both levels had taxing powers, but only the federal government could impose tariff and excise duties. Loss of these revenues, which were the major source of government funding, would be compensated by federal per capita grants to the provinces.

None of the Fathers of Confederation were democrats. They avoided any discussion of expanding political rights and strove to establish a framework that would mute the influence of an increasingly politically conscious citizenry. They were, however, obliged under responsible government to debate and pass the Quebec Resolutions in their legislatures. With their coalition government, the Canadians managed this feat easily enough, but opposition to the Quebec "scheme" mounted quickly in the Atlantic colonies. Anti-unionists argued that the Canadians, by virtue of their population, would dominate the House of Commons and even the Senate was stacked in favour of the Canadas.

The dominoes quickly began to fall. With no railway debt to encumber their treasury and a militant Tenant League stirring up trouble, Islanders withdrew from the negotiations on a union that offered them only five seats in the House of Commons. Newfoundlanders, who had little interest in railways and westward expansion, were equally unimpressed by the Canadian proposals. In New Brunswick Leonard Tilley's Liberal government, which championed Confederation, was defeated by a coalition headed by A.J. Smith in a hotly contested election in January 1865. Resistance to the Quebec Resolutions in Nova Scotia developed so quickly under Joseph Howe's leadership that Tupper thought better about introducing them in the assembly.

With the union in jeopardy, pro-Confederation forces swung into action. New Brunswick's lieutenant governor, Arthur Gordon, pushed the boundaries of his constitutional powers by forcing the resignation of his recently elected government and calling another election. This time the timber merchants, facing the end of Reciprocity, were more disposed to support a union that might offer alternative markets. The Roman Catholic hierarchy, originally opposed to a union that included the rabid Protestants from Canada West, was also persuaded to take a more positive view. For those who were still wavering, money supplied by the Canadians and their Grand Trunk allies worked wonders. In the days leading up to the election, an American wing of the Fenian Brotherhood, in a harebrained scheme designed to entangle Great Britain and the United States in a war that would give Ireland an opportunity to assert its independence, launched raids on New Brunswick and Canada West. Although easily deflected, the attacks added emphasis to the pro-Confederate position that defence could be better handled by a strong federal government. In May 1866 Tilley's pro-union party won a resounding victory.

By this time, economic prospects in Nova Scotia were so bleak with the end of Reciprocity that annexation to the United States was gaining support. Tupper was unable to convince his party to approve the Quebec Resolutions, but with the help of the Nova Scotia–born lieutenant governor, Sir William Fenwick Williams, he persuaded the Nova Scotia assembly to authorize further negotiations on union. At meetings in London, the Canadians agreed to include a clause in the British North America (BNA) Act providing for the "immediate" construction of the Intercolonial Railway "by the Government of Canada," to make the fisheries an exclusively federal responsibility, and to improve provincial subsidies, but the Canadians refused to countenance any adjustments to the lopsided power structure of the union. Pressure from the Roman Catholic hierarchy for protection of separate schools outside of the Canadas was addressed by including guarantees to separate schools in existence at the time the act went into effect and by adding the right of appeal to the federal government for remedial legislation should the laws be violated.

In March 1867 the BNA Act passed in the British Parliament, to take effect on 1 July 1867. It united the Canadas (divided into the provinces of Ontario and Quebec), New Brunswick, and Nova Scotia as the Dominion of Canada (Map 6.1). The architects of the union referred to their edifice as a "confederation" rather than a "federation," on the unfounded grounds that the latter term implied a looser structure such as the one that prevailed in the now-discredited United States. Ottawa, chosen as the capital of the United Canadas in 1857, became the capital of Canada, and the existing civil service staffed the federal offices. Even the name of the new nation underscored the prevailing power relations. It

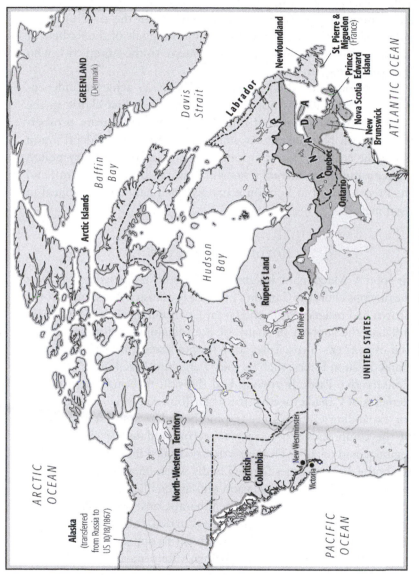

Map 6.1 Canada in 1867

was suggested that Canada should be ranked as a kingdom or vice-royalty, but in the end it became a "dominion," a term drawn, at Tilley's suggestion, from a biblical reference in Psalm 72: "He shall have dominion also from sea to sea, and from the river unto the ends of the earth." It reflected the ambitious goals of the Fathers of Confederation and would be less offensive to the Americans, who frowned on monarchies.

It is a common misconception that Canada achieved independence in 1867. This is not so. Significantly, the first clause in the BNA Act of 1867 declared that "the present and future prosperity of British North America will be promoted by a federal union under the crown of Great Britain." Foreign affairs, military policy, and constitutional amendments still required British approval, and the Privy Council in London remained the final court of appeal in legal matters.

HOLDING IT TOGETHER

Sir John A. Macdonald, knighted for his role in Confederation, was the obvious choice as Canada's first prime minister. Although George Brown had resigned from the Great Coalition in 1865, Macdonald still had the support of many of the remaining Reform members and of Cartier's Bleus. Tilley and Tupper agreed to bring their pro-Confederation forces, such as they were, into Macdonald's Liberal-Conservative Party. If anyone had the skill to bring the disparate elements of Canada together it was Sir John A. He had a bold vision for expanding Canada's geographic boundaries and a good sense of the compromises necessary to accommodate the class, ethnic, regional, and religious cleavages that bedeviled the colonies. Fond of the bottle, he sometimes faltered badly when on a binge, but he had remarkable powers of persuasion and unequalled political savvy.[8]

In the first national election, the Liberal-Conservative Party (commonly called the Conservative Party) carried 108 of the 180 seats, but almost half of the popular vote went to opposition candidates. Among the latter were George Brown's Reformers, A. A. Dorion's Rouges, and the Maritime anti-Confederates. In time, they would form a coalition that would become the basis of the Liberal Party, but for the moment opposition forces were in disarray.

Macdonald's first challenge was to address a separatist movement in Nova Scotia, where anti-Confederate candidates carried every seat except Tupper's in the 1867 federal election. Hostility to the Quebec scheme and the slippery process by which it had been implemented was so intense that a Repeal League quickly took shape, and Joseph Howe was dispatched to London to secure Nova Scotia's withdrawal from Confederation. Meeting a frosty reception, Howe began negotiating with the Canadians for better terms for his province. In 1869 Ottawa agreed to pay an additional $1 million of Nova Scotia's debt, to increase the province's annual grant by $82,698 per year for ten years, and to provide cabinet posts to two anti-Confederates. With repeal sentiment morphing into an annexation movement, Howe urged his colleagues to move quickly on the construction of the Intercolonial and to press for a new reciprocity treaty.

Macdonald hoped that negotiations between the United States and Great Britain to resolve difficulties resulting from the Civil War would provide an opportunity to negotiate free trade. In 1871 he represented Canada in a British delegation that met with their American counterparts in Washington, but the protectionist Republican Congress had little interest in reducing tariffs. The Treaty of Washington only granted free trade in fish and offered financial compensation, to be decided by arbitration, in return for American access to Canada's inshore waters. There were cries of "sellout" in Nova Scotia, but much of the energy had gone out of the repeal movement.

ANNEXING THE NORTHWEST

The transfer of the Northwest to Canadian jurisdiction created a number of challenges. In 1869 an agreement was reached with the Hudson's Bay Company to sell its territorial claims for £300,000 and a grant to the company of one-twentieth of the best agricultural land. This deal proved lucrative to the financiers who had recently bought control of the company, but others were not so well served. Consulted by neither the company nor the Canadians, the Métis feared the worst when, in August 1869, Canadian road builders and surveyors arrived in Red River.

By October a Métis National Committee had been established to confront Canadian imperialism. After stopping the work of the surveyors and blocking entry of the newly appointed lieutenant governor at the United States border, they seized control of Upper Fort Garry and established a Provisional Government. Twenty-five-year-old Louis Riel served as secretary of the National Committee and co-president of the Provisional Government. Literate and articulate, he had spent nearly a decade in Roman Catholic educational institutions in Quebec and could negotiate with the Canadians on their own terms.[9] Riel had the support of Roman Catholic missionaries in Red River, who feared, with justification, that annexation to Canada would swamp Red River with Protestant settlers from Ontario.

The small immigrant population in Red River included Canadian land speculators, who were highly unpopular in the community. In their newspaper, the *Nor'wester*, the "Canadian party" made little effort to disguise their disgust with both Roman Catholics and Aboriginal peoples. When a group of Canadians tried to overthrow the Provisional Government in February 1870, their leaders were thrown in jail, and one of the most outspoken, Thomas Scott, was executed by a firing squad. Scott was an Orangeman from Ontario, where an instant cry arose for revenge.

Concerned that the United States would use the crisis in Red River to seize control of the region, Macdonald reluctantly agreed to negotiate with representatives of the Provisional Government, who were led by Abbé N. J. Ritchot. An agreement was reached in May 1870, which met most Métis demands. The Red River area became the province of Manitoba, where both English and French would be officially recognized in legislative and court proceedings; denominational schools, both Protestant and Catholic, would be maintained. In contrast to other provinces, in Manitoba land remained under Ottawa's control, but the Métis were offered title to lands on which they farmed and 1.4 million acres to be distributed to their children.

What seemed like a reasonable conclusion to the confrontation quickly turned sour. Macdonald sent a military force of four hundred British troops and eight hundred militia led by Colonel Garnet Wolseley to impose order in Manitoba. Its ranks included Ontario Orangemen who inflicted a reign of terror on the Métis. With immigrants, most of them from Ontario, pouring into the province, many Métis decided to move further west. Riel was elected to represent Red River in Ottawa, but he was unable to take his seat because the Ontario government had issued a warrant for his arrest. He eventually fled to the United States, for fear of his life.

In an effort to avoid a repetition of the Red River experience, Ottawa negotiated seven treaties with the approximately thirty-four Aboriginal peoples living on the Prairies. Threatened by the disappearance of the buffalo and the influx of settlers, they agreed to treaties that offered land reserves; promised implements, seed, and training to launch them in agricultural pursuits; and recognized hunting and fishing rights. As with the Métis, the Aboriginal people who signed the treaties got much less than they bargained for. Assistance with farming was slow in coming, but settlers and military might were not. In 1872 the Dominion Lands Act granted free homesteads of 160 acres to any farmer who cleared 10 acres and built a home within three years of registering his claim. In 1873 the North-West Mounted Police (NWMP) was established to counter threats from disgruntled Aboriginals and American expansionists.

In 1876 the federal government consolidated its policies with respect to Aboriginal peoples in the Indian Act. Its basic premise was that First Nations needed to be segregated until they learned to farm and govern themselves in ways acceptable to the new liberal order. The act introduced elected chiefs and councils to replace traditional band structures and subjected all reserve activities to the supervision of white bureaucracies. In defining Indian status, wives, widows, and children of registered men were accorded Indian status even if they had no Aboriginal heritage, while an Aboriginal woman who married a non-status man lost her status, as did her children. Later revisions of the act denied Status Indians the right to drink alcohol or to perform traditional ceremonies such as potlatch and the sun dance. Under what was essentially an apartheid regime, Canada's First Nations faced a dismal prospect in a Confederated Canada.

ROUNDING OUT CONFEDERATION

British Columbia was also on Macdonald's expansionist agenda. After the gold rush ran its course, Vancouver Island and British

Columbia chalked up public deficits, and the Colonial Office engineered their union in 1866. Here, too, immigrants from the eastern colonies played a central role in the Confederation movement. Finding Crown colony government dominated by appointed officials, they argued that Confederation would bring with it responsible government and save the area for the British Empire: the United States had purchased Alaska from the Russians in 1867, and a pincer operation could bring the entire Pacific coast under American control.

One of the champions of Confederation was Amor de Cosmos, a Victoria-based newspaper editor whose adopted name – he was William Smith from Nova Scotia – reflected his flamboyant style. In 1868 de Cosmos and his allies established the Confederation League to mobilize support for their cause. The Colonial Office sent Lieutenant Governor Andrew Musgrave to British Columbia in 1869 to promote Confederation. The legislative council's terms for union were manageable: a wagon road connecting New Westminster to Fort Garry, with a railroad to follow in due course; the assumption by Canada of British Columbia's debt; and a generous annual grant. During negotiations held in June 1870, the Canadian delegation, led by Cartier, accepted British Columbia's conditions and even agreed to complete the railway within ten years. An election in November 1870 gave every seat in the legislature to supporters of Confederation, and in June 1871 British Columbia became the sixth province of Canada. Aboriginals, who still formed the majority of British Columbia's dwindling population of thirty-six thousand people, had no seat at the negotiating table, and no land guarantees were offered. In assuming responsibility for Indian affairs, Ottawa agreed to continue "a policy as liberal as that pursued by the British Columbia Government," which said it all.[10]

Prince Edward Island, with its own land issues, soon followed British Columbia's example. When the Conservatives under James Pope took office in 1870, they approved a costly rail line to link the Island's communities. Subsequently faced with huge public debt, Pope argued that only by joining Canada could Islanders avoid financial disaster. With American annexationists on the scene, Macdonald agreed not only to assume the railway debt and establish year-round communications between the Island and the mainland, but also to provide funds and ultimately legal support to encourage the remaining landlords to sell their land so that tenants could become freeholders. Prince Edward Island became the seventh province of Canada in 1873.

For a time it looked as if Newfoundland might also reconsider its rejection of Confederation. Conservative Premier Frederick Carter supported union, and in the months preceding the 1869 election, he negotiated a generous agreement with Canada. Newfoundland voters were not persuaded. Led by St. John's merchant Charles Fox Bennett, anti-Confederates won more than two-thirds of the legislative seats. In the 1880s railway mania swept Newfoundland with the accompanying public debt, and Canada again put out feelers, but local politicians were not interested.

As the foregoing suggests, Ottawa had become the holding company for British imperial interests in North America. Nowhere is this metaphor more apt than in the Arctic. Following an American request for mineral rights on Baffin Island, the British government issued an order-in-council in 1880 adding the Arctic Archipelago, as the District of Franklin, to Canadian jurisdiction. There was no thought of settling the region on the part of British or Canadian authorities.[11] Canadians were so uninterested that they neglected to register the order-in-council until 1895, and Ottawa refused to take responsibility for the Inuit until obliged to do so by the courts in 1939.

THE MACKENZIE INTERLUDE

Macdonald managed to win the 1872 election, but he soon ran into trouble. In May 1871 the government had introduced legislation offering financial and land incentives to the successful bidder for the Pacific railway contract. Hugh Allan, president of Allan Steamship Lines in Montreal, contributed generously to the Conservative election effort, presumably in the hope of securing the contract over his Toronto rivals. When the government announced in February 1873 that Allen's bid was successful, Liberal MP Lucius Huntington charged in the House of Commons that Allan had bought the contract with $360,000 in donations to the Conservative Party – and he had the telegrams to prove it. On 5 November 1873 Macdonald resigned as prime minister.

Opposition members came together to form a government under the leadership of Alexander Mackenzie.[12] With the Conservatives discredited, Mackenzie's Liberal coalition won a majority of seats in every province except British Columbia in the January 1874 election. Canada's second prime minister, like Macdonald, was a Scotsman and lived in Ontario, but there the similarities between the two men ended. A stonemason and newspaper editor, Mackenzie was a highly principled Baptist and teetotaler who, in keeping with his democratic ideals, three times turned down a knighthood for his services to Canada. His Liberal administration, which lasted only one term, was hamstrung by a worldwide recession. When the United States rejected renewed efforts to negotiate a reciprocity treaty, the government produced no economic strategy other than retrenchment. Many Canadians voted with their feet by moving to the United States.

The Mackenzie administration has earned its place in Canadian history for efforts to reform political and legal processes. In addition to legislating simultaneous voting, the secret ballot, and trial of disputed elections by the courts, Minister of Justice Edward Blake established the Supreme Court of Canada in 1875. To his regret, he was unable to make it the final court of appeal, which remained the Judicial Committee of the Privy Council until 1949. The Liberals also supported the demand for prohibition with the Canadian Temperance Act (1878), which enabled municipalities to hold a plebiscite to determine whether liquor could be sold within their boundaries.

MACDONALD'S NATIONAL POLICY

In 1878 the Conservative Party swept back to power. During the election campaign, Macdonald advocated a development program that became known as the National Policy. It included high tariffs to stimulate manufacturing, the rapid completion of the Pacific railway, and the encouragement of population growth through immigration. With minor modifications, these policies would form the framework of Canadian development under both Conservative and Liberal administrations until the 1930s.

The Macdonald government moved quickly to put the necessary legislation in place to achieve its goals. In 1879 Finance Minister

Tilley raised the tariff from 15 percent to levels ranging as high as 35 percent, much to the delight of manufacturers eager to fend off foreign competition. In 1880 the government approved a new Canadian Pacific Railway (CPR) company, headed by George Stephen, president of the Bank of Montreal, and financed by American, British, and Canadian capital. The Macdonald government offered the CPR syndicate generous support, including $25 million in cash, 25 million acres of land, and a twenty-year monopoly on western rail traffic. More grants were required before the line was completed in 1885, and in 1888 the government guaranteed a $15 million bond issue in return for dropping the monopoly clause. Construction across the mountain ranges in British Columbia required a Herculean effort, accomplished under the supervision of two energetic Americans – CPR general manager Cornelius Van Horne and subcontractor Andrew Onderdonk – with the labour of thousands of men, among them Chinese working under contract for a third of what was paid to their co-workers.[13]

The Macdonald government was less successful in growing the population. Although more than nine hundred thousand immigrants arrived in Canada in the 1880s, a million people left. Manitoba and the territories attracted settlers, but the numbers were disappointing to those hoping to transform the Prairies into an agricultural paradise. Yet there were promising signs. In the 1870s Icelanders, escaping volcanic eruptions and economic uncertainty at home, settled in Manitoba. German-speaking Mennonites from Russia and Jews escaping oppression in many European countries were also prepared to try their luck in western Canada, as were adherents of the Church of Jesus Christ of Latter-Day Saints, who began arriving from their base in Utah in the 1880s.

Although the rights of workers were not explicit in the National Policy, Macdonald had introduced a Trade Unions Act in 1872, which removed common law prohibitions against unions as combinations in restraint of trade. The act served as a signal to skilled labour at home and abroad that their rights would be protected. It also served as an affront to Macdonald's nemesis, George Brown, who had recently prosecuted Toronto printers for seditious conspiracy when they went on strike to impose a nine-hour day. Brown's difficulties with labour did not end there. He died in 1880 after being shot by a disgruntled former *Globe* employee who had been fired from his job.

The importance of the National Policy in promoting industrial growth has long been debated. Detractors of the policy charge that the tariff benefitted producers at the expense of consumers, encouraged the development of a sluggish industrial economy dominated by branches of American companies, and favoured development in central Canada to the detriment of the Maritimes and the west. Supporters of the National Policy, meanwhile, have argued that, as in the United States, protection was necessary to allow infant industries to succeed against competition from established companies in other countries. What is clear is that the National Policy did little to reduce Canadian dependence on foreign countries for capital and technology, or to protect it from international economic trends.[14]

TAMING THE NORTHWEST

Despite the slow development of the Northwest, its transformation was well under way by 1885. Outside of Manitoba, whose boundaries were extended in 1881, the region remained under federal government control. The Northwest Territories Act of 1875 gave power to an appointed council until such time as the population warranted representative government. The act guaranteed denominational schools, and, by an amendment in 1877, French and English were made the official languages of the courts and council.

After the last buffalo hunt in 1879, First Nations faced starvation and were desperate for help. Instead of getting much-needed assistance, they found their rations cut to save rapidly dwindling government coffers. In 1884 two thousand Cree gathered outside the territorial capital of Battleford in an attempt to put pressure on local and distant bureaucracies, which predictably dithered. Young militants called for armed protest. This development merged with growing discontent among the Métis living between the South and North Saskatchewan rivers, who demanded the same support for their communities as immigrants were receiving. When Ottawa ignored their petitions, the Métis invited Louis Riel, now driven by messianic visions, to return to Canada from exile in the United States to lead his people. Riel pressed the Macdonald government for concessions, but Ottawa refused to respond. On 18 March 1885 Riel proclaimed a Provisional Government and demanded that Ottawa grant the moderate demands outlined in a Bill of Rights.

Many Métis, including Riel's military adviser, Gabriel Dumont, argued that militant action was necessary. Confrontations between Métis and the NWMP at Batoche and Duck Lake resulted in more than forty deaths and prompted the federal government to send a militia under Major General Frederick Middleton to the scene. Within two weeks, the first detachment arrived on CPR trains. When word of the Métis rebellion reached the Cree, militants attacked the settlement at Frog Lake, killing nine people, and two farming instructors were murdered in the Battleford district. Riel withdrew his supporters to Batoche, where they held out against Middleton's forces for six weeks.

Overall, thirty-five Aboriginals and Métis and fifty-three non-Aboriginal people lost their lives in the rebellion. Eighty-one rebels were arrested and forty-four were convicted, most of them on charges of felony treason. Even Big Bear and Poundmaker, Cree chiefs who had tried to prevent violence, were sentenced to three-year prison terms. After the uprising, Aboriginal people were controlled through the bureaucratic processes of the Indian Act, while the Métis, dispersed across the Prairies, were destroyed as a political force for more than a century. Aboriginal and Métis women, no longer essential to the fur trade, became increasingly represented as deviant and degraded.[15]

Louis Riel was convicted of high treason in a blatantly rigged trial and hanged in Regina on 16 November 1885. Nine days earlier, at a ceremony at Craigellachie, British Columbia, the last spike was driven in the CPR (Images 6.3 and 6.4). This is how the Canadian West was won.

CONCLUSION

In the period between 1850 and 1885, British North America was reinvented. For those seeking economic opportunities, the infrastructure was now in place to support their efforts. Shortly after the CPR was completed, sisters Jessie and Annie McQueen from Pictou County, Nova Scotia, boarded the train to British Columbia,

Image 6.3. Following his sentencing, Louis Riel, shown here at his trial, spoke for more than an hour. By this time he was clearly mentally unstable, preoccupied more by religious visions than by political ones. (By permission of Library and Archives Canada/C-1879)

Image 6.4. While the completion of the Canadian Pacific Railway was officially commemorated at a ceremonial driving of the last spike by Donald Smith (Lord Strathcona), the workers, shown here, staged their own photographic moment – though none of the Chinese labourers were present for the occasion. (By permission of Library and Archives Canada/C-14115)

where they taught school for three times the wages that they could make in their native province. Encouraged to make the move by a Presbyterian pastor already on the scene, the McQueen sisters brought their Maritime and Protestant values with them and soon were actively engaged in Canadianizing what their brother living in New York described as "the wild west."[16]

7

Making Progress, 1885–1914

Between 1885 and 1914, Canada's development strategy began to yield dividends. The population doubled, economic growth skyrocketed, and the "last best west" came into its own (Image 7.1). With cities emerging as buzzing hives of activity, nearly 40 percent of Canada's 8 million inhabitants lived in urban areas by 1914. Such a massive transformation inevitably brought new tensions and exacerbated old ones. The even more spectacular growth of the United States in this period prompted some Canadians to argue for annexation as a solution to the nation's ills, but the British connection served as a powerful countervailing force and was the reason why Canada, still a colony politically and psychologically, became engulfed in a European war in 1914.[1]

CULTURAL CONFLICT

National unity remained a major challenge for Canadian prime ministers. In Quebec, where the Northwest uprising was perceived as a struggle for French language and Catholic religious rights, Riel's execution in 1885 was widely condemned and brought an astonishing fifty thousand people out in protest in Montreal. Drawing on this discontent, Liberals and disaffected Conservatives in Quebec founded the Parti national under the leadership of Honoré Mercier. The new party's success in the 1886 provincial election signaled the collapse of the political alliance between the Conservative Party and the Roman Catholic Church that had prevailed since the 1850s. In

164

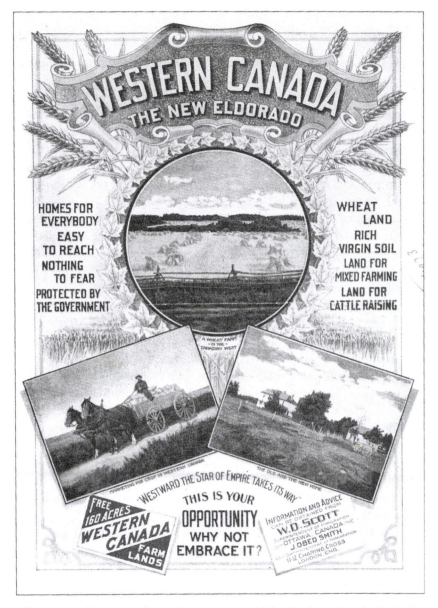

Image 7.1. Posters such as this one were widely distributed in the United States and Europe to encourage immigration to Western Canada. (By permission of Library and Archives Canada/C-85854)

the federal election of 1887, the Liberals won nearly half the seats in Quebec, where nationalist feelings continued to gain ground. In the Maritimes, Acadians also embraced the discourse of nationalism, attempting in a series of congresses to distinguish their identity from that of their francophone cousins in Quebec.

Deciding whether denominational schools were eligible for public funding and which languages of instruction were permitted in the classroom produced controversy across the land. After Confederation, the education question was first joined in New Brunswick, where the Common Schools Act of 1871 excluded Roman Catholic schools from provincial funding. When the courts declared the legislation valid, Ottawa was called upon to take action under the remedial provisions of the BNA Act. This became unnecessary when a violent confrontation in the Acadian community of Caraquet, in January 1875, resulted in two deaths. The tragedy prompted a compromise whereby the provincial government permitted religious orders to teach Roman Catholic students where numbers warranted.

Denominational schools in Ontario were protected by the BNA Act, but French linguistic rights were not. In the nasty aftermath of the Northwest Rebellion, the Ontario government limited hours of instruction in languages other than English. Local school boards often ignored this regulation, but Protestant zealots were determined to impose compliance. The issue merged with the uproar over Quebec's Jesuit Estates Act of 1888, which offered compensation for the Order's properties confiscated following the conquest. When the Quebec government invited Pope Leo XIII to arbitrate among the contending claimants, an Ontario-based organization calling itself the Equal Rights Association launched a campaign to rid the nation of papal and French-Canadian influences.

The Ontario assault on minority rights was echoed in Manitoba, where the population was increasingly English and Protestant. In 1890 Thomas Greenway's Liberal government abolished official bilingualism and the separate schools system guaranteed by the Manitoba Act. Lawyers were summoned. When the Judicial Committee of the Privy Council ruled that the federal government had the powers to restore public funding for denominational schools, the Conservatives were torn between assisting the aggrieved

minority and upholding education as an exclusively provincial matter. Either way, the Conservatives would lose votes.

CANADA IN QUESTION

As the foregoing suggests, provincial rights had emerged as a thorny
issue in the years following Confederation. Oliver Mowat, Liberal
premier of Ontario from 1872 to 1896, led the charge against
Macdonald's efforts to augment federal powers by, among other
things, disallowing provincial legislation. In Mowat's view of federalism, the provinces retained the jurisdiction they held prior to
Confederation except for specific responsibilities granted to the central government. Macdonald was determined to keep the provinces
subordinate to Ottawa. When he attempted to restrict Ontario's
expansion by awarding the resource-rich territories north of Lake
Superior to Manitoba, Mowat personally fought the case in the
courts all the way to the Judicial Committee of the Privy Council
and won. Empire Ontario was not to be denied.

Following his victory at the polls, Mercier convened a meeting
of premiers to discuss matters of common interest. Mowat supported this initiative, as did the Liberal premiers in the Maritimes,
who were experiencing difficulty managing on their federal subsidies. Fed up with being ignored by Ottawa, Nova Scotia premier
William. S. Fielding introduced a resolution in 1886 calling for
repeal of the British North America Act and the establishment of a
Maritime union. New Brunswick's premier, Andrew G. Blair, was
not prepared to go that far, but he was willing to discuss constitutional issues with his provincial counterparts. The Conservative
administration in Manitoba, led by John Norquay, Canada's first
premier of Métis descent, also had grievances to air, most notably the monopoly clause in the CPR contract, which frustrated his
plans to build a railway to the United States. At their meeting in
Quebec City in October 1887, these five premiers – Conservative
premiers in British Columbia and Prince Edward Island declined
to attend – agreed on a number of matters, including the need for
increased provincial subsidies, provincial selection of half of all
senators, and provincial consent before local projects could be
placed under federal control. Macdonald treated the meeting as

an exercise in partisanship, which it was, but provincial grievances were real.

While provincialism festered, relations with the United States continued to spark controversy. The Liberal Party, under the leadership of Edward Blake from 1880 to 1887, included free trade in its election platforms, a policy that appealed to primary producers seeking American markets. Radicals in the Liberal ranks went even further, supporting commercial union with the United States, a policy that would harmonize tariff structures. For the liberal iconoclast Goldwin Smith, a British-born academic living in Toronto, annexation to the United States seemed the best option for Canada. In his book *Canada and the Canadian Question*, published in 1891, Smith argued that annexation would consolidate North America's peoples into one progressive nation, enhance the global power of English-speaking peoples, and submerge French Canadians into an American melting pot.

Union with the United States was not on the agenda for most Canadians, and even free trade was losing some of its lustre. Not only would free trade threaten industries protected by the National Policy tariff, but it might also endanger the British connection, which offered a "sense of power" that Canadians could never mobilize by themselves.[2] Great Britain's renewed interest in imperialism in the closing decades of the nineteenth century was warmly embraced by many anglophone Canadians, who basked in the glory of Queen Victoria's long reign over an empire "where the sun never set." In an effort to give structure to their sentiments, imperial enthusiasts called for a common imperial tariff, colonial representation in an imperial parliament, and cooperation in imperial defence. These policies never fully materialized, but the British connection was widely celebrated in commemorative ceremonies, classrooms, and literary expression.

Canada's future seemed to be clearly on the line in the 1891 election. While Macdonald ran on the slogan "The old flag, the old policy, the old leader," the Liberals, under Wilfrid Laurier, declared their support for "unrestricted reciprocity." This position appealed to the radical wing of the Liberal party, but not to most voters. When Macdonald died three months after the election, his party dissolved into squabbling factions that took their toll on four Conservative prime ministers – John Abbott, John Thompson, Mackenzie Bowell, and Charles Tupper – in rapid succession. Canadians elected a Liberal majority in 1896.

LAURIER'S LIBERALISM

Canada's seventh prime minister was a French-speaking Roman Catholic. Trained in law, Laurier had joined the Rouges as a young man and edited a newspaper, *Le Défricheur*, in Quebec's Eastern Townships. He initially opposed Confederation, but gradually became reconciled to the new political order. After a term in the Quebec assembly, he won a federal seat in 1874 and served briefly as minister of inland revenue in the Mackenzie cabinet. Laurier's principled opposition to conservative forces in Quebec endeared him to liberals everywhere. Under Laurier's leadership, the Liberal Party reformed its organizational structures and, to the relief of business interests, retreated from its rigid free-trade position. Playing to the power of the provinces, Laurier invited Blair, Fielding, and Mowat to serve in his first cabinet.[3]

Laurier was a man of principle, but his success as prime minister had much to do with his ability to compromise. This trait was reflected in his approach to the Manitoba Schools Question. Obliged to uphold his party's provincial rights position, he allowed the Manitoba legislation to stand, but he negotiated a compromise whereby the province agreed to permit religious instruction and instruction in languages other than English where student numbers warranted. A similarly clever manoeuvre on tariffs, applying lower tariffs to any country admitting Canadian products on a preferential basis, automatically granted Great Britain preference but did little to threaten Canadian manufacturers whose main competition came from the United States.

Good luck as much as good management characterized Laurier's term in office. In 1896 global economic conditions began to improve, and they remained relatively buoyant until 1912. The discovery of gold in the Klondike encouraged forty thousand people to make the difficult trek to the Yukon, but they were not the only ones who turned to Canada as a land of opportunity. Under the supervision of Clifford Sifton, appointed minister of the interior in 1897, immigration was vigorously pursued, with spectacular results. Nearly 3 million people came to Canada between 1896 and 1914, many of them settling on the Prairies. In 1905 the Laurier government created two new provinces out of the Northwest Territories. As in Manitoba, the public lands and natural resources remained under federal control in Alberta and Saskatchewan, a policy guaranteed to be a cause for grievance until 1930, when the wishes of the Prairie provinces finally prevailed. Laurier's efforts to extend the privileges of Roman Catholic schools in the new provinces were undermined when Sifton abruptly resigned over the issue.

Encouraged by expansionist euphoria, the Laurier government supported the efforts of the eastern-based Grand Trunk and the western-based Canadian Northern railways to complete transcontinental lines. Like the CPR, the two new railways were riddled with extravagance, patronage, and political corruption, but unlike the CPR, they failed to make a profit and became serious drains on the public purse. In 1918 the federal government assumed control and rolled them, along with the Intercolonial and other failing railway companies, into Canadian National Railways.

NATION AND IMMIGRATION

The impact on Canada of the arrival of 3 million immigrants in the space of one generation cannot be overestimated. In addition to expanding the geographical range of settlement and performing much of the labour required in a dynamic economy, they brought new ideas and cultural diversity. Two-thirds of the newcomers arrived from Great Britain and the United States, but enough came from elsewhere to alter the ethnic composition of Canada and lay the foundations for a pluralistic society that continues to be a defining feature of the nation.

Immigrants flocked to Canada for a variety of reasons, including the offer of free land. By the end of the nineteenth century, the settlement frontiers in Argentina and the United States had vanished as potential homes for the ambitious, oppressed, and dispossessed populations of Europe. If Canada seemed remote and uninviting, the aggressive sales pitch orchestrated by the Department of the Interior in cooperation with private interests made Canadian opportunities

Image 7.2. Galicians at immigration sheds in Quebec City. (Courtesy of Library and Archives Canada/C-4745)

better known to prospective immigrants. In seeking settlers to farm the Prairies, Sifton targeted "peasants in sheep-skin coats" as good prospects.[4] Immigrants from the Hapsburg provinces of Galicia and Bukovyna, known today as Ukrainians, were the most numerous of the European peasant cultures to answer Canada's call. Often poor and illiterate, Ukrainians arrived in successive waves, 150,000 by 1914 and another 70,000 in the interwar years (Image 7.2).

The majority of the newcomers came to stay, but others were sojourners, planning to return home with money in their pockets. In the first decade of the twentieth century, men from the border-lands of Greece, Bulgaria, Serbia, and Albania, known today as Macedonians, found jobs in Toronto's factories, abattoirs, and construction sites, and many of them decided to stay in Canada when the Balkan wars wracked their homeland in 1912–13. Italians came both as settlers and sojourners, their numbers swelling in the first two decades of the twentieth century when more than 120,000 Italians arrived in Canada. Like the Macedonians, most of the Italian immigrants were young men, many of them recruited by Italian labour agents (*padrone*) based in Montreal and Toronto to work on contract for railway, mining, and construction companies.

Canadians had little interest in welcoming non-white immigrants, but a few managed to slip through the barriers mounted against them. Because their families in China depended upon the money they sent home, many of the Chinese men recruited to build the CPR stayed on. Responding to pressure from British Columbia, where most of the Chinese had settled, the federal government imposed a head tax on Chinese immigrants in 1885. Japanese immigrants who established themselves in farming, fishing, and trade in British Columbia also faced discrimination. When whites marched through Asian sections of Vancouver, breaking windows and shouting racist slogans in 1907, the federal government responded by negotiating a "gentleman's agreement" with Japan that restricted the number of Japanese allowed to enter the country to four hundred annually. Whether immigrant or Canadian-born, Chinese and Japanese were denied the franchise in the western provinces, barred from access to the professions, subjected to discriminatory housing covenants, and segregated in public places.

It was more difficult to impose restrictions on immigrants from India, which, like Canada, was a British colony. In 1908 the federal government passed an order-in-council requiring East Indians to arrive by continuous passage from their homeland. Since there was no direct steamship line between the two countries, this policy served its exclusionary purpose. In 1913 a group of Sikhs successfully contested the restriction, a victory that encouraged others to charter the *Komagata Maru*, a Japanese-owned freighter, to bring 376 Punjabis to Canada in 1914. Detained on board for two months in Vancouver harbour while their case was heard before the courts, the would-be immigrants were eventually ordered to leave.

Nearly one-third of the new immigrants came from the United States. Because most of them spoke English and came as individuals, they attracted little attention from Canadians. It was different for Americans with black skin. The arrival on the Prairies of thirteen hundred African American homesteaders from Oklahoma between 1910 and 1912 resulted in petitions from all three Prairie provinces

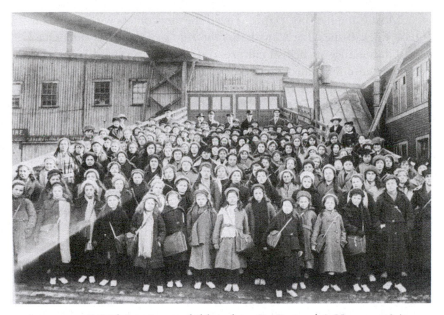

Image 7.3. British immigrant children from Dr. Barnardo's Homes arriving at the port of Saint John, New Brunswick. (By permission of Library and Archives Canada/Online MIKAN no. 3193366)

urging Ottawa to ban further admission of black immigrants. The federal government resisted a formal policy of exclusion, but border officials were rewarded for the rigourous application of immigration regulations to blacks trying to enter the country.

Despite their fondness for all things British, Anglo-Canadians were not always keen on "green Englishmen," who sometimes proved to be indifferent farmers and exhibited an annoying sense of superiority. Domestic servants were more welcome. Between 1904 and 1914, some ninety thousand British women and others from continental Europe came to Canada to work in the homes of the rapidly expanding middle class. Great Britain was also the source of nearly a hundred thousand poor and orphaned children sent to Canada between the 1860s and 1920s. Most of them were indentured to farm families as cheap labour. Known as "Home Children" – "home" was a term used for orphanage – they seldom received the care they were promised (Image 7.3).

Most Canadian-born citizens eyed the newcomers with suspicion. For English-speaking Canadians, the tide of foreigners threatened the dominance of British culture and socially accepted behaviour. Reformers complained about the political values and drinking habits of immigrants, their treatment of women, and even wedding celebrations that seemed excessively exuberant. When a radical branch of the Doukhobors, known as Sons of Freedom, destroyed their property and conducted nude protest marches, shocked government officials tried to break up their community by demanding that the strict letter of the homestead law be observed. Schools were perceived as the most likely vehicle for inculcating Anglo-conformity, and successive waves of immigrant children endured the strict tutelage of teachers, most of them young women, who believed it was their duty to Canadianize their charges.

Francophones, meanwhile, were anxious about a changing demography that made them a smaller minority in the country. Instead of moving to the Prairies, which were increasingly dominated by English-speaking Protestants, francophones in Quebec either established new farms on the rocky settlement frontier of their province or slipped across the border to New England, where factory jobs were plentiful and a Franco-American community was in place to receive them. Nationalist spokesman Henri Bourassa, the grandson of Louis-Joseph Papineau, argued for a policy of bilingualism and biculturalism to ensure the survival of French culture in Canada, but this view was rejected by English- and French-speaking Canadians alike. Both sides of the linguistic divide, however, shared Bourassa's concerns about the impact of the new industrial order on Canadian society.

THE ECONOMY ON A ROLL

Between 1885 and 1914, Canada's economy went from strength to strength. Industrial development was initially reflected in the expansion of consumer goods industries, such as textiles, clothing, footwear, and cigars, followed by a surge in capital goods industries, such as machinery and equipment, and new technologies that spurred development in mining, pulp and paper, and chemical industries. By 1921 nearly 30 percent of Canada's GNP was derived from manufacturing and construction, a proportion that remained virtually constant until the 1990s.

The development of an iron and steel industry at the turn of the century signaled Canada's arrival as an industrial nation. Located in convenient proximity to coal mines on Cape Breton Island and iron ore shipped from Bell Island, Newfoundland, Sydney became home to Nova Scotia Coal and Steel and Dominion Iron and Steel. The Hamilton Steel and Iron Company began pouring open-hearth steel in 1900 and established its dominance in the industry following its reorganization by Canadian financier Max Aitken as Stelco in 1910. By that time, American visionary Francis Hector Clergue had capped his industrial empire at Sault Ste. Marie with a massive steel and iron works. Between 1877 and 1900, Canadian iron production increased over sixfold, and it multiplied tenfold again by 1913.

With nearly 80 percent of Canada's electrical generating capacity, Ontario and Quebec dominated the second industrial revolution based on mining, chemicals, and pulp and paper, which relied on abundant energy resources. Ontario's initiative in developing Niagara Falls gave the province a massive source of hydroelectric power. In Quebec American capital developed Shawinigan Falls on the St. Maurice River. Unlike Ontario, which made hydro a government-run service in 1906, Quebec left the hydro industry to private enterprise. Whether publicly or privately owned, the abundant supply of hydroelectric power served as a powerful magnet to industries. By 1901 Ontario accounted for fully half of the gross value of Canadian manufacturing and Quebec for nearly one-third.

In this period Canada emerged as a resource frontier on a global scale. The most spectacular success story played out on the Prairies, which became the breadbasket of the world. By 1914, Canada's wheat production was second in volume only to that of the United States. On the Atlantic coast, investment poured into canning factories designed to process lobster, herring, and sardines, and into cold storage facilities to handle fresh fish, but the industry remained highly decentralized and subject to cutthroat competition. In British Columbia the lucrative salmon-processing industry was centralized under the British Columbia Packers Association in 1902. British Columbia was also Canada's new timber frontier, with Pacific coast cedar and Douglas fir meeting the demand for lumber in rapidly growing North American cities. Although the Klondike gold rush made headlines, it had less impact on the Canadian economy than other mining ventures. Coal mines in the Maritimes, Alberta, and British Columbia expanded, and when the processes for separating complex ores were developed, the nickel-copper deposits around Sudbury, Ontario, and zinc-lead-silver deposits in British Columbia were brought into production.

Like other industrializing countries, Canada spawned an expanding service sector. The bureaucracies that increasingly characterized state and private institutions required an army of clerks, lawyers, and managers to keep their operations running smoothly, while cities depended on construction workers, cabdrivers, cleaners, cooks, and other service providers. Clerical work, increasingly performed by women skilled in the use of the new mechanical typewriter, was one of the fastest-growing occupations. Retailing also blossomed, its central role in the industrial age symbolized by the meteoric rise of the T. Eaton Company from a new dry-goods and clothing store in Toronto in 1869 to a commercial empire based on catalogue sales and multiple branches throughout Canada and overseas. No longer sustained by a fur trade monopoly, the Hudson's Bay Company turned to retailing, opening the first of a chain of department stores in Winnipeg in 1881.

Canada's toothless anti-combine laws, first introduced in 1889, had little impact on corporate practices, which were aimed at controlling the market. A spate of mergers in the 1880s was followed by an even bigger merger movement in the early twentieth century. Many of the companies established in this period, among them Massey-Harris, Imperial Oil, Bell Canada, General Electric, Stelco, and the Canada Cement Company, remained household names in Canada for nearly a century. The same trends prevailed in banking, with four of the five Canadian banks that still tower over the business centres of Canadian cities – Nova Scotia, Commerce, Montreal, and Royal – establishing their position in the financial firmament.

LABOUR WOES

The gap between rich and poor was a singular feature of the new industrial order. While Canada's corporate elite indulged in conspicuous displays of their accumulating wealth, labourers often faced penury. They worked long hours for low wages under strict, sometimes tyrannical, supervision, and they had no job security. In 1886 Macdonald tried to spike criticism of labour conditions in Canadian factories by establishing a Royal Commission on the Relations of Labour and Capital. The commissioners held inquiries in Ontario, Quebec, and the Maritimes, and their report, submitted in 1889, offered damning evidence of cruel and exploitative practices. The commissioners recommended a wide range of reforms, including compensation for injury on the job and the prohibition of child labour, but the only immediate outcome of the inquiry was the declaration in 1894 of a national holiday – Labour Day – for Canada's working people.

Those hoping to eliminate the worst abuses of the factory system faced a number of hurdles, among them provincial jurisdiction over workplace conditions, which obliged reforms to proceed piecemeal. And, once passed, labour laws were rarely enforced. Factory Acts prohibiting employment in factories of boys under twelve and girls under fourteen were introduced in Ontario and Quebec in the 1880s and later replicated elsewhere, but they were often circumvented by families who relied on the labour of their children for survival. In response to the demands of an increasingly organized labour movement, the Laurier government passed an Alien Labour Act (1897) to prevent companies from importing low-paid contract labour and strikebreakers from the United States. It had little impact. Many employers tried to earn the loyalty of their employees by sponsoring company picnics, excursions to nearby tourist sites, and food baskets at Christmastime, but when such inducements failed, they used force, calling upon governments to send in police, militia, and troops to put down strikes.

Although unions were organized to press for reforms, their power was compromised by jurisdictional disputes. The Noble and Holy Order of the Knights of Labor, which had originated in 1869 among Philadelphia garment cutters, gained a foothold in central Canada in the 1880s, where it tried to organize all workers regardless of skill in "industrial" unions. In contrast, craft unions organized workers according to their trade and dominated the Trades and Labour Congress (TLC), established in 1883. The TLC adopted the policy of the American Federation of Labor (AFL) of seeking higher wages and improved working conditions rather than radical changes to the capitalist system. In 1902, at a meeting in Berlin, Ontario, the TLC formally affiliated with the AFL and then expelled industrial unions, such as the Knights of Labor, from its ranks.

Labour organizations were also fragmented along regional and cultural lines. In Quebec the Roman Catholic Church created its own, invariably conservative, labour organizations, which came together as the Confédération des travailleurs catholiques du Canada in 1921. Labour in Nova Scotia was represented by the Provincial Workmen's Association, initially a militant union that waged more than seventy strikes before 1900. By the first decade of the twentieth century, coal miners in Nova Scotia, Alberta, and British Columbia had turned to the more radical United Mine Workers (UMW) of America. Unskilled labourers, especially in British Columbia, joined the Industrial Workers of the World (IWW), an American-based organization that advocated syndicalism to overthrow the yoke of capitalism.

In 1900 the federal government established a Department of Labour and hired a university-trained labour relations expert, William Lyon Mackenzie King, as its first deputy minister. King helped to engineer the 1907 Industrial Disputes Investigation Act, which prohibited strikes and lockouts in public utilities and mines until the dispute had been investigated by a tripartite board of arbitration representing labour, capital, and government. Since the legislation offered no protection when employers retaliated against workers attempting to organize, it is not surprising that only 10 percent of the Canadian labour force was unionized in 1910.

THE AGE OF REFORM

Industrialization was accompanied by an unprecedented movement of people from rural areas to cities. In the boom years from 1901 to 1911, the populations of Montreal and Toronto doubled, and western cities such as Winnipeg, Calgary, Edmonton, and Vancouver grew even faster. Wherever they were located, cities exhibited the worst features of uncontrolled growth. Noise, overcrowding, inadequate sewerage disposal, and disease made life unpleasant for most city dwellers, and brought demands for reform.

Reform had many faces in industrializing Canada, but at its core was increasingly the recognition that social conditions, rather than individual flaws, were part of the problem. Most reformers were progressives – demanding action by the state to reform the worst outcomes of capitalism – but a few so-called radicals imagined a day when capitalism would be abolished. Whatever their focus, reform efforts were expressed in a vocabulary of morality that was widely shared in Victorian Canada. In 1886 Toronto's municipal government even created a Morality Department in the city's police force to pursue prostitutes, alcohol and drug dealers, gamblers, and vagrants. As a result of this and similar initiatives, the city was labeled "Toronto the Good," a reputation that lingered until the second half of the twentieth century.

At the forefront of the movement for progressive reform was a formidable alliance of professionals, church leaders, and hardworking volunteers. Their influence was enhanced by developments in communications, which enabled them to form nationwide organizations and draw support from their international counterparts. By the twentieth century, health professionals had become especially prominent, using new scientific evidence to marshal support for building hospitals, establishing clinics for young mothers and their babies, and teaching schoolchildren that "Cleanliness is next to Godliness." Churches, meanwhile, embraced the "social gospel," expanding their charitable activities to address the appalling conditions that characterized the industrial age. Even the Roman Catholic Church was becoming more receptive to reform ideals. In 1887 Pope Leo XIII lifted an ineffectual ban on the Knights of Labor, and in his encyclical of 1891, *Rerum Novarum*, he condemned an uncontrolled market economy.

The movement to prohibit the manufacture, sale, and consumption of alcohol continued to attract wide-ranging support. When he assumed office, Laurier ducked the issue by agreeing to a national referendum. Held in 1898, it yielded a majority for prohibition in every province except Quebec. The relatively small overall majority and a low voter turnout allowed Laurier to resist the pressure for federal legislation, but prohibitionists continued their crusade at the provincial and municipal levels and were particularly active at election time, demanding that all candidates openly declare their position on alcohol.

On other matters, Ottawa bowed to public pressure. The Protestant churches cooperated with union leaders, through the Lord's Day Alliance, to insist that the federal government impose Sunday observance laws in 1907. Buoyed by this achievement, the Methodists and Presbyterians collaborated in the founding in 1907 of the Moral and Social Reform Council of Canada (rechristened the Social Service Council of Canada in 1913) to pursue their ambitious reform agenda. On one matter most reformers agreed. The new industrial order made it easier for men to shirk their family obligations. In 1913 a federal law made it a criminal offense not to support a wife, including a common law wife.

In their quest for a better society, reformers focused on sexual practices. Reforms to the Criminal Code in 1892 included two years' imprisonment for anyone convicted of disseminating ways of preventing conception or causing abortion. Nevertheless, some progressives went even further and advocated a program of eugenics. Drawing on scientific findings relating to reproduction in the plant and animal world, eugenicists argued that society could be improved by preventing people with undesirable mental and physical traits from reproducing. The enthusiasm for social control and scientific analysis also led to same-sex relationships being labeled "homosexual" and deemed unnatural. While social purity advocates demanded jail sentences for homosexuals, the medical profession identified same-sex attraction as a form of insanity requiring confinement in a lunatic asylum.

With pollution and resource depletion proceeding at alarming rates, progressives took up the cause of environmental reform. The example of the United States inspired the federal government to create Banff Hot Springs Reserve and Rocky Mountain Park in 1885, and Ontario became the first province to follow suit with the founding of Algonquin Provincial Park in 1893. Following the North American Conservation Conference convened by President Theodore Roosevelt in 1909, the Laurier administration established a Canadian Commission of Conservation. Under the energetic direction of Clifford Sifton, the commission investigated everything from fur farming and migratory birds to power development and urban planning.

The "city beautiful" movement, with its notions of rational planning, elegant architecture, and public spaces, appealed to many progressives. Originating in Europe and the United States, the movement in Canada established voluntary associations, such as Montreal's City Improvement League, and enlisted the support of the Union of Canadian Municipalities, established in 1901. Progressive reformers pressed for government control of essential urban services, including water, power, telephones, and street railways, and the appointment of boards staffed by experts to curb the power of profit-seeking interests. In communities large and small, fraternal organizations, such as the Independent Order of Odd Fellows, the Rotary, and Chambers of Commerce, lent their energies to improving local conditions.

With most rural areas connected to the wider world through railways, regular postal service, and newspapers devoted to the farm population, reform sentiments blossomed in the countryside. Rural people shared many of the concerns of their city cousins, prohibition most particularly, but they were also alarmed by the growing power of urban-based banks and insurance companies, and by the depopulation of rural areas, which lacked many of the services cities had to offer. The flight of women from the farm to take up opportunities in the cities was a particular concern. As agriculture became more commercialized, men gradually took control over women's work in the dairy and garden, but the drudgery and isolation associated with farm life still compared unfavourably to the independence provided by a wage-paying job in the city.

Rural reform movements rolled across Canada in successive waves and varied from region to region. In eastern Canada, the American-inspired Grange Movement and the Patrons of Industry gained a wide following. On the Prairies, agrarian discontent led to the creation in 1901 of the Territorial Grain Growers' Association, which became the basis for provincial associations following the creation of the provinces of Saskatchewan and Alberta in 1905. Cooperatives, organized on the principle of cooperation rather than competition and owned by their members rather than by investors, were also popular in rural Canada. The founding in 1909 of the Cooperative Union of Canada brought cooperators together for education and lobbying activities. In the same year, Ontario farmers and western grain growers established the Canadian Council of Agriculture. The results of all this organizing activity were manifested in 1910 when a thousand farmers descended on Parliament

Hill demanding lower tariffs, better rail and grain elevator service, and legislation supporting cooperative enterprises. In 1914 the United Farmers of Ontario was formed, with direct political action on its agenda.

As elsewhere in the Western world, socialism took root. The socialist cause was advanced by the arrival of immigrants with experiences in radical politics, but this also meant that diversity prevailed. With Marxism, Christian socialism, and reformism competing for attention, no single approach or political party gained nationwide traction. The example of Great Britain, where labourers were throwing their support behind the Independent Labour Party, founded in 1893, offered an appealing option for moderate socialists. In 1900 Arthur Puttee was elected as a labour candidate in Winnipeg, Canada's most politically charged city, but few were able to emulate his success.

WOMEN IN PUBLIC

Women served as the rank and file of many Canadian reform efforts. The doctrine of separate spheres initially led women to organize separately from men and to focus their energies on the problems facing women and children. In the 1870s, Women's Missionary Aid Societies sprouted in various Protestant churches and women helped to found branches of the Young Woman's Christian Association (YWCA), beginning in Saint John in 1870, to provide accommodation for single women in urban environments. The first Canadian branch of the Woman's Christian Temperance Union (WCTU) was founded by Letitia Youmans in 1874 in Picton, Ontario, and branches spread quickly across the nation. Roman Catholic women, especially in Quebec, continued to work within the religious orders that had responsibility for education, health care, and social services. By 1901, more than 6 percent of the province's single women over twenty years of age were nuns. On the Prairies, women's auxiliaries of the Grain Growers' Association developed a busy agenda, including reform of the homestead laws that denied women the right to apply for land. Farm women were also the focus of Women's Institutes, the first one founded in 1897 by Adelaide Hoodless in Stoney Creek, Ontario, following the death of her child from drinking impure milk.

Women's activism came together in the National Council of Women of Canada (NCWC), a national federation of women's clubs, established in 1893. The brainchild of Lady Aberdeen, the wife of the governor general, it encompassed a wide range of organizations and supported causes such as temperance, child welfare, and professional advancement for women. Lady Aberdeen was also the moving force behind the Victorian Order of Nurses (1897), an organization to provide nursing services in remote areas. In 1910 the NCWC finally endorsed women's suffrage, perceived as a radical but necessary step in recognizing women as having public power in their own right.

By the end of the nineteenth century, "woman suffrage" was a reform whose time had come. The women associated with the Literary Society in Toronto felt sufficiently confident in 1883 to launch Canada's first Woman's Suffrage Association. Although the high profile of women in prohibition and other reform causes made many men nervous, the common arguments against female suffrage – that politics was too rough for "ladies" or that women were less intelligent than men – failed to carry much weight in a liberalizing society. Two perspectives dominated the argument in support of female suffrage: liberal feminists demanded the vote and the abolition of laws that discriminated against women on the principle of fairness; maternal feminists drew on the doctrine of separate spheres to claim power in their roles as wives and mothers. However one approached it, women's suffrage became central to the struggle for reform.

Female suffrage was a slow slog, but women managed to score some victories along the way. Beginning in the 1880s, laws granting married women rights over their property and children and the right to vote in civic elections passed in most provinces. Mount Allison, a Methodist institution of higher education in Sackville, New Brunswick, led the British Empire in opening its doors to women in the 1870s, and most Canadian universities gradually followed, though the new science and professional programs remained largely male preserves. Obliged to train in the United States, medical doctors Emily Stowe and Jenny Trout led the battle to force Queen's University and the University of Toronto to admit women to their medical programs. They met partial success in 1883 when medical schools for women were established in both institutions. By the turn of the twentieth century, Canadians had produced their own suffrage superstar in Manitoba's Nellie McClung, a novelist and activist whose clever repartee proved highly effective.

CANADIAN SOCIETY AND CULTURE

The same trends that sustained reform movements – the rise in literacy, advances in communication, and a sense that progress was possible – also enriched Canadian intellectual life and cultural expression. Canadians greatly benefitted from porous borders that welcomed new people and ideas and made Canada a testing ground for innovation. Scottish-born Alexander Graham Bell experimented with the telephone and airplane on Canadian soil, and the east coast became the site of Guglielmo Marconi's wireless experiments at the turn of the century. Nevertheless, Canadians often found the United States the best place to put their abilities into practice, as was the case with Reginald Fessenden, who experimented with radio transmission, and James Naismith, who invented the game of basketball, in Massachusetts.

As more Canadians gravitated to cities, the rural environment began to take on a rosy hue among those who did not live there. Urbanites joined organizations such as the Field-Naturalists' Club and established foundations to fund summer vacations in the countryside for children from city slums. With urban life increasingly defining what it meant to be a man, boys became the particular focus of reformers who saw nature as the vehicle for inculcating masculine virtues. Naturalist and animal-story writer Ernest Thompson Seton inspired the Woodcraft Club movement dedicated to teaching boys the skills of tracking, camping, canoeing, and woodcraft. Similar skills were taught by the Boy Scouts, founded in Britain in 1908 by South African War veteran Robert Baden-Powell, who also launched the Girl Guides in 1909. Urbanites who could afford to do so boarded trains in the summer months for rural retreats such as Muskoka, Murray Bay, St. Andrew's-by-the-Sea, Cavendish Beach, the Bras d'Or Lakes, or one of the new national or provincial parks. For those seeking "authenticity," hunting and fishing with an Aboriginal guide provided the ultimate "wilderness experience."

Sporting activities were also reshaped by the opportunities and values of the industrial age. Competitive games, the codification of rules regulating play, and commercialization paralleled trends in the marketplace and sparked debates about the purpose of sports. While the middle class clung tenaciously to the amateur ideal, with its prohibition of payment to participants and its gentlemanly codes of conduct, professionalism increasingly prevailed. In 1893 Governor General Lord Stanley donated a cup to the Canadian amateur hockey champions. After winning the Stanley Cup in 1908, the Montreal Wanderers immediately turned professional and the trophy followed suit. The Grey Cup, donated in 1909 by Governor General Earl Grey for football, experienced a similar trajectory. Professional baseball emerged as the most popular spectator sport, attracting a huge working-class audience throughout Canada. By 1914, the prevalence of school and college athletics and the multitude of programs run by voluntary groups had given sports an unprecedented place in the lives of most young Canadians.

The arts also flourished in the age of industry, with local and touring theatre companies, literary clubs, and poetry readings attracting large audiences.[5] As with sports, governors general were often instrumental in encouraging cultural endeavours, none more so than the Marquis of Lorne, who inspired the founding of the Royal Canadian Academy of Arts (1880), the National Gallery of Canada (1880), and the Royal Society of Canada (1882). Of the thirty-six organizations affiliated with the Royal Society in 1900, two-thirds were historical in their focus, and they included a group from the Six Nations and two women's historical societies.[6] Canadian historians, both amateur and university-trained, drew selectively and romantically on past events to support nation-building efforts. In schools, children learned about the heroic feats of Champlain, Dollard des Ormeaux, Madeleine de Verchères, Isaac Brock, and Laura Secord, among others. Commemorations such as the one held to mark the tercentenary of Quebec City in 1908 were attended by thousands of people and left in their wake statues, monuments, and plaques to serve as signposts to collective historical memory.

Canadians were enthusiastic consumers of fiction, and a few Canadian writers achieved international status. After winning first prize for her manuscript in an American Humane Society competition, Margaret Marshall Saunders sold more than a million copies of *Beautiful Joe* (1893), the story of a dog rescued from a brutal master. Lucy Maud Montgomery's first published novel, *Anne of Green Gables*, about a spunky orphan, became an instant success when it appeared in 1908. With its idealization of rural life, the peasant novel, a popular European genre, took firm root in Canada. Its most enduring example, Louis Hémon's *Maria Chapdelaine* (1913), evoked the difficult choice for many French Canadians of moving either to New England to find work or to communities on Quebec's agricultural frontier. International audiences were fascinated by Aboriginal peoples, who figured prominently in many Canadian works. Readings by E. Pauline Johnson, Canada's "Mohawk Princess," on stages in and outside Canada drew on her hybrid background for dramatic effect. For Archie Belaney growing up in England, an Aboriginal heritage proved so appealing that he moved to Canada in 1906 and assumed an Aboriginal identity, becoming famous as a writer and environmentalist under the name of Grey Owl.

The new realism was reflected in the work of Sara Jeannette Duncan, a disciple of the American novelist Henry James. In her novel *The Imperialist* (1904), she dissected small-town Ontario and explored the need to balance British sentiment with the reality of North American life. Canada's most popular humourist, Stephen Leacock, taught economics at McGill University, a discipline that helped him to expose the foibles of North American capitalism in such books as *Sunshine Sketches of a Little Town* (1912) and *Arcadian Adventures of the Idle Rich* (1914). A Canadian counterpoint to American and British magazines could be found in *Saturday Night* (1887), *Canadian Magazine* (1893), and *Busy Man's Magazine* (1905), which became *Maclean's Magazine* in 1911.

Canadian artists followed trends defined elsewhere and remained wedded to representational works that sold well. In Ontario the men who would eventually be known as the Group of Seven – Lawren Harris, J. E. H. MacDonald, Frank Carmichael, Frank Johnston, Arthur Lismer, Fred Varley, and A. Y. Jackson – began applying new approaches to art in their sketches of Algonquin Park, where one of their earlier collaborators, Tom Thompson, drowned in 1917. On the west coast, Emily Carr worked in splendid isolation to hone a powerful, postimpressionist style to convey the majesty of the British Columbian landscape and its Aboriginal inhabitants. For most people, the Brownie camera, introduced in the United States by Eastman Kodak in 1900, produced the best pictures and at a cost they could afford. The "movies," which first appeared on the scene in the late 1890s and usually cost a nickel to view, drew both enthusiastic crowds and moral condemnation.

ABORIGINAL PEOPLES IN THE AGE OF PROGRESS

Aboriginal peoples throughout industrializing Canada adjusted as best they could to the forces swirling around them. It was not that they were ignored. Residential schools, most of them run by the churches that pioneered in Aboriginal missions, took root in this period,[7] while Frank Oliver, Sifton's successor as minister of the interior, introduced measures facilitating the expropriation of reserve lands that stood in the way of "progress." Aboriginal peoples tried to fight back by petitioning London and contesting the loss of their land in court but with little success.

Like many other Canadians, Aboriginal peoples found jobs in the industrial economy. The Iroquois of Kahnawake, near Montreal, became widely known as skilled construction workers, especially on the new skyscrapers that dominated the downtown core of major cities. In areas where railways were being constructed, Aboriginal women did laundry and cleaning for wages while men worked on the lines. On the Pacific coast, Aboriginals worked in the lumber mills, mines, canneries, and the commercial fishery, even as access to traditional salmon-fishing sites was being denied them. A few, including Riel's lieutenant Gabriel Dumont, who joined Buffalo Bill's Wild West show in 1886, performed what were perceived as traditional Aboriginal cultural practices for audiences becoming hooked on fictional narratives built around cowboys and Indians.

With the discovery of gold in the Yukon, the federal government moved quickly to assert its authority in the Northwest Territories, signing treaties with the Dene in 1898. Aboriginals living in the territories had no say when the boundaries of Quebec, Ontario, Manitoba, Saskatchewan, and Alberta achieved their present configuration early in the twentieth century. Because Canada's claim to its Arctic sector was called into question by other nations, the federal government sponsored forays into the north by Captain Joseph Bernier between 1906 and 1911 and Vilhjalmur Stefansson in 1913. The Inuit of the eastern Arctic remained largely outside European influences, but the inhabitants of the central and western Arctic bore the brunt of diseases and the slaughter of whales and walrus. As a result the Inuvialuit were almost wiped out by the Alaskan Inuit.

LAURIER'S CHALLENGES

Laurier was a popular prime minister and continued to win convincing victories in federal elections. Like Macdonald, Laurier built his success on support in Quebec and Ontario, but the western provinces, increasingly a force to be reckoned with, complicated the political scene by championing free trade and railing against eastern influences. International developments also raised troubling questions about where Canadian interests lay.

In 1899 Britain declared war against Dutch settlers – called Boers – in South Africa. Many anglophone Canadians felt that it was their war too and pressured Laurier to send a Canadian contingent to South Africa, a policy supported in London and by the British commander of the Canadian militia. In sharp contrast, Bourassa and other French-Canadian nationalists, who identified with the embattled Boers, were determined that Canada not be involved in the conflict. Laurier's compromise – Ottawa would equip and raise volunteers, but once in South Africa they would be paid and deployed by the British – cost him politically. It was perceived as too little by jingoistic imperialists and too much by Bourassa, who resigned from the House of Commons in protest. More than 7,000 Canadians volunteered for service and 244 of them died in the South African War. At home women joined the Imperial Order Daughters of the Empire founded in 1900 to support the war effort.

Laurier's attempts to find a middle ground between subordination to imperial authorities and total independence were made more complicated by the United States, which had entered another expansionary phase. In 1898 the Americans defeated Spain in a war over

Cuba and then occupied Puerto Rico, Guam, and the Philippines. The disputed boundary between Alaska and the Yukon seemed to present the opportunity for another takeover. With the discovery of gold in the Klondike, the width of the Alaska Panhandle suddenly became relevant for determining who owned the ports through which people and goods entered the goldfields. Canada's dependence on Britain in foreign affairs was underscored when the British appointee to the tribunal established in 1903 to decide the boundary sided with the United States.

As a result of the meddling of British officers in Canada's affairs during the South African War and the bad feelings lingering from the Alaska boundary decision, the Laurier government insisted in 1904 that the officer commanding the Canadian militia be appointed by Canada rather than by Britain. Canada theoretically also assumed greater responsibility for its own defence in 1906 when Britain withdrew its troops from Halifax and Esquimalt, the last two British bases in Canada. In 1909 John A. Macdonald's former secretary, Joseph Pope, was charged with the task of establishing a Department of External Affairs. Although Great Britain was still technically in control of Canada's external relations, the growing volume of paperwork surrounding trade, boundary disputes, the fisheries, and other matters pointed to the need for bureaucratic surveillance over the nation's international interests.

The problem of naval defence proved especially problematic. Given the escalating Anglo-German rivalry, Canadians were pressed either to make a direct financial contribution to the British Admiralty or to establish their own navy. Laurier typically took a compromise position. His Naval Service Bill, introduced in 1910, proposed a Canadian navy that, in times of war, could be placed under imperial control. United in their disdain for Laurier's "tinpot navy," the Conservatives were nevertheless deeply divided between an English-Canadian majority in their party demanding a direct contribution to the British Admiralty and French Canadians who opposed any money being spent on naval defence. In 1910 Henri Bourassa, the undisputed spokesman for the nationalist cause in Quebec, launched a new newspaper, *Le Devoir*, which trumpeted his anti-imperialist views on the matter.

THE BORDEN ADMINISTRATION, 1911–1914

As the 1911 election neared, the combination of nationalist forces in Quebec, alienation on the Prairies, and charges of corruption threatened to undermine Laurier's administration. Its chances for success suddenly brightened when the United States, under Republican President William Howard Taft, made an offer that seemed too good to refuse: a comprehensive trade agreement that allowed the free entry of a wide range of natural products and lower rates on a number of manufactured goods, including the agricultural implements and machinery so necessary for Canadian farms. The Liberals made the much-sought reciprocity treaty the central plank in their campaign platform (Image 7.4).

For once Laurier's political acuity failed him. Enraged by the prospect of reciprocity, eighteen prominent Toronto businessmen and financiers, along with the Canadian Manufacturers' Association, deserted the Liberal Party, denouncing reciprocity as a threat to Canada's survival as a nation. At the same time, Laurier's Quebec stronghold crumbled as Bourassa's nationalists damned the naval policy as a sellout to English Canada. The popular vote in the hard-fought 1911 election was close, but Liberals won only 13 of Ontario's 86 constituencies and altogether captured only 87 ridings; the Conservatives took 134 seats, including 27 in Quebec.

Robert Laird Borden, federal Conservative Party leader since 1901, had little of the charisma that clung to Laurier. An earnest, hardworking, and decent man, Borden had built a large legal practice in Halifax and had broken his ties with the Liberals in 1891 over the issue of reciprocity. He ran for office as a Conservative in 1896 and was Tupper's choice as his successor. Borden worked doggedly to rebuild a party shattered by the divisions in the 1890s and to bring a progressive perspective to its platform. In the 1908 and 1911 elections the party championed policies such as free rural mail delivery, civil service reform, public ownership of utilities, and federal assistance to technical education.[8]

Borden had a rough ride as prime minister. A little over a year after he took office, the leader of the Quebec contingent in the cabinet, Frederick Debartzch Monk, resigned over the naval question. Like other Quebec nationalists, he was opposed to Borden's policy

Image 7.4. Prime Minister Wilfrid Laurier is shown here at a ceremony to lay the cornerstone for the College Building at the University of Saskatchewan on 29 July 1910. His visit to the Prairies that year convinced him that a free-trade treaty with the United States would clinch Liberal support in the western provinces. (Courtesy of University of Saskatchewan Archives, A-8)

to make an "emergency" $35 million contribution to Great Britain's efforts to build up the imperial navy. When the Conservative Party's Naval Aid Bill was introduced into the House of Commons, it encountered such fierce opposition from the Liberals that the government invoked closure, a manoeuvre designed to limit debate. This was the first time that such a procedure had been used in Canada, and Laurier pointed to it as justification for instructing the Liberals in the Senate to defeat the bill.

Legislation creating a tariff commission and providing subsidies to provincial highways also fell victim to the Senate's powers to veto and amend bills. In justifying their obstructionism, Liberal

senators argued that the Borden administration was usurping powers that were not authorized by the BNA Act. Even the Grain Act of
1912, which created a Board of Grain Commissioners and gave the
federal government the power to own and operate terminal grain
elevators, had to be carefully administered so as not to invoke the
wrath of the Liberal senators.

Not all programs foundered on the rock of Senate intransi-
gence. In the Prairie provinces, Borden's popularity soared when
he agreed to support the construction of a railroad to Hudson
Bay. Farmers were pleased when many of the provisions of the
aborted free-trade agreement of 1911 were made available in the
Underwood Tariff adopted by the United States in 1913. In 1912
Borden made good on his promise to Canada's most powerful
provinces – Quebec, Ontario, and Manitoba – that he would grant
them huge sections of federally administered territories on their
northern borders. And many Canadians, including bankers and
brokers, were relieved when the federal government stepped in to
save the nation's two faltering railway companies from impending
bankruptcy.

When an economic recession descended in 1912, the downside of
the industrial economy became manifest. The federal government
responded by appointing a commission on the cost of living in 1913
and by urging the railways to maintain high levels of employment.
In the larger cities, municipal governments established employment
bureaus. These efforts proved inadequate for the many people facing
destitution, including the hundreds of thousands of immigrants still
pouring into the country. In August 1914 the economic crisis was
eclipsed by an even larger one – the outbreak of war in Europe.

CONCLUSION

If Borden's first three years in office proved challenging, the next
four years would test his endurance to the limit. The outbreak of
the First World War in the summer of 1914 only added to the class,
cultural, and regional tensions that made governing Canada so difficult. Despite impressive economic growth and successful political
compromises, Canada was still a fragile nation-state. Alternative

destinies, including provincial independence, union with the United States, and imperial federation, continued to attract those who were disappointed in what Canada had to offer. It was anything but certain that the country could survive the pressures of fighting an all-out war.

8

Hanging On, 1914–1945

Between 1914 and 1945, two world wars, an influenza pandemic, and economic collapse touched the lives of all Canadians. Each of these crises enhanced the role of the state and deepened the fault lines that bedeviled the nation. As political parties sprouted left and right to address perceived problems, it was an intensely political time, fraught with danger and potential. It was also a period in which mass consumer culture called into question old verities and made automobiles, fashions, household appliances, radios, and movies the standard-bearers of status and well-being. With no place to hide from global trends, security – economically, politically, and militarily – became the overriding obsession.

DESCENT INTO THE ABYSS

As a member of the British Empire, Canada was automatically at war when Great Britain declared its intention on 3 August 1914 to intervene in the madness unfolding in Europe.[1] The assassination of Austrian Archduke Franz Ferdinand and his wife in Sarajevo by a Serb nationalist set off a chain reaction among European military alliances that drew one country after another into the conflict. In the end, Great Britain, France, and Russia – and eventually Italy, Japan, and the United States – were aligned against Germany, Austria-Hungary, and the Ottoman Empire. On 4 August, members of the Canadian House of Commons, in a rare moment of unanimity, approved the War Measures Act, giving the federal government authority to do anything deemed "necessary for the security, defence, peace, order, and welfare of Canada."

The Great War, as it was initially called, touched the lives of all Canadians and marked a major turning point in how they viewed themselves in the world. Starting with a standing army of 3,110 men and a navy consisting of two aging vessels, Canada emerged as a military power of some consequence and paid the price for its commitment to the conflict. Of the more than 600,000 Canadians who experienced military service, nearly 65,000 of them died, and another 170,000 were wounded, many of them maimed for life. For those who remained at home, production quotas, rationing, voluntary labour, and constant worry dominated daily life.

The First Division of the Canadian Expeditionary Force was assembled at Valcartier, near Quebec City, and dispatched to England on 3 October. In addition to 31,000 men – the majority of them British-born – the ships carried 101 Canadian Nursing Sisters, the first of more than 3,000 women who served in the only military unit open to them. Canadian soldiers initially fought as "imperials" under Britain's Army Act and were led by a British commander, Major General E. A. H. Alderson. In April 1915 they faced their first real test at Ypres, when they were subject to a chlorine gas attack.

In the early years of the war, Canada's military planning was plagued by inadequate facilities, bottlenecks in supplies, and the ineffective administration of Minister of Militia Sam Hughes. He was finally dismissed from his portfolio in 1916, but not before he had earned the ill will of many men on the front for insisting on the use of Canadian-made Ross rifles, which had a tendency to jam in the heat of battle. Borden gradually brought more efficiency to wartime planning by creating a variety of committees, many of them staffed by businessmen such as Joseph Flavelle, general manager of the William Davies Packing Company of Toronto. As chair of the Imperial Munitions Board (IMB), Flavelle managed more than six hundred factories employing 150,000 workers. Not everyone was impressed. Critics noted that most contracts were awarded to companies in Quebec and Ontario and that businessmen prospered while servicemen's families were often forced to rely on charity.

As the war production got under way, labour shortages, spiraling costs, and inflation became serious problems. The federal government created the National Service Board in 1916 to mobilize manpower for the war effort and recruited women into transportation and metal trades, which had hitherto been closed to them. With wages frozen and prices escalating, labour unrest increased, prompting the government to prohibit strikes and lockouts in 1918. Efficiency and economy served as the rationale for nationalizing several of Canada's failing railways and for establishing a Civil Service Commission to bring merit into the federal government's hiring practices. In addition to suspending the gold standard and expanding the money supply, Ottawa raised money by selling Victory Bonds, War Savings Certificates, and War Savings Stamps. Two "temporary" levies were also imposed: a war profits tax in 1916 and personal income taxes in 1917. In departures from pre-war trends, Canada extended credit to Great Britain and secured loans in the New York bond market.

ON THE FRONT

Most of Canada's enlisted men served in muddy, flea-infested trenches that stretched from the Swiss border to the English Channel. In these unsanitary conditions, death was ever-present, not only from enemy fire but also from such afflictions as dysentery, pneumonia, and "trench fever." The six thousand Canadians killed or injured at Ypres in April 1915 were only the first in a long list of battle casualties. During the Somme offensive, twenty-four thousand Canadians were among the more than six hundred thousand killed or wounded in the Allied forces. The Newfoundland Regiment, which fought at Beaumont Hamel on the first day of the battle, 1 July 1916, was almost entirely wiped out (Image 8.1).

In April 1917 the Canadian Corps took Vimy Ridge after a fiercely fought battle that resulted in more than ten thousand Canadian casualties. It was the first time that all four Canadian divisions had fought together and a pivotal moment in Canada's efforts to move beyond its colonial military status. In the fall of 1916 Borden had created a Ministry of Overseas Military Forces and redefined the Canadian Expeditionary Force (CEF) as an overseas contingent of

Image 8.1. These mud-splattered Canadian soldiers were among the lucky survivors of the Battle of the Somme in 1916. (By permission of Library and Archives/Canada PA-000832)

the Canadian militia. British officers were gradually replaced by Canadians, and on 9 June 1917 Arthur Currie, the Canadian commander of the First Canadian Infantry Division, took over from Major General Julian Byng as commander of the Canadian Corps.

While the vast majority of Canadian military personnel joined the army, significant numbers also served at sea and in the air. The need for expanded sea power was underscored early in the war when German U-boats proved highly effective in sinking civilian and merchant shipping. Most of the Canadians who served in the Canadian navy operated antisubmarine craft on the east coast, where German U-boats ranged widely. Canadians also joined the Royal Flying Corps, the Royal Naval Air Service, or the Royal Air Force. The expertise that Canadians gained in the British flying units and advances in aircraft technology led to the establishment of the Royal Canadian Air Force in 1924.

THE INDIGNITIES OF WAR

During his visit to England and France in the spring of 1917, Borden became convinced that conscription was necessary to replenish the thinning ranks of the Canadian Corps. The Military Service Act, introduced in June 1917, imposed compulsory military service on single men between the ages of twenty and thirty-five. Introduced in the House of Commons by Solicitor General Arthur Meighen, the bill passed, with French Canadian members voting against it, on 29 August 1917. A new chapter in Canada's culture wars had begun.

Most Canadian men managed to avoid military service, but it quickly became obvious that few of the volunteers – only fifteen thousand – were French-speaking. Although initially sympathetic to the Allied cause, French Canadians felt isolated in a military dominated by English- speaking commanders and recruits. As accusations circulated that francophones were shirking their duty, several provincial governments intensified their efforts to abolish French-language education. Nationalists in Quebec wondered aloud why they should bother going overseas when they had their own battles to fight at home.

Borden had postponed calling an election in wartime, but conscription forced his hand. Fearing the loss of Quebec to Bourassa's nationalists, Laurier rejected Borden's offer to join him in a coalition. A rump of Liberals, most of them from the western provinces and Ontario, joined the Conservatives to create a Union government that campaigned on a platform of conscription, prohibition, and abolition of party patronage.

To ensure a victory for the shaky coalition, the Borden administration introduced a Military Voters' Act enfranchising every man and woman in the CEF, and a Wartime Elections Act that gave the vote to mothers, wives, and sisters of soldiers and denied it to conscientious objectors and citizens of enemy origin naturalized after 1902. Running scared during the election campaign, Borden promised that sons of farmers would be exempted from conscription. The Union government won a majority of seats in the 17 December election, but the Liberals took all but three of the seats in Quebec and won nearly 39 percent of the popular vote.

Whether conscription made much difference to the war effort has been much debated, but there is little disagreement about its impact on the home front.² Nationalism in Quebec was greatly advanced by what was perceived as yet another example of English-Canadian perfidy, and the Liberal Party, which had stood by Quebec in 1917, reinforced its power in the province to such an extent that it became the governing party of Canada for much of the twentieth century.

French Canadians were not the only Canadians who felt victimized during the war. The more than half a million people in Canada who traced their origins to enemy countries were forced to register with police, and 8,579 were interned in one of the twenty-six camps scattered across the country. After the Bolshevik Revolution in Russia in the fall of 1917, the government issued an order-in-council making it an offence to print or possess any publication in an enemy language without a license from the secretary of state; "foreign" organizations, the Industrial Workers of the World among them, were banned, as were meetings in which enemy languages were used.

Despite the need for manpower, visible minorities were initially excluded from military service in what recruiting officers sometimes claimed was "a white man's war."³ Galvanized by this latest affront, African Canadians in Nova Scotia and Japanese in British Columbia formed their own segregated units. Aboriginal men were often admitted despite official restrictions, but they, along with most Asians, were exempted from conscription because they were disenfranchised.

On the morning of 6 December 1917, the devastation caused by war was brought home to Canadians when the French munitions ship *Mont Blanc*, laden with explosives, collided with the Belgian relief ship *Imo* in Halifax harbour. More than sixteen hundred people were killed outright, and another nine thousand were injured in the blast or the subsequent fires and tidal wave that engulfed the city. As word of the calamity spread, help arrived from across Canada, from Newfoundland, and from Massachusetts, where many Maritime-born Canadians lived and worked. More than $30 million, over half of it from the federal government, was provided to help Halifax and the town of Dartmouth on the other side of the harbour to recover from the devastation.

The Allies continued to suffer heavy losses in Europe – the Battle of Passchendaele in 1917 was another bloodbath – but the arrival of American troops at the front in the fall of 1917 provided a much-needed boost to war-weary Allied forces. The Hundred Days leading to the armistice on 11 November 1918 began with the battle of Amiens, spearheaded by the Canadian Corps, which suffered another forty-five thousand casualties in the final months of the war.

WINNING THE PEACE

From the beginning of the war, Borden pressed British authorities to give the dominions a stronger role in war planning. He got his wish when Prime Minister David Lloyd George created an Imperial War Cabinet in 1917 – the British War Cabinet with dominion representation. Canada was represented in the British Empire delegation to the Paris Peace Conference and, along with other dominions, separately signed the Versailles Treaty. Canada also became a member of the new League of Nations, established to keep the peace, and the International Labour Organization, designed to maintain international labour standards. Despite these successes, Canada was still technically a colony, a point that American President Woodrow Wilson raised when he opposed the status accorded to the British dominions at Versailles.

In the final months of the war, Canadians were forced to deal with yet another crisis. What at the time was called the Spanish flu – because uncensored newspapers from neutral Spain first revealed information about the pandemic – initially arrived in eastern Canada in September 1918 with recruits from the United States en route to the Allied offensive in Europe. It was then efficiently dispersed westward by the Canadian Siberian Expeditionary Force, which the federal government assembled to support the "White" Russian forces against the Bolsheviks.[4] Before the pandemic ran its course, it took the lives of a hundred million people worldwide, among them fifty thousand Canadians.

Demobilization and reconstruction brought more challenges. When the lack of ships caused delays in getting Canadian soldiers home following the Armistice, riots erupted. British authorities scrambled to find enough ships to rid themselves of the troublesome

Canadians, most of whom were back home by the summer of 1919. Canadian veterans emerged as a major new political force following the war, their influence channeled through the Great War Veterans' Association (GWVA), founded in Winnipeg in 1917 and reorganized as the Canadian Legion in 1925. Before hostilities ended, the federal government had created a Department of Soldiers' Civil Re-Establishment, under Senator James Lougheed, to coordinate various programs for the returned men, many of them mentally or physically disabled. In the interwar years, the costs of hospital care, disability pensions, and survivor benefits for veterans ranked second after the national debt in government expenditure.[5]

Having fought a war to defend democracy, Allied governments were obliged to reflect on their own political inadequacies. The Union government followed up the Wartime Elections Act with legislation in 1918 giving the federal franchise to women on the same basis as men. In 1916 the three Prairie provinces had adopted female suffrage, and all provinces but Quebec – a holdout until 1940 – soon followed. By 1920, most of the property and income restrictions placed on voting rights had been eliminated, so that only Status Indians, Asians, women in Quebec in provincial elections, conscientious objectors, prisoners, and people under twenty-one were denied the right to vote.

Although some of the policies advocated by women's groups, including prohibition and mothers' allowances, were implemented at the provincial level, political party organizations remained dominated by men. Women also continued to be denied access to some professions and to privileges such as Senate appointments. Determined to eliminate the remaining barriers to equality, five Alberta suffragists pursued what became known as the *Persons* case through the courts. In 1929 the Judicial Committee of the Privy Council concluded that women were "persons" under the law not only in pain and penalty but also in rights and privileges. This decision had major implications for the status of women in Canada and throughout the British Empire, but more battles would be fought before the legal victory was put into practice.[6]

Canadian workers also had reform on their minds. By 1918 plans were afoot in the western provinces to create One Big Union (OBU) that would focus the power of labour in Canada. This context helps to explain what happened when the Winnipeg Trades and Labour Council called a general strike on 15 May 1919 following the breakdown of negotiations in the city's metal and building trades. Only twelve thousand workers in Winnipeg belonged to unions, but thirty thousand people joined the strike and sympathetic general strikes erupted across the country. Convinced that they had a revolution on their hands, the federal government dispatched the Royal North-West Mounted Police to Winnipeg. On "Bloody Saturday," 21 June, the Mounties fired into the crowd of protesters; two men were killed and others injured. Recognizing the state's determination to crush the strike, its leaders capitulated on 26 June. The federal government then moved quickly to suppress radical protest, passing Section 98 of the Criminal Code, which outlawed any organization whose professed purpose was to bring about "governmental, industrial or economic change" by force. Labour radicalism nevertheless continued to flourish, and the Communist Party of Canada was founded at a secret meeting in Guelph, Ontario, in 1921.

Agrarian discontent also coalesced into political action. In 1916 the Canadian Council of Agriculture produced the Farmers' Platform, which included a call for free trade; graduated income, inheritance, and corporation taxes; and nationalization of railway, telegraph, and express companies. Farmer candidates in the 1917 election supported the Union government, but when Borden cancelled the exemption from conscription for farmers' sons in April 1918, five thousand protestors converged on Ottawa. Later that year, the Farmers' Platform was rechristened the New National Policy, which served as the platform for the Progressive Party of Canada, launched in 1920. Under the leadership of Manitoba's Thomas A. Crerar, a former Liberal who had severed in the Union cabinet, the Progressive Party quickly gathered momentum.

POLITICS TRANSFORMED?

The 1921 federal election offered voters more options than ever before and resulted in Canada's first minority government. Under its new leader, Arthur Meighen – Borden retired from political life in 1920 – the Conservative Party won only 50 seats. The Liberal Party, which chose William Lyon Mackenzie King as leader following Laurier's death in 1919, won all of Quebec's 65 constituencies and a sprinkling elsewhere for a total of 116. To the surprise of many, Crerar led the Progressive Party to a second-place finish, winning 65 seats, most of them in Ontario and the Prairie provinces. Its ranks included Agnes Macphail from Grey County, Ontario, the first woman to be elected to the House of Commons. Two Independent Labour Party members also warmed the opposition benches: J. S. Woodsworth, briefly imprisoned for editing a strike newspaper during the Winnipeg General Strike, was elected to represent Winnipeg's working-class north end, and William Irvine, a Scottish-born Unitarian minister, won a seat in Calgary. King managed to form a government with the tacit support of the Progressive Party, which refused to function as the official opposition.

Canada's new prime minister was a charter liberal through his mother, the granddaughter of William Lyon Mackenzie. Ambitious in the extreme, King boasted five university degrees, including a PhD from Harvard, and had accumulated impressive experience in his roles as deputy minister of labour, as minister of labour from 1909 to 1911, and as an industrial consultant to John D. Rockefeller during the war. King had lost his seat in the 1911 election and ran unsuccessfully as a Liberal in 1917, a move that paid dividends in Quebec. In 1918 he published *Industry and Humanity*, in which he emphasized the role of the state in reconciling what he saw as the ultimately common interests of labour and capital. Liberals at the end of the Great War were ready for such idealism, and King easily edged out W. S. Fielding, his only competitor at the party's leadership convention.

What was not widely known until after his death was that King indulged his Presbyterian belief in the afterlife by dabbling in the new spiritualism that had become popular in Victorian Canada. He consulted Ouija boards, held séances with his much-idealized dead mother and various deceased political figures, and kept a secret diary in which he chronicled in mesmerizing detail his public and private lives.[7] Whatever his personal quirks, King had a sixth sense politically, a trait that enabled him to establish the record as Canada's longest-serving prime minister.

King's first objective was to bring the Progressive Party into the Liberal fold. Arguing that Progressives were only "Liberals in a

hurry," he courted moderates in the party, obliging them by lower-
ing tariffs on farm equipment, completing a rail link to the port of
Churchill, and restoring favourable freight rates on grain. By the time
of the 1925 election, the Progressive Party had lost much of its political steam, but the Liberals carried only 101 seats, while the resurgent
Conservatives won 115. Again, King teamed up with the Progressives,
now reduced to 24 seats, and earned the support of the two Labour
MPs by conceding a means-tested old-age pension. The fragile alliance collapsed in June 1926 following a Conservative motion of
censure of widespread corruption in the Customs Department.

When King asked Governor General Julian Byng to dissolve
Parliament, Byng exercised his prerogative by asking Arthur
Meighen to form a government. Meighen's ministry lasted only
three days, but it gave King the election issue he needed – Byng's
violation of the principle of responsible government in refusing
King's request to call an election. The national trump card played
well in enough constituencies to enable the Liberals to win the most
seats in the September 1926 election. King now turned his attention
to the Maritime Rights Movement, which had erupted just in time
to deny him a majority government.

Never able to get much traction in Ottawa, the Maritime provinces fell increasingly behind the rest of the country in the race for
industrial development. Manufacturing in the Maritimes declined
by 40 percent between 1917 and 1921 and never recovered to
its prewar levels. With the merger of the Intercolonial into the
Canadian National Railway system in 1918, freight rates increased
dramatically and Saint John and Halifax were abandoned as major
terminals for international trade. Even the region's coal and steel
industries failed to prosper and were rocked by a series of protracted
strikes. With King's attention focused on the western provinces and
Quebec, leading business and professional interests in the region
aligned with the Conservative Party and launched a campaign for
"Maritime rights." The movement made modest demands, among
them larger federal subsidies, national transportation policies that
took the region's needs into account, and tariff policies that offered
protection for the Maritime coal and steel industries (Image 8.2).[8]

King's response was to establish a Royal Commission on Maritime
Claims, chaired by British lawyer-industrialist Sir Andrew Rae

Image 8.2. This stark image by Lawren S. Harris of a miner's family, shown against a backdrop of company housing in Glace Bay, Nova Scotia, appeared on the cover of the July 1925 issue of the *Canadian Forum*, a progressive magazine founded in 1922. (Courtesy of Stew Sheppard)

Duncan. Although Duncan's recommendations supported most of the region's demands, King moved cautiously. The Maritime Freight Rates Act of 1927 helped the region's producers compete more effectively in central Canadian markets, but the crucial issue, the inadequacy of revenues in the smaller provinces to cover the rapidly expanding demands on their treasuries, was ignored. Maritimers continued to limp along until 1929, when Canadians everywhere got a taste of the east coast economic experience.

THE ECONOMIC ROLLER-COASTER

Between 1914 and 1945, the Canadian economy experienced breathtaking highs and lows. The wars stimulated economic growth, but the overheated economy of the late 1920s collapsed following the crash of the New York stock market in October 1929. Both the good times and the bad times left indelible marks on Canadians.

Like most nations involved in the Great War, Canada had trouble adjusting its economy to peacetime production. The federal government slashed its spending, and export markets contracted sharply. As the effects of these developments rippled throughout the economy, bankruptcies and unemployment increased and many people moved to the United States, where economic recovery began sooner. By 1924 conditions had improved in most regions of Canada, buoyed by a renewed global demand for wheat, pulp and paper, and minerals, and by an insatiable desire for consumer products, which flooded the market.

Despite dramatic cyclical swings, the second industrial revolution, based on the internal combustion engine, electrical power, and new chemical processes, rolled merrily along, and the service sector expanded to account for 50 percent of GNP. Much of Canada's growth in this period resulted from American investment, which as early as 1924 surpassed that of Great Britain. The automobile symbolized the new consumer economy. By the 1930s the output of the Ontario-based branch plants of Chrysler, Ford, and General Motors was second in value only to that of the United States.

Inevitably, many people fell victim to the intense economic restructuring that characterized the age of mass consumption. Some lines of work became obsolete – blacksmithing and subsistence farming, for example – while others expanded to accommodate new technologies. Even in hard times, people found employment as automobile mechanics, bush pilots, and radio announcers, jobs that could scarcely have been imagined a generation earlier.

During the Dirty Thirties, investment and consumption stalled. High American tariffs and unprecedented competition in international markets brought disaster to Canada's primary producers. By 1933, the worst year of the Great Depression, the value of Canadian exports was less than half of what it had been in 1929. The economic crisis was compounded on the southern Prairies by an environmental disaster in the form of a decade-long drought, which was exacerbated by wheat monoculture. Nearly 20 percent of the labour force was officially classified as unemployed in 1933, but the real figure was much higher. While some of the unemployed retreated to family farms, most people no longer had this option. Their only hope was social assistance, commonly called "the dole," which was not only inadequate to cover the costs of food and shelter but was also circumscribed by demeaning regulations.

THE POLITICS OF CHAOS

Politicians were at a loss as to what to do. During the 1930 election campaign, King responded in a partisan way to demands from the provinces, announcing that he would not provide so much as "a five-cent piece" to any Tory government seeking assistance. Conservative Party leader Richard Bedford Bennett made political hay out of the "five-cent piece speech" and, promising "to blast" his way into international markets, led his party to a resounding victory.[9]

Born in Albert County, New Brunswick, Bennett was raised by his Methodist mother to be sober and industrious. He experienced firsthand the economic trends in the Maritimes, which had brought hard times to his father's shipbuilding operations. After teaching school, Bennett studied law at Dalhousie University and, in 1897, was lured to Calgary to work as a junior partner in Senator James Lougheed's legal firm. Bennett became involved in local politics, made profitable investments in stocks and real estate, and participated in a variety of successful business ventures. In 1911 he won the Calgary seat in the House of Commons. Opposed to Borden's decision to form a Union government, he refused to run in the 1917 election, but Meighen enticed him back into politics in 1925. A "progressive" Conservative who supported both old-age pensions and unemployment insurance, he was chosen as party leader at a convention held in Winnipeg in 1927.

A man of action, Bennett called a special session of Parliament shortly after the June 1930 election to deal with the economic crisis. His government earmarked an astounding $20 million to provide jobs for unemployed men in public works and embarked on a program of tariff increases to protect Canadian industries from foreign competition. By the end of September, Bennett was in London, urging his startled listeners at the Imperial Conference to return to a policy of imperial preference. Great Britain, also brought to its knees by the economic crisis, abandoned the gold standard in 1931 and, following an Imperial Conference held in Ottawa in 1932, granted preferential treatment for a variety of Canadian commodities, including automobiles, agricultural produce, and timber. None of these initiatives reversed the trends. Breadlines lengthened, prices continued to plummet, and municipal and charitable organizations collapsed under the weight of the demands placed upon them. As conditions worsened, Bennett found the political ground slipping from under his feet.

The Depression intensified political radicalism of both the right and the left that had been gaining momentum since the Great War. As fascism became the reigning ideology in Italy and Germany, the Canadian Union of Fascists, based in Winnipeg, was founded, and Adrien Arcand led a similar organization, the Parti National Social Chrétien, in Quebec. When the various fascist parties came together in 1938 as the National Unity Party of Canada, Arcand, a declared anglophile, was chosen as its leader.

While authorities paid little attention to the rise of fascism – indeed, Bennett sought Arcand's support – they were not so complacent about communism. The Bennett government declared the Communist Party illegal in 1931 and, the following year, established relief camps under military control to house the single, unemployed men who were believed to be the most susceptible to communist ideology. Ultimately, nearly 170,000 transient men were herded into camps, where they worked on a variety of public projects in return for their board and twenty cents a day. Not surprisingly, this draconian measure had the opposite effect of what was intended. Working under the umbrella of the Workers Unity League, the Communists organized the Relief Camp Workers Union (RCWU), which led several thousand of its members in British Columbia on a strike for "work and wages" in the spring of 1935. More than a thousand of the strikers then boarded eastward-bound freight trains, picking up support along the way. Their goal was to confront the prime minister, but they were stopped in Regina by the Royal Canadian Mounted Police. In the end, eight trekkers, including their spokesman, Arthur Evans, met with Bennett in Ottawa, but the discussions ended in a shouting match (Image 8.3). A new and

Image 8.3. Unemployed men joining the On-to-Ottawa Trek at Kamloops, British Columbia. (Courtesy of Library and Archives Canada, 029399)

more aggressive union, the Committee of Industrial Organizations (CIO), was founded in the United States in 1935 and soon spread into Canada. The CIO and its successor, the Canadian Congress of Labour, continued the activities of the Workers Unity League in organizing industrial workers in Canada.

Hard times proved to be a powerful catalyst for unity among Canada's democratic socialists. In 1932 left-wing Progressives, Labour Party supporters, social gospellers, and socialist intellectuals came together in Calgary to form the Co-operative Commonwealth Federation (CCF), choosing J. S. Woodsworth as their leader. The party's policy manifesto, adopted at a convention in Regina the following year, included nationalization of key industries and universal welfare programs. The CCF won seven seats in the 1935 election and, by 1939, formed the opposition in British Columbia, Saskatchewan, and Manitoba. In 1944 the CCF produced the first democratic socialist government in North America when the Scottish-born Tommy Douglas led the party to victory in Saskatchewan.

Other provinces also embraced new political parties. In Alberta radio evangelist William "Bible Bill" Aberhart became a convert to the doctrines promoted by a British engineer, Major C. H. Douglas, who advocated reforms to monetary policy and the distribution of "social credit" to keep the economy running smoothly. Aberhart offered voters a social dividend of twenty-five dollars a month and led his Social Credit Party to a convincing victory in the 1935 provincial election. Once in office, Aberhart dragged his feet on dispensing social credit, and most of his party's efforts to control banking and money supply were disallowed by the courts because they invaded federal jurisdiction. The Social Credit Party nevertheless remained popular and continued to hold office in Alberta until 1971.

In Quebec a group of dissident Liberals, eager to inject reform into the long-serving administration of Premier Louis-Alexandre Taschereau, joined forces with the Conservatives led by Maurice Duplessis to form a government in Quebec in 1936. Under Duplessis, the newly christened Union Nationale moved steadily to the right. With clerical and corporate backing, Duplessis introduced legislation to suppress Communist and other troublesome organizations and collaborated with the Liberal premier of Ontario, Mitchell Hepburn, to keep unions in their place and to stonewall federal programs that threatened to infringe on provincial rights.

BENNETT'S NEW DEAL

Duplessis and Hepburn had good reason to be worried. In his efforts to stem the crisis, Bennett pushed at the edges of federal jurisdiction, passing legislation to address problems relating to housing, marketing, and municipal funding. He also provided relief to hard-pressed farmers through the Farmers' Creditors Arrangement Act and established the Bank of Canada to bring central control over credit and currency. Facing an election, Bennett announced in a series of live radio broadcasts in 1935 that he planned to introduce legislation to regulate hours of work, set minimum wages, and establish a program of unemployment insurance. "The old order is gone," Bennett announced. "If you believe things should be left as they are, you and I hold irreconcilable views. I am for reform. And in my mind, reform means government intervention.... It means the end of laissez-faire."[10]

Bennett's "new deal," modelled on that of popular American president Franklin D. Roosevelt, was a belated response to a growing rift in his party on how to manage the spectre of poverty in the midst of plenty. As capitalist restructuring took its course, corporate executives made as much as $25,000 a year, while ordinary workers, if they had jobs, made only a fraction of that sum. In February 1934 Bennett reluctantly authorized his minister of trade and commerce, Henry H. Stevens, to investigate corporate price-fixing and market manipulation. Testimony before the Commission on Price Spreads revealed damning evidence of how companies such as Canada Packers and Eaton's gouged their suppliers and swindled consumers. When Bennett resisted taking action on these findings, Stevens resigned and established the Reconstruction Party. The party of "the little man" won only one seat – Stevens won his Vancouver riding – in the 1935 election, but it split the Conservative vote in constituencies across the country.

Resisting pressure to present bold new policies, King campaigned under the slogan "King or chaos," and won the largest majority of his political career, but attracted almost the same popular vote as in 1930 (44.7 percent to 44.0 percent). The Social Credit, CCF, and others new parties syphoned off enough votes to reduce the Conservatives to 39 seats. Since most of Bennett's New Deal program and even his marketing board legislation were declared unconstitutional by the courts, King moved cautiously. He signed a trade agreement with the United States that had been negotiated by his predecessor, closed the relief camps, and established two commissions: a National Employment Commission to recommend policy on unemployment and relief and a Royal Commission on Dominion-Provincial Relations to investigate ways of resolving the constitutional impasse.

Many Canadian provinces faced bankruptcy in the 1930s, but they managed to hang on with a little help from Ottawa. Newfoundland was not so lucky. Like the Maritimes, Newfoundland struggled through the 1920s, its fisheries crippled by a sagging international market. In 1927 the Judicial Committee of the Privy Council ruled in Newfoundland's favour in the long-standing dispute over the border between Labrador and Quebec, but the government was so overexposed that it tried, without success, to sell its resource-rich windfall. When the Depression descended, fish, forestry, and mineral sectors collapsed and Newfoundland could neither pay its mounting debt nor provide social assistance to destitute citizens. In August 1932 a demonstration of unemployed workers in St. John's deteriorated into a riot that gutted the legislature and forced Liberal Prime Minister Richard Squires to call an election. The United Newfoundland Party won an overwhelming victory and turned to Great Britain for help, which came in the form of a commission of inquiry into the colony's future. Headed by Lord Amulree, the commission recommended that Newfoundland surrender self-government to a British-appointed commission headed by a governor. It was a humbling moment for Britain's oldest North American colony, but there seemed to be no other option.

SOCIETY IN TRANSITION

As with political and economic developments, social trends had their antecedents in the prewar period: cities continued to grow at the expense of the countryside, mortality and fertility rates maintained their steady decline, and people became more secular in their orientation. Hastened by the shock of the Great War, Canadians began to question the Victorian values on which they had been raised. English Canadians came to terms with the sacrifice of so many young men by idealizing the ordinary soldier through monuments in town squares and reflections on the war that highlighted its role in fostering a national spirit, but many veterans adopted a devil-may-care attitude. Women who had shouldered weighty responsibilities while men served overseas were no longer prepared to be the "angels in the house." They, too, wanted to earn money, drink alcohol, drive cars, and fly airplanes. Who could stop them?[11]

A communications revolution, represented by radio, recordings, movies, and magazines, played a central role in promoting new lifestyles. In each of these media, American productions swamped Canadian content and brought demands for government intervention. The federal government created the Canadian Broadcasting Corporation in 1936 to establish its own stations and supervise private stations, but short of jamming the airwaves, nothing could lure audiences away from American programming. Similarly, the National Film Board, founded in 1939, developed into one of the world's great documentary production facilities, but Canada's movie theatres remained dominated by Hollywood. And tariff protection for Canadian magazines, introduced by the Bennett administration, was soon whittled away in trade agreements.

While the American dominance of the popular media bothered Canadian nationalists, most people paid little attention to where their songs and stories came from. The dream of many Canadians was to make it "big time" south of the border, and a few of them managed to do so. In the interwar years, Canadians Mary Pickford and Louis B. Mayer pursued successful careers in Hollywood, Guy Lombardo and his Royal Canadians played "the Sweetest Music This Side of Heaven" from their base at the Roosevelt Hotel in New York, and Nova Scotia–born country singer Wilf Carter delighted his listeners as Montana Slim. Popular cultural expression in Canada, like the corporations that sponsored it, was a North American–wide phenomenon, of which Canadians were enthusiastic consumers and sometimes creators.

Often brash and provocative, the new popular culture brought thunderous criticism from watchdogs of Canadian morality. Censor boards appeared in most provinces, including Quebec, where the Roman Catholic Church was particularly effective in ensuring that depictions of sex, burglaries, gambling, divorce, suicide, and unpatriotic behaviour were rigourously excised from movies. Evangelical churches were comprehensive in their criticism of the new worldly pleasures, condemning as sinful smoking, drinking, swearing, dancing, doping, and gambling. In 1925 the Methodist, Presbyterian, and Congregationalist churches merged to form the United Church of Canada in an effort to support the cause of ecumenism and to increase their influence. While some might argue that the United Church had little success in achieving either goal, there is little doubt that it exerted a strong moral influence on Canadian social and political life for the next half century.

Prohibition was one of the victims of the new age of secular pleasures. Between 1920 and 1933, all provinces except Quebec adopted prohibition, as did the United States. Fewer people drank alcohol under prohibition, but the difficulty of policing the legislation and the criminal activities that developed to circumvent it soon had governments scrambling to find an alternative. In the United States, gangsters operated bootlegging rings that were North American in scope, enabling many Canadians to make fortunes by running alcohol, produced locally or brought in from Europe and the Caribbean, across the border. By 1930, all provinces except Prince Edward Island had abandoned prohibition for government-regulated liquor sales that could be taxed to pay for the costly new roads demanded by motorists.

The new media played a prominent role in promoting and commercializing romantic relationships between women and men. In this period, a white dress for the bride and a honeymoon after the marriage ceremony became popular. While some women proved themselves good sports by agreeing to a camping trip after their nuptials, others longed to travel to the ultimate honeymoon destination, Niagara Falls. The media stressed the attractiveness of the bride, and women generally became objectified through beauty contests. Even babies were submitted to such indignities. Men wanted to be tall, dark, and handsome, like movie heartthrobs Rudy Valentino and Clark Gable. Companionable marriage remained the ideal, but the number of divorces, difficult to get because they required an act of parliament in most provinces, began to rise.

Family life evolved to accommodate the new consumerism. By the 1930s, electricity had become widely available even in many rural areas, and those who could afford to do so purchased household appliances to make domestic chores easier. Since modern conveniences were often acquired to substitute for domestic help, the old adage "women's work is never done" continued to ring true. In many rural families, men insisted that farm machinery, which inevitably included a car or truck, took precedence over the kitchen ranges and iceboxes promoted in the Women's Institute's model kitchens and available for all to admire in illustrated catalogues from Eaton's and Simpson's. The Depression forced women everywhere to "make do," but some of them broke under the pressure, as did the men in their lives who were unable to conform to the breadwinner ideal.[12]

Women continued to have fewer children, especially during the 1930s when the age of marriage increased and limiting family size became a survival strategy. The average number of children per family dropped to 2.5 during the Great Depression, the lowest in recorded history. By that time, popular opinion was beginning to soften on the issue of birth control. Legal restrictions remained on the books, but birth control advocates won an important victory in 1937 when Dorothea Palmer, a field-worker for the Parents' Information Bureau in Ottawa, was found not guilty of violating the law because she was acting "for the public good."

In this period, medical science went from strength to strength. Canadian pride swelled when a team based at the University of Toronto, under Dr. Frederick Banting, discovered insulin and he, along with co-discoverer John Macleod, received a Nobel Prize in 1923 for their efforts. At McGill University, Maude Abbott and Wilder Penfield made breakthroughs in dealing with congenital heart disease and neurosurgery. Mothers, meanwhile, became the focus of dubious advice on how their babies should be raised. The lucky infants had mothers who ignored suggestions that toilet training begin at the age of two weeks, that bottled formula replace breast milk, and that bad habits be discouraged through systematic corporal punishment.[13] With birth medicalized, more women had their children in hospitals than at home. Fewer children and better medical treatment led to a lower death rate for both mother and child, but at the expense of the practice of midwifery and of a woman's control over her own body.

Many of these social trends were reflected in one of the few Canadian stories that grabbed international attention: the birth of five identical girls to a poor, rural, francophone couple, on 28 May 1934, in Corbeil, Ontario. The media immediately focused on the Dionne quintuplets, who, a few months after their birth, were made wards of the Crown. Raised under the supervision of Dr. Allan Roy Dafoe, who had helped two midwives to deliver them, they were subject to the latest thinking in child-rearing practices and were a source of amusement to the nearly 3 million people who visited their compound between 1936 and 1943. As a tourist attraction, they added $51 million to the Ontario treasury. They also inspired four Hollywood films. After a long custody battle, the girls were returned to their family, but they continued to be exploited. The girls left home as soon as they were legally able to do so, and later in life they revealed that they had been sexually abused by their father.

For racialized minorities, the interwar years brought little respite from discrimination, despite efforts to organize against it. Frederick Loft, a Mohawk veteran of the Great War, was the moving spirit behind the League of Indians in 1918, but he was placed under police surveillance for his efforts. When Mi'kmaq Grand Council chief Gabriel Sylliboy argued in 1927 that he had the right to hunt out of season based on eighteenth-century treaty rights, he lost his case. The courts were equally deaf to African Canadians who challenged laws requiring blacks to sit in segregated areas of theatres and practices excluding them from professions, from many areas of paid labour, and even from restaurants. During the Depression minorities were often the last hired and the first fired from available jobs and had difficulty securing welfare.

STORM CLOUDS ON THE HORIZON

Canada's hybrid status as both nation and colony was addressed by the Statute of Westminster, passed by the British Parliament in 1931. In accordance with decisions made at imperial conferences held since the Great War, Great Britain renounced its right to legislate for the dominions. Self-governing nations choosing to stay in the British Commonwealth would be tied to Great Britain only by the Crown and any other constitutional arrangements that individual countries decided to retain. Canada was cautious in abandoning such remnants of colonialism as legal appeals to the Judicial Committee Council and the power to amend the British North America Act. Until 1945, other pressing matters took precedence over constitutional reform, which inevitably created federal-provincial tensions.

Canada was also cautious in its approach to international affairs. When Walter Riddell, Canada's representative at the League of Nations, called for stronger measures against Italy after its fascist leader, Benito Mussolini, invaded Ethiopia in 1935, he was informed by the King administration that Canada should not be taking a lead on the world stage. Canada was not alone in its caution, with the result that the League became ineffective in stopping the aggressive foreign policies adopted by Germany, Italy, and Japan. A few Canadians – including the medical doctor Norman Bethune and twelve hundred volunteers in the Mackenzie-Papineau Battalion – supported the republican cause in the Spanish Civil War (1936–39), but Ottawa remained silent on developments in Spain and also in Germany, where Adolph Hitler absorbed Austria and dismantled Czecheslovakia in 1938.

War could not be avoided. On 3 September 1939, Great Britain and France finally decided to stop Hitler, who, with the approval of the Soviet Union's Joseph Stalin, had invaded Poland two days earlier. The Axis alliance eventually included Japan, which took advantage of the war in Europe to pursue its imperial designs in the Pacific.

No longer a colony of Great Britain, Canada declared war on its own behalf on 10 September, after Parliament was recalled to vote on the matter. Canadians might have followed the American example of remaining neutral in 1939, but the King government, sensing the strong pro-British sentiment in Canada and the potential economic opportunities, had little hesitation in joining the Allied cause. Few could argue that it was not a "just war" against aggressive dictators determined to dominate the world. American neutrality ended on 7 December 1941, when the Japanese bombed Pearl Harbor in Hawaii.[14]

In taking the country to war, King promised that his government would not impose conscription for overseas service. This was not enough for Quebec Premier Maurice Duplessis, who called a snap election and made Canada's involvement in the war the major campaign issue. Quebec's federal ministers, led by King's powerful Quebec lieutenant, Justice Minister Ernest Lapointe, threatened to resign if Duplessis won. Fearing that without its Quebec contingent, the cabinet might refuse to honour King's anticonscription promise, Quebecers elected a Liberal government. A resolution passed in the Ontario legislature criticizing Ottawa's lacklustre war effort prompted King to call a national election in March 1940, which the

Liberals won handily, but the promise not to invoke conscription would soon come back to haunt them.

Within a few weeks of the election, Hitler's forces overwhelmed Denmark and Norway and then conducted a blitzkrieg through the Netherlands, Belgium, and France. The surrender of France early in June 1940 and the evacuation of more than three hundred thousand Allied troops from Dunkirk raised fears that Great Britain might soon be invaded. The Canadian government promptly enacted the National Resources Mobilization Act (NRMA), which provided for the conscription of soldiers for home defence. Arguing that the legislation meant "not necessarily conscription but conscription if necessary," King called a plebiscite for 27 April 1942, asking Canadians to decide whether the government should be released from its pledge not to impose conscription for overseas service. While nearly 65 percent of Canadians voted yes, 72 percent of Quebecers said no. The threat of conscription sparked the formation of the Bloc populaire canadien, a new nationalist political party in Quebec led by André Laurendeau, and returned the Union Nationale to power in a 1944 provincial election.

King made every effort to avoid imposing conscription, including firing pro-conscription Defence Minister J. L. Ralston in the autumn of 1944. When his replacement, General A. G. L. McNaughton, failed to secure the necessary voluntary enlistments, the government authorized sending sixteen thousand NRMA soldiers overseas. This decision resulted in fierce resistance among the conscripts – many of whom quickly deserted from their Canadian bases – and added further fuel to the feelings of betrayal in Quebec. Since King had clearly done all he could to avoid this unpopular policy, he managed to escape the hostility that had been heaped on Borden.

Military service quickly solved Canada's unemployment problem. Nearly 1.1 million men and women joined the forces, from a population estimated at 11.5 million in 1941. Most served in the army. About 250,000 joined the Royal Canadian Air Force and nearly 100,000 enlisted in the Royal Canadian Navy. The Canadian government also established a Merchant Navy at the beginning of the war to provide a workforce for wartime shipping. Although only men participated in combat, 50,000 women served in the Canadian armed forces, organized as auxiliaries in each of the three armed services branches. More than 42,000 Canadians died in wartime service and another 54,000 were injured. These numbers paled in comparison to the overall tally. Casualties in the Second World War reached 55 million, many of them civilians killed or wounded by bombs, invading armies, or concentration camp personnel, who exterminated an estimated 6 million Jews, along with untold numbers of homosexuals, gypsies, and other people deemed unworthy by the Nazi government. Timothy Snyder estimates that at least 14 million people were killed in what are now Poland, Belarus, Ukraine, Estonia, Latvia, and Lithuania as Nazi and Soviet armies crisscrossed their territories.[15]

CANADA'S WAR

Following the collapse of France, Germany bombed London and other British cities and stepped up its highly successful U-Boat campaign against Allied shipping in the Atlantic. At times, it seemed that only the stirring rhetoric of Winston Churchill, who had become prime minister in May 1940, kept the British going. Canadian support, including capital, food, and war materiel, played a crucial role in helping Britons to triumph in their "darkest hour." With the fate of North America now in question, Roosevelt and King met in August at Ogdensburg, New York, where they established a Permanent Joint Board on Defence for North America. The following month, the American and British governments agreed in principle that, in return for fifty aging destroyers and other military equipment, the United States could build military bases in Newfoundland, Bermuda, and the Caribbean.

The Canadian government took measures against enemy aliens and others perceived as potential troublemakers. Again, the targets of security measures were sometimes questionable, most notably Canada's seven thousand Jehovah's Witnesses, declared illegal because of their unpopularity, especially in Quebec. When the Soviet Union switched sides in 1941, Canada was obliged to lift proscriptions against Communist organizations. In 1942 Canada removed twenty-two thousand people of Japanese ancestry – nearly

Image 8.4. Japanese Canadians being relocated in the interior of British Columbia. (By permission of Library and Archives Canada/C-46350)

three-quarters of whom had been born in Canada or were naturalized Canadians – from coastal British Columbia to abandoned
mining towns in the interior, to construction projects, or to farms
on the Prairies (Image 8.4). Even refugees from Europe were
treated shabbily. In the 1930s Canada's doors remained closed to
Jews fleeing Nazi regimes, and Canada accepted only about thirty-
five hundred refugees from enemy countries during the war, the
result of anti-Semitic views that were widely held in Canada, even
at the highest level of the civil service.

The war intensified in 1941 as Hitler turned his army against
the Soviet Union, and Japan destroyed the British and American
fleets in the Pacific, overran Malaysia and Singapore, and captured
the American army in the Philippines. In December 1941 almost
1,300 Canadians died and another 1,700 were taken prisoner in a
futile attempt to defend the British colony of Hong Kong against
the Japanese. After Hitler invaded the Soviet Union, Stalin brought
pressure to bear on his new allies to open a second front in the west.

An unsuccessful landing on French beaches at Dieppe in August 1942 left 907 Canadians dead and 2,000 prisoners. Then the tide began to turn. In November the British Eighth Army broke through the German and Italian lines in northern Africa, and, the following month, the Soviet army stopped Hitler's army near Stalingrad.

In 1943 Canadians forces, which remained largely outside the main action in the early years of the war, became involved in the Allied invasion of Sicily and mainland Italy. Canadians also participated in the invasion of France at Normandy on D-Day, 6 June 1944, which finally established a western front. The Third Canadian Division led the assault on Juno Beach, one of the five main landing sites.

As in the First World War, the Royal Canadian Navy's primary responsibility was escorting the Atlantic convoys that transported food and supplies to the Allied nations in Europe. The RCN had its hands full both on the high seas and in Canadian waters, which were threatened by German U-Boats. During the war, nineteen merchant ships were sunk in the lower reaches of the St. Lawrence River and along the Atlantic coast, among them the ferry between Cape Breton and Newfoundland, which went down in October 1942 with the loss of 237 passengers.

Soon after war was declared, Canada agreed to host the British Commonwealth Air Training Plan (BCATP), which trained almost half the total aircrews supplied by Great Britain and the Commonwealth for the war effort. Canada was also central to the delivery to Britain of planes built in North America in an operation known as Ferry Command, flying nearly ten thousand aircraft from bases such as Gander and Goose Bay, Labrador, to Great Britain. Since long-distance flights were still chancy, five hundred people lost their lives in this operation. The death rate was also high in the Allied bomber offensive against Germany. In 1942 only one airman in three survived a thirty-mission tour of duty. By 1944, the success rate had improved owing to better training and new aircraft, but critics, both then and now, argued that the money and manpower committed to Bomber Command could have been better spent elsewhere.[16]

In an effort to avoid the experience of the First World War, the King administration exercised tight control over the wartime economy. Under its energetic minister, C. D. Howe, the Department of Munitions and Supply expanded existing industries, created new ones, and seconded members of Canada's business community to keep industrial processes running efficiently. Twenty-eight Crown corporations were added to Canada's industrial capacity, almost all of them in central Canada, which was the major beneficiary of the wartime industrial boom. To deal with the labour shortage, a massive campaign was launched to recruit women, and in Quebec and Ontario, temporary child-care centres were established to enable married women to answer the call. With the federal civil service more than doubling in size between 1939 and 1945, the era of Big Government had arrived. By 1944, Ottawa's expenditures accounted for nearly 40 percent of GDP, much of it funded through personal and corporate taxes and the sale of Victory Bonds.

The United States loomed large in Canada's wartime planning. At a meeting between Roosevelt and King at Hyde Park, New York, in April 1941, Canada was included in the Lend-Lease arrangement between Great Britain and the United States, which made available $7 billion for the purchase of American equipment and supplies. When the Japanese occupied the Aleutian Islands in the summer of 1942, the United States, with Canada's permission, built a two-thousand-kilometer overland route through Canada to Alaska. The Americans also built the Canol pipeline from Whitehorse in the Yukon to Norman Wells in the Northwest Territories and developed northern airstrips to transport bombers and fighter planes to Europe and the Soviet Union. In recognition of the evolving relationship, the Canadian government upgraded its diplomatic presence in Washington to embassy status.

Facing a growing number of strikes, Ottawa made an accommodation with labour, whose organized power could no longer be ignored. In February 1944, Order-in-Council PC 1003 guaranteed workers the right to organize and to bargain collectively, established procedures for the certification and compulsory recognition of trade unions, defined unfair labour practices, and created an administrative apparatus to enforce the order. When a wave of strikes following the war threatened to create the kind of standoff that occurred in 1919, the principles of PC 1003 were enshrined in peacetime legislation.

The war also provided the opportunity to introduce social policies that many Canadians had long been demanding. In 1940 the federal government introduced a national unemployment insurance program, after seeking provincial agreement to a constitutional amendment. Since the policy applied primarily to industrial workers, it affected only a small proportion of the labour force, but the principle of federal leadership in social planning was established. The Royal Commission on Dominion-Provincial Relations, which reported in 1940, was supportive of new constitutional arrangements that would enhance federal powers, but its recommendations, not surprisingly, met resistance in provincial capitals.

Most Canadians had become impatient with constitutional wrangling. Having watched the federal government mobilize resources to increase production and eliminate unemployment, and fearing another postwar slump, they demanded the kind of reforms being trumpeted by the CCF, which was growing in popularity. Even the Conservative Party had seen the writing on the wall. In 1942 the party adopted a new name – Progressive Conservative; a new leader – the former Liberal-Progressive premier of Manitoba, John Bracken; and a progressive platform. The Liberals got the message. At a meeting of the National Liberal Federation in September 1943, the party followed the CCF and the Progressive Conservatives in adopting a program supporting social security. King moved quickly to establish three new departments – Reconstruction, National Health and Welfare, and Veterans Affairs – to preside over postwar planning and, in 1944, introduced universal family allowance legislation. The theories of British economist John Maynard Keynes relating to the role of governments in maintaining balanced economies influenced officials in the department of finance and had a significant impact on planning for postwar Canada.

The end of the war brought other challenges. Halifax became the scene of another calamity, this one prompted by seamen and civilians who looted liquor stores, trashed a tramcar, and created two days of general mayhem when the war ended in Europe. Overseas, delays in bringing 350,000 members of the armed forces home again resulted in rioting in July 1945, including a two-night fracas at Aldershot. In addition to service personnel, Canadians welcomed nearly forty-five thousand war brides (and a few war husbands) and their children, numbering nearly twenty-two thousand. Canadian soldiers also left behind an estimated twenty-three thousand so-called war children, the result of relationships – some brief, others longer term, some even bigamous – with local women.[17]

This fast footwork on the part of the Liberals enabled them to win a majority of seats in an election held on 11 June 1945. By that time, the war in Europe had finally ended. Early in 1945, the Canadians in Italy joined their comrades in the Netherlands for the final campaign. Overrun from all sides, Hitler committed suicide and the Germans surrendered on 5 May. The Japanese surrendered on 14 August after the United States dropped atomic bombs on Hiroshima and Nagasaki. Rich in uranium, Canada was represented by C. D. Howe in the top-secret discussions with the British and Americans that ushered in the atomic age.

Determined to make a successful transition to peacetime conditions, the King administration passed legislation in 1942 requiring companies to rehire servicemen in their former jobs and put plans in place to give veterans more generous benefits than those available in 1919. C. D. Howe, appointed minister for reconstruction in 1944, gave tax breaks to companies converting their factories to consumer production. Export markets were initially slow to develop but were buoyed by sales made possible under the Marshall Plan, a generous aid program established by the United States in 1947 to keep war-torn European countries from falling to Communist parties. Instead of the postwar recession predicted by many economists, Canada experienced growth, its GNP rising from $11.8 billion in 1945 to $18.4 billion in 1950.

Canada participated actively in the creation of the United Nations, the International Monetary Fund (IMF), and the World Bank as vehicles for preventing another war and stabilizing the global economy. Despite the wishes of people everywhere, growing tension between the Soviet Union and the West made consensus impossible, leading to the partition of Germany (and later Korea and Vietnam), and to a Cold War that would dominate international relations until the 1990s. Canadians got their first taste of

Cold War politics in the fall of 1945, when a defecting clerk from the Soviet embassy, Igor Gouzenko, revealed that a ring of Soviet spies was operating in Canada.

CONCLUSION

The Second World War clarified many of the issues that remained unresolved during the Depression. Impressed by what the federal government could do under the War Measures Act, most Canadians, if not their provincial governments, were eager to see Ottawa assume more powers, especially in the areas of economic development and social welfare. Canadians were also prepared to assume an expanding role in international affairs. In a new world order where the United States rather than Great Britain was the leader of the Western democracies, Canadians found themselves in familiar territory, but they still needed to tread carefully.

9

Liberalism Triumphant,
1945–1984

Canada is a poster child for the "golden age" of economic growth and social transformation that occurred in the three decades following the Second World War.[1] Blessed with a (mostly) booming economy, the country embraced a range of human rights and social welfare legislation, making it possible for more Canadians to access political power and material well-being. No longer taking their cue from Great Britain, Canadians began to develop a distinct – if discordant – national voice and engaged in lively discussions on how to accommodate the overwhelming influence of the United States. Optimism about the future began to fade in the 1970s under the pressure of economic crises and centrifugal forces, but Canada remained a beacon of hope for people around the world struggling to survive in a steadily shrinking "global village."

THE RIGHTS REVOLUTION

The movement for human rights, expressed in various ways for more than two centuries, coalesced in the Universal Declaration of Human Rights adopted by the United Nations in December 1948.[2] Penned with the assistance of Canadian legal scholar John Humphrey, the declaration asserted that everyone, "without distinction of any kind, such as race, colour, sex, language, religion, political or other opinion, national or social origin, property, birth or other status," was entitled to life, liberty, and security; to freedom of speech, thought, and assembly; and to "security in the event

226

of unemployment, sickness, disability, widowhood, old age or other lack of livelihood."[3]

Putting these entitlements into practice was a tall order, but many Canadians were ready for the challenge. As the war came to an end, activists added new organizations, such as the Nova Scotia Association for the Advancement of Coloured People (1945) and the Council of Christians and Jews (1947), to the ever-expanding roster of voluntary groups pushing for human rights reforms. Governments responded and sometimes took the lead. In 1947 Saskatchewan adopted a Bill of Rights, and in 1951 Ontario introduced legislation relating to fair practices in employment, housing, and public services. Meanwhile, the federal government abolished most of Canada's discriminatory franchise laws in the years immediately following the war and introduced its own fair practices legislation in 1956. Between the adoption of a federal Bill of Rights in 1960 and the constitutionally entrenched Canadian Charter of Rights and Freedoms in 1982, human rights steadily developed legal muscle.

Social policy also advanced piecemeal. After the 1945 election, the King administration proposed a comprehensive suite of nationwide social services, but the provinces, led by Ontario and Quebec, argued that they could not fulfill their obligations if they surrendered their taxing powers to pay for the program. As a fallback position, Ottawa signed tax rental agreements with provinces willing to follow its lead. Most of them eventually relented. Canadians quickly realized that social programs paid huge dividends. When family allowances began arriving in 1945, many children enjoyed better diets, local retailers benefitted, and, since payment was conditional on children remaining in school, education levels rose dramatically.

Other programs gradually followed. The minister of health and welfare, Paul Martin Sr., introduced universal old-age pensions in 1951 and a hospital insurance program, cost-shared with the provinces, in 1957. Saskatchewan, which had adopted a public insurance plan for hospital services in 1947, extended health benefits to include physician services – after a noisy protest from doctors – in 1962. In 1966 the federal government passed its own Medical Care Act and a Canada Assistance Plan to cover welfare services. The way had been paved for poorer jurisdictions to participate in cost-shared programs in 1956 when Ottawa adopted an equalization formula that provided payments to provinces whose tax revenues fell below those of the two wealthiest provinces, British Columbia and Ontario.

To sustain the costs of these and other initiatives, the Department of National Revenue increased its demands and its efficiency, making tax filing a dreaded annual ritual for a growing number of Canadians. Public spending at all levels increased from 30 percent of GDP in 1960 to 48 percent in 1985. Although critics complained about the costs of welfare programs, which rose to nearly 33 percent of GDP by the 1970s, Canada spent considerably less on social welfare than most European countries.[4] Nor were social services always the most costly item in the national budget. The military initially had pride of place in Cold War Canada, accounting for 45 percent of federal spending in 1953 before dropping to about 23 percent in 1961 and further still thereafter.

LIBERALISM IN COLD WAR CANADA

The legislation relating to human rights and social services was championed primarily by the Liberal Party, which held power in Ottawa for most of the time between 1945 and 1984. When in office from 1957 to 1963 and briefly in 1979, the Progressive Conservatives made little effort to change policy direction. Parties with other political agendas remained on the scene, but they never came close to holding power in Ottawa and rarely challenged the overarching liberal consensus. Even the CCF shed much of its radical rhetoric in 1961 when it allied itself with labour unions, rebranded itself as the New Democratic Party (NDP), and chose popular Saskatchewan premier Tommy Douglas as party leader. In this period, the success of the two mainline parties in Ottawa was determined more by personalities and regional interests than by major ideological differences. The Liberals relied on voters in Ontario and Quebec to maintain power – never choosing a national leader from any other province – while the Progressive Conservatives drew much of their electoral support and most of their leaders from outlying provinces.

King shuffled off the political stage in 1948, satisfied that he had been a good steward of liberalism and national unity. By that time, he had groomed his successor, Louis St. Laurent, who had been brought into the cabinet in 1941 as minister of justice. Of French and Irish descent, St. Laurent was a successful lawyer, closely associated with Canada's business community. His strong commitment to federalism and his courageous support of conscription in November 1944 earmarked him as prime ministerial material. In 1946 King relinquished his external affairs portfolio to St. Laurent, who easily bested his rivals at a leadership convention in August 1948. He proved popular on the campaign trail, exhibiting a common touch that earned him the sobriquet "Uncle Louis." The Liberal Party won the largest majority in its history in the 1949 election.[5]

St. Laurent served on the front lines of the Cold War, which dominated the international scene.[6] In Europe and elsewhere, the Soviet Union and the United States vied for the ascendancy of their respective systems – capitalism and communism. Initially, the United States, with the atomic bomb at its disposal, had the upper hand in the standoff, but by 1949 the Soviet Union had its own nuclear weapons and mainland China had a Communist government, which the Americans – and Canada – refused to recognize. Since an all-out war was unthinkable, both sides jockeyed for position in hotspots around the world. The United Nations, on which many Canadians had pinned their hopes for security in the atomic age, was immediately compromised by the ideological battle.

In this context, Canada followed the American lead. The Permanent Joint Board on Defence, established in 1940, was supplemented in 1949 by the North Atlantic Treaty Organization (NATO), a military pact that included the United States and Britain as well as Western European nations. When the Communist regime in North Korea invaded South Korea in 1950, Canada agreed to contribute troops to United Nations forces, most of them American, sent to defend the thirty-eighth parallel boundary between the two Koreas. The conflict threatened to escalate when the People's Republic of China became involved. An armistice was reached in July 1953, but not before 2.5 million people were killed, wounded, or abducted. In all, more than 25,000 Canadians served in the Korean War.[7]

As the Cold War rumbled on, Canada dropped all notions of downsizing its military commitments. The federal government built new and refurbished existing armed forces bases, sent a brigade to Europe as part of Canada's NATO obligations, and invested heavily in rearmament. As new weaponry made a Soviet attack over the North Pole a distinct possibility, Canada and the United States constructed three radar defence systems on Canadian soil – the Pine Tree, Mid-Canada, and Distant Early Warning lines. To bolster its shaky sovereignty in the north, Ottawa began in 1953 to relocate Inuit families from northern Quebec and the Northwest Territories to remote areas of the Arctic, leaving them to fend for themselves in Grise Fiord and Resolute Bay.

The United States was ubiquitous in Canada's emergence as a warfare state. With its industrial economy booming, the Americans invested heavily in Canadian minerals, oil, and timber and collaborated in developing the St. Lawrence Seaway, completed in 1959, to move goods efficiently to and from the continent's industrial heartland. When it became clear that Canada's balance of payments was being seriously undermined by expenditures on American military equipment, the United States acceded to a Defence Production Sharing Agreement that led to more American purchases from Canadian-based firms.

As with social welfare, a consensus emerged that military security transcended political differences. In 1958 the Progressive Conservative government signed the defence production agreement and the North Atlantic Air Defence Treaty (NORAD) to produce a unified air command for North America, both initially negotiated by the Liberals. The Progressive Conservatives also cancelled Canada's efforts to build its own interceptor aircraft, the costly Avro Arrow, which the Liberals had planned to do after the election, and agreed to the installation of long-range BOMARC antimissile bases in Ontario and Quebec.[8]

In diplomatic circles, Canadians often played the role of moral arbiter, demanding, for example, that economic and social outcomes be added to military commitments in the NATO agreement and that the United States moderate its goals in the Korean War. Both of these interventions were initiated by Minister of External Affairs Lester Pearson, who further enhanced Canada's image as helpful fixer in 1956 when British, French, and Israeli forces attacked Egypt following its nationalization of the Suez Canal. Pearson's solution to the ensuing crisis – that a United Nations force be sent to maintain the peace – allowed the aggressors to save face, went down well with the Americans, and won Pearson a Nobel Peace Prize. After Suez, Canadian military forces became publicly identified with various UN peacekeeping missions around the world.

Newfoundland and Labrador's decision to join Canada in 1949 was orchestrated in the context of the Cold War. Since the colony's location was pivotal in the sea-lanes and air routes of the North Atlantic, its status was of more than local significance. During the Second World War, the colony emerged from bankruptcy to unprecedented prosperity, eliminating the rationale for commission government. Ottawa, fearing that the strong American military presence that took root in the colony during the war might draw it into the orbit of the United States, worked behind the scenes with British authorities to encourage Confederation with Canada.

Delegates were elected to a National Convention, which met in June 1946 to discuss the colony's future. Through radio broadcasts of the convention proceedings, Joseph Smallwood – farmer, trade unionist, radio personality – emerged as the champion of Confederation. He argued that by becoming a Canadian province the colony would benefit from social security programs, improved community services, and economic stability. In the outports this message had wide appeal. Elites in St. John's and the Roman Catholic Church preferred a return to the status of a self-governing dominion, while a minority, who valued the efficient administration of the British commission, was content with the status quo. After two hotly contested referenda, a majority of 52.4 percent opted for Confederation. On 31 March 1949 Newfoundland – its name officially changed to Newfoundland and Labrador in 2001 – became Canada's tenth province.

THE ECONOMY ON A ROLL

A decade of economic growth following the Second World War enabled the federal government to fund welfare, warfare, and infrastructure projects, including an eight-thousand-kilometer

Trans-Canada Highway completed in 1962. With its economic prosperity dependent on exports, Canada was an enthusiastic signatory in 1947 of the General Agreement on Tariffs and Trade (GATT) designed to reduce trade barriers. Global free trade proved an elusive goal, so tinkering with the tariff continued to be a staple of international relations.

In the postwar period, products such as plastics, pesticides, and pharmaceuticals, which had been developed during the war, joined new consumer durables such as televisions, agricultural machinery, and snowmobiles to boost secondary industry. As in earlier periods, innovation in communications – television, transistors, computers, and satellites – played a major role in advancing productivity in what would become known as the Information Age. Canada's television network was the longest in the world when it was completed in 1958, and *Alouette 1*, launched in September 1962, made Canada the third nation in space after the Soviet Union and the United States. With its *Anik* (the Inuit word for "brother") series, operative by the 1970s, Canada led the world in the use of satellites for commercial communications.

Economic activity remained concentrated in the St. Lawrence–Great Lakes heartland, but outlying regions also benefitted from public and private investment. Buoyed by consumer and military demand, oil from Alberta, potash from Saskatchewan, iron ore from the Ungava-Labrador border, and uranium from the Northwest Territories, Ontario, and Saskatchewan were brought into production. Huge hydroelectric developments on Churchill Falls, the Columbia River, James Bay, and the St. Lawrence Seaway, along with CANDU nuclear reactors, produced power for an energy-hungry North American market.

Under the impact of new machinery and processes, agriculture, fisheries, and forestry became more productive, while drastically reducing the number of workers in these sectors. This restructuring contributed to the growth of cities and service industries. By the 1980s three out of four Canadians were classified as living in urban areas. Most Canadians moved voluntarily from their rural homes, but others became the focus of government programs to hasten the process. In Newfoundland thirty thousand people were relocated to "growth centers" from their outport communities,

250 of which disappeared completely. Similarly, Inuit scattered throughout the North were moved to communities where services could be more easily provided. Inevitably, there was much resentment about the abandonment of familiar landscapes, especially since the new communities often failed to provide the promised services and employment.

Between 1941 and 1981 Canada's population soared from 11.5 million to nearly 25 million. This growth was fuelled by a baby boom following the war and rising levels of immigration. Until the 1960s, when the focus of immigration policy shifted from ethnicity to skills, the majority of immigrants came from Europe, many of them refugees who were now more welcome than they had been during the war. Population growth was also propelled by a lengthening life expectancy – seventy years for men and seventy-seven years for women by the 1970s – the result of better nutrition, preventive medicine, and the availability of "miracle drugs" such as antibiotics and polio vaccines.

While grateful to be living in a land of relative peace and prosperity, many immigrants found themselves at the bottom of a rigid ethnic hierarchy. In 1965 the sociologist John Porter published *The Vertical Mosaic*, in which he revealed that an economic elite of fewer than a thousand men – mostly of British and Protestant background, and graduates of private schools – dominated Canadian political and economic life. Even in Quebec, where francophones made up nearly 80 percent of the population, a small clutch of privileged anglophones controlled the economy.

ROGUE TORY

In the postwar decade, welfare, warfare, and consumerism kept the economy humming and enough Canadians happy to give the Liberals another majority at the polls in 1953. St. Laurent, who functioned much like the chairman of a board in cabinet meetings, allowed his ministers considerable leeway, and they, in conjunction with a highly skilled civil service, did their jobs reasonably well. The determination of C. D. Howe, "Minister of Everything," to proceed quickly with federal funding for a gas pipeline from Alberta to the St. Lawrence heartland in 1956 finally convinced Canadians that the Liberals had become too arrogant. When the government invoked closure on the pipeline debate, the opposition parties complained loudly not only about the muzzling of Parliament but also about the extent of American investment in the project. Canada was changing and the Liberal Party had missed the signals.

In the 1957 election, the Progressive Conservatives won by a slim margin, and in another election the following year, they captured 208 out of 265 seats. The hero of the hour was John G. Diefenbaker, a Baptist lawyer from Prince Albert, Saskatchewan. A member of Parliament since 1940, he twice ran for party leadership before his successful bid in 1956. Unlike most federal party leaders, Diefenbaker came from relatively humble origins and took pride in being a champion of the underdog. A powerful orator, he was, his biographer Denis Smith suggests, "one of the last pre-television democratic leaders, who sought direction and self-confidence by face-to-face and intuitive connection with voters rather than by polls, focus groups, and opinion management."[9] Yet it was television that brought Diefenbaker's message to Canadians in 1957 and 1958, and they liked what they saw.

Diefenbaker's rhetoric caught a wave of nationalism and empowerment that was gaining momentum in postwar Canada. Unlike his predecessors, Diefenbaker was able to convince voters that the Tories meant it when they said that they would support the welfare state and extend its logic by investing in underdeveloped areas of the country. In recognition of the support he received from the outlying regions, Diefenbaker drew the majority of the ministers in his first cabinet from the Atlantic and Western provinces. He also appointed Canada's first female cabinet minister (Ellen Fairclough), first minister of Ukrainian heritage (Michael Starr), and first Aboriginal senator (James Gladstone). The 1960 Bill of Rights was Diefenbaker's special project, paving the way for enfranchising Status Indians and for dropping the ethnic hierarchy that prevailed in Canada's immigration policy.

While Diefenbaker's cultural and populist sensibilities endeared him to many, he failed to connect with francophone Canadians, and he lacked the leadership skills to reconcile the progressive and conservative wings of his party. Divisions within the cabinet were exacerbated by an economic downturn that descended as the Progressive Conservatives assumed office. Spending freely to achieve its rural and regional goals, the government was obliged to present a series of deficit budgets, causing alarm among fiscal conservatives. In 1960 a public row erupted between the minister of finance, Donald Fleming, and the governor of the Bank of Canada, James Coyne, who kept a tight reign on monetary policy. This was followed by a monetary crisis, which coincided with the June 1962 election campaign. As confidence in the Canadian dollar waned, the government pegged the floating Canadian dollar at 92.5 cents (U.S.), a reasonable move to forestall a collapse of the currency, but the opposition made political hay out of the compromised "Diefendollars."

The Progressive Conservatives survived at the polls, but just barely, capturing only 116 seats to 100 for the Liberals. Diefenbaker was devastated by the result and inconsolable about having to govern with the support of the 30 members of the Social Credit Party, 26 of them from the Quebec wing of the party, under the leadership of Réal Caouette. Following the election, there was another run on the dollar and a balance-of-payments crisis, which forced the government to impose tariff surcharges, reduce spending, and borrow from the IMF and other sources to keep the economy on an even keel. Diefenbaker, who had a deep-seated distrust of Ottawa bureaucrats, of financial interests, and of the United States, especially under its popular new president, John F. Kennedy, felt that Canada was being unfairly targeted. He retreated into a sulk and his ministers scrambled to pick up the pieces.

Conditions deteriorated further when the United States moved to stop the Soviet Union from installing missiles in Cuba, which had embraced communism under its revolutionary leader Fidel Castro. For a few days in October 1962 it seemed that a war between the two superpowers was unavoidable. The Soviets finally blinked, but not in time to save the Canadian government from criticism when Diefenbaker dragged his feet in responding to the American demand that Canada put its NORAD defences on a state of alert. In addition to adding considerable stress to a Canadian public terrified by the threat of nuclear war, the Cuban Missile Crisis drew the ire of the Americans, blew the lid off the cabinet, and precipitated a long-overdue debate on defence policy.

Image 9.1. The Canadian Voice of Women for Peace (VOW), established in 1960, brought middle-class women, such as the ones shown here, to a demonstration in Ottawa in the fall of 1961 against arming BOMARC missiles with nuclear warheads. (By permission of Library and Archives Canada/ Duncan Cameron fonds/PA-209888)

The issue that divided the cabinet and the nation was whether Canada should install nuclear weapons in its BOMARC missile bases and F-104 aircraft. In the years since the Diefenbaker government had signed the NORAD agreement, the consensus around defence policy had begun to unravel. New and credible initiatives, such as the Pugwash Conference and Voice of Women, demanded an end to nuclear madness. In the cabinet, Howard Green, secretary of state for external affairs, supported a policy of disarmament and urged the prime minister to reconsider Canada's agreement to acquire nuclear warheads as part of its defence strategy. The minister of defence, Douglas Harkness, felt that Canada had no alternative but to cooperate fully with its powerful ally (Image 9.1).

While the cabinet dithered, the United States acted. American General Lauris Norstad, the retiring supreme commander of NATO, let it be known during an Ottawa press conference in January 1963 that Canada would be shirking its international commitments if it failed to accept nuclear weapons. The American State Department then publicly contradicted Diefenbaker's claims that BOMARC missiles were effective without being equipped with nuclear weapons. Pushed to his limits, Harkness resigned from the cabinet early in February, and Social Credit support of the government evaporated. In the ensuing campaign, Diefenbaker maintained enough support to deprive the Liberals of a majority government in the April 1963 election.

CANADA'S AMERICAN PROBLEM

On the surface, Lester Pearson, the diplomat's diplomat, appeared to be the ideal leader to heal the breach with the United States.[10] The son and grandson of Methodist ministers, Pearson grew up in southern Ontario, where many people shared his Irish Protestant roots. He earned degrees at Toronto and Oxford, taught history at the University of Toronto, and in 1928 moved to the Department of External Affairs, where his diplomatic skills blossomed. In 1946 King appointed him undersecretary of state for external affairs and encouraged him to run for political office in a 1948 bi-election. As minister of external affairs from 1948 to 1957, Pearson developed a high profile in international circles and tried to deal evenhandedly with American senator Joseph McCarthy's witchhunt against communism, which spilled over into Canada and even smeared Pearson himself.[11] The obvious choice as successor to St. Laurent, he moved quickly after the party's dismal showing in 1958 to recapture the political middle ground lost to Diefenbaker. The American favourite going into the 1963 election, Pearson put the defence issue behind him by accepting nuclear weapons, but concerns about the dominance of the United States in Canadian affairs would not go away.

The Americanization of Canadian culture, especially with the advent of the hugely popular medium of television, led to the appointment in 1949 of a royal commission on the arts, letters, and sciences. Chaired by Vincent Massey, a member of one of the founding families of the farm-implements giant Massey-Harris (after 1953 Massey-Fergusson), the commission recommended government programs to strengthen Canadian cultural production, including state control over television stations, federal grants to universities, and increased funding to cultural institutions such as the

National Film Board and the National Museum. The St. Laurent government acted on this advice and, in 1957, created the Canada Council, a government agency to support the arts. Initiatives such as the Stratford (Shakespeare) Festival and the Royal Winnipeg Ballet benefitted, as did the struggling Canadian publishing industry.

Despite these efforts, popular culture remained dominated by American television, magazines, movies, and recordings. In 1968 the Pearson government established the Canadian Radio-Television Commission (CRTC) to regulate broadcasting and created a Canadian Film Development Corporation to encourage a Canadian-based movie industry. After the adoption of tougher Canadian content regulations in 1970, Canadian talent had more opportunities to find an audience on radio and television. The combined efforts of the CBC and its francophone counterpart Radio-Canada, Radio-Québec (established 1968), the Canada Council, and various regulatory bodies spurred an outpouring of film, art, music, drama, and print that is one of the most significant developments in postwar Canada (Image 9.2).

The Canadianization movement gained momentum in the late 1960s as Canadians began to imagine themselves as a better version of the North American dream.[12] In an effort to slow the Americanization of university faculties, the federal government supported policies to hire qualified Canadians over foreign applicants and responded positively to many of the recommendations of *To Know Ourselves: The Report of the Commission on Canadian Studies* (1975), authored by the president of Trent University, Thomas H. B. Symons. With the help of federal government funding, Canadian Studies programs sprouted not only in Canadian universities but also internationally in an effort to cultivate a higher profile for what journalist Bruce Hutchinson dubbed "The Unknown Country."[13]

Canadians also vowed to demonstrate their excellence in sports. In 1961 Ottawa passed the Fitness and Amateur Sports Act, which provided funding to encourage physical fitness and to make a better showing at the Olympics. Postwar prosperity and urbanization brought larger audiences to professional team sports, especially hockey. Aired on Saturday night television as well as radio, games between teams in the American-dominated National Hockey League (NHL) produced popular heroes such as Maurice "Rocket" Richard, whose skills on the ice helped the Montreal Canadiens to win a string of Stanley Cups in the 1950s and 1960s. When the

Image 9.2. Canadian literature, art, and film flourished everywhere in the second half of the twentieth century, including among the Inuit living in the Canadian North. Their artwork was often marketed through community cooperatives, as was the case with this image of *Walrus Hunters on Sea Ice*, 1967, by Parr (1893–1969). Printed by Eegyvudluk, Pootgoogook (1931). Stonecut. (Collection of the West Baffin Eskimo Co-operative Ltd., on loan to the McMichael Collection, by permission)

Rocket was suspended in 1955 as a penalty for brawling, fans at the Montreal Forum took to the streets in riotous indignation. The legendary competition between the Montreal Canadiens and the Toronto Maple Leafs reflected long-standing tensions between anglophones and francophones. In 1972, Canadians all cheered together when Paul Henderson scored the winning goal for Canada in a Summit Series game against the Soviet Union.

The influence of the United States on what passed as Canadian culture drew criticism from Canadian intellectuals. At the University of Toronto, Harold Innis and Marshall McLuhan expressed concerns about the technological imperative bearing down on Canada, but there seemed to be little that anyone could do to shape media that were controlled by powerful American corporations. In 1965 philosopher George Grant published *Lament for a Nation*, in which he argued that the homogenizing forces of liberalism, modernity, and technology had undermined "defining particularisms" that made Canada distinct in North America. For Grant, Diefenbaker represented "the last gasp of Canadian nationalism" that finally succumbed to Kennedy's Camelot. Grant's book became a best seller in a country whose anglophone citizens were searching desperately for reasons why they should have a separate identity from the United States.

While Grant lamented the loss of what he believed were the admirable features of Canada's British heritage, the Liberal government continued to remove the ties that bound Canadians to Great Britain. The Canadian Citizenship Act (1946) enabled immigrants, for the first time, to become citizens of Canada as well as "British subjects," and appeals to the Privy Council were abolished in 1949. Three years later, the Canadian rather than the British government appointed Canada's governor general, Vincent Massey, who was also the first native-born Canadian to hold the post. In 1964 the Pearson government decided to adopt a distinctive Canadian flag to replace the British Red Ensign and the Union Jack, which had hitherto been used on ceremonial occasions. After six months of heated debate in the House of Commons and across the nation, the government finally invoked closure, and a new Maple Leaf flag was hoisted over the Parliament Buildings in Ottawa on 15 February 1965.

The flag debate was a tempest in a teapot compared to the controversy that surrounded the growing American dominance of the Canadian economy. While it was clear by the 1920s that the United States was replacing Great Britain as Canada's major source of investment and markets, the Second World War and Cold War accelerated the trend. This and other economic issues prompted the St. Laurent government to establish a Royal Commission on Canada's Economic Prospects in 1955. Chaired by Toronto-based accountant Walter Gordon, the commission produced a report expressing concerns that American branch plants, which dominated many sectors of the Canadian economy, blunted Canada's potential and contributed to a balance-of-payments problem as capital flowed out of the country in the form of interest and dividends.

The Diefenbaker government took these concerns seriously, introducing tax incentives for Canadian-based industries, and defying the
United States by trading with Communist countries such as China,
Cuba, and the Soviet Union. Pearson went even further, appointing his friend and benefactor Walter Gordon as minister of finance.
Backed by a small team of purposeful advisers outside the civil service, Gordon introduced a budget in 1963 that included a 30 percent "takeover tax" on the sale to foreigners of shares in Canadian
companies and a 20 percent withholding tax on dividends paid to
nonresidents from foreign subsidiaries operating in Canada. These
policies brought howls of protest from the business community,
forcing the withdrawal of some of the budget recommendations.
Their friendship strained by Gordon's nationalist stance, Pearson
accepted his finance minister's resignation after the 1965 election,
which produced another minority government. By that time, a solution to the balance-of-trade problem was found in the Automotive
Products Trade Agreement between Canada and the United States,
concluded in January 1965. The Auto Pact created an integrated
continental market for automobiles and automobile parts and guaranteed levels of production and investment in Canada. Ontario,
where most of the automobile industry was located, boomed.

Relations with the United States nevertheless remained fragile.
In April 1965 Pearson voiced his support for a negotiated peace
in Vietnam while speaking at Temple University in Philadelphia.
President Lyndon B. Johnson, who in February had stepped up
bombing in the divided country, was furious, berating Pearson at
a luncheon following his speech. Despite this glitch in Canadian-
American relations, Canada continued to pursue diplomatic efforts
on behalf of the United States to end the war in Vietnam and benefitted by supplying the American military under the defence sharing
agreement.

QUEBEC IN QUESTION

Standing up to the United States was popular in Quebec, which was
experiencing a stunning transformation. While Duplessis continued
to dominate the provincial political scene until his death in 1959,
urban secular values had long been undermining the rural, Roman

Catholic, and antistate worldview promoted by his regime.[14] In 1948 a group of avant-garde Quebec artists and intellectuals, led by Paul-Émile Bourduas, released *Refus global*, an indictment of the narrow orthodoxy that prevailed in the province. More criticism followed and was fuelled by the advent of French-language television. When Jean-Paul Desbien, a Marist Brother, anonymously published harsh criticism of the province's Church-controlled education system in 1960, under the title *Les insolences du Frère Untel*, the book sold a hundred thousand copies.

The extent of new thinking in Quebec became clear when the Liberal Party, led by former federal cabinet minister Jean Lesage, was elected to office in June 1960. Campaigning with the slogan *Le temps que ça change* (It's time for a change), the Liberals introduced state control of education, hospitals, and social welfare, and signaled their intent to challenge anglophone dominance of industry in Quebec by nationalizing private power companies. Instead of spurning federal initiatives as Duplessis had done, the Lesage administration insisted that federal monies available for cost-shared programs such as the Canadian Pension Plan be administered by a Quebec Pension Plan, thereby making available a major new source of funds for investment in the province. Under Lesage, the provincial bureaucracy expanded dramatically and modernization developed at a dizzying pace.

The sense of agency that infected francophones in Quebec meant that the state actually accomplished what it set out to do. Within little more than a decade, education levels improved dramatically, the average income of francophones rose from near the bottom to the top of the ethnic hierarchy, Québécois women registered the lowest birth rate in Canada, and Québécois, more than Canadians elsewhere, eschewed marriage for common law relationships. After the province's Catholic unions formally ended their affiliation with the Church in 1960, the Confédération des syndicats nationaux (CSN), along with international unions and organizations representing teachers and civil servants, became a major force in Quebec politics. Taking advantage of state policies at the provincial and federal levels, francophone cultural expression flourished as a counterpoint to homogenizing North American influences. It was "a fantastic time to be young," the historian Jean Bélanger concludes, "to have ideas and ideals, to be alive, to wish to do things, to want to improve the world, to be a Québécois."[15]

Accompanying the "quiet revolution" inaugurated by the Lesage administration was a much noisier outburst of francophone nationalism. Nationalist expression in Quebec was not new, but it took on new forms, some of them inspired by militant postwar independence movements throughout the world, especially in the French colony of Algeria.[16] In 1960 supporters of independence for Quebec formed the Rassemblement pour l'indépendance nationale, and on the eve of the Liberal Party assuming federal office on 22 April 1963, a bomb planted by radical separatists exploded in an army recruiting office in Montreal, killing a janitor. More explosions followed. The "Quebec question" instantly became the dominating force in Canadian political life.

Recognizing the threat of separatism both to the nation and to the fortunes of the Liberal Party, Pearson established a Royal Commission on Bilingualism and Biculturalism under co-chairs André Laurendeau and Davidson Dunton to advise on policy, and he paid close attention to Quebec representation in his cabinet. Troubled by a string of scandals relating to several of his francophone ministers, Pearson recruited three new faces from Quebec – journalist Gérard Pelletier, union leader Jean Marchand, and public intellectual Pierre Elliott Trudeau – to run on the Liberal ticket in 1965.

The Liberals in Quebec lost the 1966 election to the Union Nationale, led by Daniel Johnson, but the changes kept coming. Under Lesage, the Quebec government had established formal diplomatic relations with France, a policy encouraged by President Charles de Gaulle, condemned by Ottawa, and embraced by the Johnson administration. During his visit to Canada in 1967, de Gaulle prompted a diplomatic row with Canada by shouting "Vivre Québec libre" from the balcony of Montreal City Hall, to the delight of sovereignists. In 1968 René Lévesque, a former Radio-Canada talk-show host and member of Lesage's cabinet, cobbled together an alliance of social democratic pro-sovereignty forces to create the Parti Québécois (PQ).

As francophones reinvented Quebec, anglophones in the province began to feel the chill. Many of them moved to Toronto, as did head offices of banks and insurance companies. In 1967 Montreal, still the largest city in Canada but no longer its economic capital, hosted the World's Fair, Expo 67, as part of Canada's centennial celebrations. This highly successful event based on the theme "Man and His World" attracted 50 million visitors and signaled that Canada had arrived as one of the world's great nations.

SOCIETY IN TRANSITION

While Quebec generated the most *sturm und drang*, other areas of Canada experienced the same dizzying trends. The civil service expanded in every province to manage new state responsibilities, unions emerged in the burgeoning white-collar sector, and secularization and social programs challenged the centrality of church and family. Across Canada, rural areas hollowed out as "baby boomers" moved to cities to find work and excitement. The boomers grew up with television, embraced the Enlightenment ideal of progress, and experienced state policies that conveniently supported their need for public schooling, university education, employment, and social security. With sex, drugs, rock 'n' roll, short skirts, and long hair creating controversy everywhere, the old Canada suddenly vanished.[17]

Few postwar trends went as deep and had such a profound impact as the changing status of women.[18] While many Canadians attempted to restore the family ideal disrupted by the Depression and Second World War, the ideal in practice left something to be desired. Middle-class women often felt isolated in their suburban homes, while the pressure to own modern conveniences meant that most women needed a job to pay for them. Ignoring all swings in the business cycle, women's labour-force participation rate doubled between 1951 and 1981. Wage-earning women soon discovered that they were working a "double day" – at home and on the job – and facing a "double standard" in the workplace. Not only were they barred from many areas of employment and most managerial positions, they received less pay than men for doing the same work. After prodding by a formidable alliance of club women, led by Laura Sabia, president of the Canadian Federation of University Women, and Judy LaMarsh, the only female cabinet minister, Pearson established a Royal Commission on the Status of Women, chaired by journalist and broadcaster Florence Bird, in 1967.

Nothing influenced the status of women more than changing attitudes toward sex. During and after the Second World War men experienced increasing sexual freedom, and this was encouraged through magazines such as *Playboy*, founded in 1953, which circulated easily in Canada after the relaxing of obscenity laws in 1959. Women, meanwhile, still agonized about being virgins when they married and often paid the price if they were not, forced by pregnancy into an unwanted marriage or single motherhood. With the advent of the birth control pill, approved for contraceptive use in the United States in 1960, women's sense of agency took a giant leap. Ignoring Canadian laws against the dissemination of birth control, women sought the pill, doctors prescribed it, and both the birth rate and the marriage rate began to plummet.

The law was also a laggard in removing same-sex relationships from the criminal code. Fledgling gay rights organizations pressed for an end to this and other forms of discrimination, and for recognition that sexual orientation was neither a psychological defect nor a moral failing. They faced an uphill battle. In the early 1960s, the RCMP developed a useless devise, crudely labeled a "fruit machine," to detect homosexuality in applicants for civil service jobs.

Bureaucratic processes were becoming more prevalent in labour relations – contract negotiations could be especially time-consuming – but Canadian workers were still obliged to fight battles on the picket lines. The anti-Communist hysteria that accompanied the Cold War made radical unions subject to special forms of intimidation. Following the Second World War American labour leader Harold "Hal" Banks used gangs of thugs to break up the Communist-controlled Canadian Seamen's Union while governments looked the other way.

Workers in Quebec were dogged by a government determined to keep them in their place, a situation that only encouraged activism. In 1949 five thousand workers in the town of Asbestos, Quebec, conducted an illegal four-month strike against the American-owned Johns-Manville Company. As violence between strikers and provincial police escalated, young intellectuals such as Pierre Elliott Trudeau and Gérard Pelletier took up the cause of the strikers, and even Archbishop Joseph Charbonneau of Montreal expressed his sympathy publicly. The striking workers were ultimately defeated by superior force, but the Asbestos strike was yet another signal that attitudes in Quebec were changing.

In 1956 the two major labour organizations in Canada, the Trades and Labour Congress and the Canadian Congress of Labour, merged into the Canadian Labour Congress, a move precipitated by a similar development among their counterparts in the United States. Like the industries in which they organized, Canadian unions were often branches of American organizations, a situation that created growing resentment. A distinctly Canadian perspective was bought to the union movement in the 1960s when public service workers, who were denied the right to unionize, refused to accept this dictum. The Canadian Union of Public Employees was founded in 1963, the same year Ontario civil servants gained bargaining rights. Other jurisdictions soon followed, as did a rash of strikes in the public sector. Boosted by the unionization of white-collar workers, among them teachers, nurses, and clerical staff, the proportion of Canada's labour belonging to unions rose from 17 percent in 1946 to nearly 38 percent in 1981.

JUST WATCH ME

While Pearson managed to dodge many of the social tensions percolating in postwar Canadian society, his successor, by either choice or necessity, met them head on. Pierre Elliott Trudeau emerged triumphant in the leadership convention that followed Pearson's retirement early in 1968 and, in a wave of "Trudeaumania," led the Liberal Party to a majority victory.[19] The son of a mother with English heritage and a francophone father who made his first million selling a chain of gas stations to Imperial Oil in 1932, Trudeau studied at the Université de Montréal, Harvard, the Sorbonne, and the London School of Economics. In his youth, he travelled widely and was attracted to a variety of ideologies, including Quebec nationalism, fascism, anti-Semitism, personalism, and socialism, before his liberalism congealed. Coeditor with Gérard Pelletier of the influential journal *Cité Libre*, he earned the wrath of Duplessis and other conservatives in Quebec with his trenchant critiques and even skewered Pearson in 1963 for bowing to the United States in accepting nuclear weapons. Pearson nevertheless welcomed Trudeau into the Liberal fold, appointing him minister of justice in 1967. From this platform, he launched a comprehensive review of the criminal code and set the wheels in motion to reform the constitution. Legislation to relax laws relating to abortion, birth control, divorce, gambling, homosexuality, and suicide were passed in 1969, but constitutional reform remained an elusive goal.

In the 1968 campaign, Trudeau captured the public imagination by promising to create a "Just Society" and by exhibiting a youthful image that belied his forty-eight years. Driving a sports car, wearing sandals and a leather jacket or a rose in his lapel, he was clearly a sixties man. Trudeau was also seen as the man who could deal with Quebec. Claiming that *nationalistes* were reactionaries posing as revolutionaries, he fearlessly opposed special status for the province. Instead, he was determined to make francophones feel at home across Canada. Under his leadership, Parliament passed the Official Languages Act in 1969, which gave French the same status as English in areas of federal jurisdiction. New Brunswick, with its growing Acadian population and popular Acadian premier Louis J. Robichaud, also adopted bilingual legislation in 1969.

Not everyone was impressed. Diefenbaker led a rump of Progressive Conservatives from western Canada against bilingualism, and Canadians whose backgrounds were neither French nor English wondered where they fit into a bilingual Canada. In 1971 the Trudeau government announced its intention to create a secretary of state for multiculturalism to stem criticism from ethnic minorities, whose numbers were expanding dramatically under the impact of the revised Immigration Act of 1967.

Trudeau's liberal credentials were called into question on many occasions but never more sharply than in October 1970, when two cells of the Front de libération du Québec (FLQ) abducted James Cross, the British trade commissioner in Montreal, and Pierre Laporte, the Quebec minister of labour and immigration. Consisting of only a few members, the FLQ had been associated with many of the bombings in Quebec and was determined to bring about a regime change in the province. In return for release of their hostages, the kidnappers demanded the freeing of twenty-three

Image 9.3. *O.K. Everybody Take a Valium!* Terry Mosher, aka Aislin, the gifted cartoonist of the *Montreal Gazette*, captured the anxiety that prevailed in Canada when the Liberal Party under Robert Bourassa lost the 1976 election to the Parti Québecois, led by René Lévesque. (*Montreal Gazette*, reproduced with the permission of McCord Museum/P090-A_ ✓ 50-1004)

"political prisoners," broadcasting of the group's manifesto, providing $500,000 in gold, and arranging sanctuary for the terrorists in Cuba or Algeria.

Trudeau took decisive action, fearing that the kidnappings might spark a general uprising in Quebec, where university students, union leaders, and many left-wing politicians agreed with the goals, if not the methods, of the FLQ. When probed by CBC interviewer Tim Ralfe on how far he would go to maintain law and order, Trudeau quipped, in his typical offhanded way, "Well, just watch me." On 16 October, the federal government, at the request of the government of Quebec, proclaimed the War Measures Act, imposed martial law on the entire nation, and began rounding up hundreds of suspected terrorists and their alleged sympathizers. The next day, Laporte's body was found in the trunk of an abandoned car. After two anxious months, the crisis ended when Cross was finally released in return for safe passage of the kidnappers to Cuba. At the time, an overwhelming majority of Canadians, both in and outside Quebec, approved of the federal government's aggressive stance.

The impact of Ottawa's handling of the crisis is still debated, but it seems safe to conclude that it helped to end a cycle of violence threatening Canadian democracy and that it fuelled support for independence in Quebec. The Liberals, led by Robert Bourassa, won elections in Quebec in 1970 and 1974, but they failed to keep pace with growing nationalist sentiment in the province. When the Parti Québecois won the provincial election in 1976, Trudeau met his match. A purposeful René Lévesque promised even tougher language laws in Quebec than those introduced by his Liberal predecessor, and he planned to hold a referendum on sovereignty. Canadians held their collective breath (Image 9.3).

REAPING THE WHIRLWIND

Quebec nationalism was not the only issue stirring the political pot. On expanding university campuses, the "New Left" was being transplanted from the United States, helped along by American draft dodgers who sought sanctuary in Canada during the Vietnam War (Image 9.4). The American Black Power, Native Rights, and Women's Liberation movements also quickly took root in Canada, and gay rights and environmental activists joined hands across the border. Governments were obliged to pay attention.

In defining his goals for a Just Society, Trudeau focused on Canada's First Nations, who were becoming increasingly vocal in demanding redress for their shameful condition. Minister of Indian

and Northern Affairs Jean Chrétien released a White Paper in June 1969, the main thrust of which was to abolish Indian status and transfer responsibility for Indian Affairs to the provinces. The National Indian Brotherhood (NIB), founded in 1968 to represent Status Indians, was not impressed, demanding Aboriginal self-government and respect for Aboriginal treaty rights, not assimilation. In a stinging critique, entitled *The Unjust Society* (1969), the young Cree chief Harold Cardinal outlined a much different agenda for his people.

Ottawa withdrew the White Paper and embarked on the long, difficult process of addressing Aboriginal grievances. During the 1970s, pressures from the NIB – reorganized as the Assembly of First Nations in 1982 – led the government to begin closing residential schools. In a landmark decision relating to the Nisga'a in British Columbia, six of the seven Supreme Court judges ruled in 1973 that Aboriginal title existed before colonization began, but they were split (3–3–1) on whether subsequent legislation in the province had extinguished that title. This led Trudeau to concede that Ottawa was obliged to negotiate comprehensive land claims with First Nations not covered by treaties. In Quebec the Cree and Inuit drew upon this principle to insist that their rights be recognized before the massive James Bay power development could proceed. A proposed pipeline in the Mackenzie River valley to bring oil from

---

Image 9.4. Anti–Vietnam War protest at the Toronto Consulate, October 1968. Anti–Vietnam War protests began escalating in the United States in 1964 and quickly spread to Canada, as did draft resisters, military deserters, and people generally opposed to American foreign policy. Although the figures are difficult to determine because the Canadian government declared in May 1969 that immigration officials could not ask would-be American immigrants about their military status, estimates suggest that as many as thirty thousand draft resisters and deserters arrived in Canada. Roughly the same number of Canadians volunteered to fight with the American military in the Vietnam War. As this image suggests, many of the anti–Vietnam War protesters were young people. Antiwar sentiment was especially strong on university campuses, where both students and professors openly expressed opposition to American imperialism. (By permission of York University Libraries, Clara Thomas Archives & Special Collections, Toronto Telegram fonds, ASC04607)

Prudhoe Bay was postponed after an inquiry conducted by Justice Thomas Berger from 1975 to 1977 heard testimony from the Dene and Inuit in the region. Meanwhile, local authorities throughout Canada sometimes faced direct action, as was the case in Kenora, Ontario, where protestors occupied a park between 1972 and 1974, claiming that it, like much of Kenora, belonged to the Anishinabek Nation.

Women also included direct action among their strategies for change. In 1970 the Royal Commission on the Status of Women submitted its report, offering 167 recommendations to kick-start the process of eliminating the discriminatory laws and practices relating to women. When the government was slow to respond, club women and activists attracted to more radical feminisms mobilized to demand a national day-care program, reform of family law, an end to family violence and harassment in the workplace, and programs to address women's poverty. Restrictions on abortion rights that remained in the 1969 legislation prompted five hundred women to join an Abortion Caravan that began in British Columbia and ended in Ottawa, where thirty of the protestors shut down Parliament in May 1970 by chaining themselves to seats in the visitors' gallery and shouting "Abortion on Demand!" In 1979 Sandra Nicholas Lovelace, a Maliseet from the Tobique First Nation who had lost her Indian status under the Indian Act when she married a white man, took her case to the United Nations, which in 1981 found Canada in breach of the International Covenant on Civil and Political Rights. By then, feminism in all its manifestations had become one of the most widespread and powerful social movements in Canada.

Encouraged by Civil Rights and Black Power movements in the United States, African Canadians became more assertive in their struggle against discrimination. In the Maritimes and Ontario, separate schools were gradually abolished after a 1954 American court ruling outlawed racial segregation in public education on the grounds that separate was never equal. A decision by the Halifax city council in 1962 to relocate people living in the black community of Africville galvanized resentment and led to a visit to the city by Stokely Carmichael, leader of the Black Panthers. In Toronto and Montreal, where many of the recent immigrants from the West Indies and Africa had settled, racism became the focus for a number of confrontations with authorities. One of the largest student protests in Canadian history occurred in the winter of 1969 at Sir George Williams University (now Concordia), when the university was slow to redress accusations of racism.

The environmental movement in North America reached a new level of awareness in 1962 when Rachel Carson published *Silent Spring*, in which she revealed the dangers posed by the "tide of chemicals born of the Industrial Age." As with the other movements, voluntary organizations became the catalyst for action. A group of American and Canadian activists adopted the name Greenpeace and conducted highly visible campaigns against nuclear testing, dumping of toxic wastes into lakes and oceans, and the slaughter of whales, dolphins, and baby seals. In 1972 a United Nations Conference on the Human Environment met in Stockholm to discuss the decaying state of the planet. Chaired by a Canadian, Maurice Strong, the conference produced a declaration of environmental rights and established a program to fund and coordinate investigations into environmental problems. The Trudeau administration, meanwhile, passed the Arctic Waters Pollution Prevention Act, designed to assert Canadian sovereignty against claims by the United States that their supertankers carrying oil from Alaska had the right to travel through the Northwest Passage.

Long a critic of American imperialism, Trudeau was less inclined than his predecessors had been to take a conciliatory position in relations with the United States. He cut Canada's NATO commitments and departed from the United States in officially recognizing the People's Republic of China in 1970. His government also pursued the recommendations of a Task Force on the Structure of Canadian Industry, chaired by University of Toronto economist Mel Watkins, to encourage Canadian ownership and management in vital sectors of the economy. As a result of these initiatives, President Richard Nixon made no exceptions for Canada when he decided to impose import controls on manufactures in 1971.

PROGRESS ON THE ROPES

The polls suggested another Liberal victory in the October 1972 election, but the result was a cliff-hanger, 109 seats for the Liberals to 107 for the Progressive Conservatives, led by former Nova Scotia premier Robert Stanfield. The Liberal administration survived with the support of the NDP, led by David Lewis, which won 31 seats. Even the presence during the campaign of Trudeau's new wife, Margaret Sinclair, twenty-nine years younger than her famous husband, and their son, Justin, failed to charm the disenchanted electorate.

In the months following the election, the Arab members of the Organization of Petroleum Exporting Countries (OPEC) placed an embargo on oil exports during yet another war with Israel. When the United States simultaneously tried to cool down an economy overheated by the Vietnam War, the result was high unemployment and inflation coming together in "stagflation." Initially, the economic crisis played into the hands of the federal Liberals. They engineered their own defeat in May 1974 by introducing a budget that they knew the opposition would reject. With stagflation as the main issue, the Progressive Conservatives promised to implement wage and price controls. The Liberals campaigned successfully against such a draconian measure and then introduced the very policy advocated by their opponents. Voter cynicism spiked and trust in the competence of the state began to dwindle.

Nowhere was cynicism more evident than in Alberta, where Trudeau's efforts to establish a national energy policy, including a freeze on oil prices, were deeply resented. In 1973 Ottawa created Petro-Canada, a Crown corporation with a broad mandate to develop a Canadian presence in an industry that was controlled by foreign corporations. The Foreign Investment Review Agency (FIRA), established in 1974, seemed to Albertans to be yet another program designed to keep the oil-rich province from taking advantage of global trends. The other western provinces joined Alberta in resisting what they perceived as an unwarranted attempt to deprive the west of resource revenues for the benefit of the east.

As western alienation mounted, the Progressive Conservative Party chose Joseph Clark, a young MP from Alberta, to succeed Stanfield as their leader in 1976. Clark understood the growing discontent in the western provinces, but he, like the premier of Alberta, Peter Lougheed, was a "progressive" Conservative and thus offered no threat to postwar liberal consensus. Although he led his party to just a few seats short of a majority government in the May 1979 election, his government was defeated in December on a budget that included an increased tax on gasoline. Trudeau, who had planned to step down as leader of the Liberal Party, was thrust into another election, which he won handily, but only two seats west of Ontario elected Liberal members.

Trudeau's last term in office established his reputation, which remains highly controversial. In the fall of 1980, his government introduced a National Energy Policy (NEP), designed to promote oil self-sufficiency, establish lower-than-world prices for oil in Canada, increase Canadian ownership, and enhance federal government revenues. The Canadian petroleum industry had expanded rapidly since the 1970s, not only in Alberta but also in Saskatchewan and increasingly off the Atlantic coast, where the declaration of a two-hundred-mile (370 km) limit in 1977 added significantly to Canada's already impressive oil and gas endowment. Initiated in the spirit of earlier measures designed to spread wealth beyond producing provinces, Ottawa's assertion of control over natural resources invoked the wrath of provincial premiers. Foreign companies, which stood to lose under the new rules, also cried foul. When the price of oil began to drop with the onset of a recession in the early 1980s, bankruptcies ensued and westerners blamed Ottawa.

The Trudeau government was also heavy-handed when it came to Quebec, taking an active part in the "non" campaign in the province's referendum on sovereignty held on 20 May 1980. When the "oui" side garnered less than 40 percent of the vote, Trudeau pushed ahead with constitutional reform. It was a risky move, especially since twenty years of constitutional wrangling had yielded little. As in the past, most provinces resisted the initiative. Only Ontario and New Brunswick were initially onside. The Trudeau cabinet then decided to proceed without unanimous provincial approval. In the final negotiations, all provinces save Quebec eventually agreed to support Ottawa's constitutional package. The British Parliament passed the Canada Act in March 1982, ending its power to amend the British North America Act and replacing it with the Constitution Act, 1982, which included the renamed British North America Act, an amending formula, and a Charter of Rights and Freedoms (Image 9.5).

The Canada Act is wonderfully revealing, not only about the compromises required to "bring the constitution home," but also

Image 9.5. Prime Minister Trudeau and Queen Elizabeth II sign Canada's constitutional proclamation in Ottawa, 17 April 1982. (By permission of The Canadian Press/Ron Poling)

about the nation that had developed in the postwar period. In the amending formula finally agreed upon, the federal government could change the constitution with the approval of the Parliament plus two-thirds of the provinces representing a combined population of at least 50 percent of all Canadians. Unanimous consent of all provinces as well as both houses of Parliament was required for amendments affecting representation in the House of Commons, Senate, and Supreme Court and for changes affecting the use of the French and English languages. Any province believing that its rights were compromised by an amendment could declare that amendment null and void within its boundaries. As a concession to the smaller provinces, section 36 of the constitution committed Canadian governments to the principle of equalization to "ensure that provincial governments have sufficient revenue to provide reasonably comparable levels of public services at reasonably comparable levels of taxation."

The Charter of Rights and Freedom guaranteed democratic, mobility, and legal rights and prohibited discrimination on the basis of race, ethnic origin, colour, religion, sex, age, or mental or physical disability. Fearing that the principle of gender equality would be compromised in the various saw-offs among provinces, feminists across Canada organized a highly effective lobby to insert section 28, which declared that "notwithstanding anything in this Charter, the rights and freedoms referred to in it are guaranteed equally to male and female persons." Aboriginal pressure to have the right to self-determination enshrined in the constitution failed, but the Charter guaranteed that nothing in the document would affect "any aboriginal, treaty or other rights and freedoms," including those recognized by the Royal Proclamation of 1763 and by land claim agreements. The Charter also confirmed Canada's and New Brunswick's bilingual status and stated that the Charter "shall be interpreted in a manner consistent with the preservation and enhancement of the multicultural heritage of Canadians."

Through its provisions, the constitutional package made it more difficult to change legislation relating to human rights, bilingual institutions, the equality of provinces, and the supremacy of Parliament. It also greatly enhanced the powers of the Supreme Court of Canada, which would inevitably be required to rule on contested constitutional matters. This, without question, is Trudeau's most enduring legacy.

CONCLUSION

In the four decades following the Second World War, Canada was essentially reinvented as a modern nation-state. The old cleavages remained, of course, especially the French-English divide, but here, too, there were seismic shifts. In Quebec the "quiet revolution" intensified a preoccupation with the francophone majority in the province, while Canadians of British heritage experienced what the historian José Igartua calls "the other quiet revolution" as they moved from an ethnic-based to a rights-based notion of citizenship, and tried to produce a set of symbols and policies that would bind all Canadians together as a nation.[20] The new constitution was a start in that direction, but by the time it passed into law, the gods of Canadian liberalism decided to roll the dice.

10

Interesting Times, 1984–2011

Neoliberal forces that had been gathering strength since the 1970s found a champion in Canada when Brian Mulroney led the Progressive Conservatives to a landslide victory in the 1984 federal election. Confronted with mounting economic challenges, Mulroney and his successors fixed their attention on new liberal orthodoxies, among them global economic competitiveness and a reduced role for the state in sustaining social welfare. As Communist regimes in Europe collapsed under the weight of their fossilized bureaucracies, efforts to create a new world order based on free-market capitalism advanced rapidly. Canada and the United States signed a Free Trade Agreement in 1988, and the World Trade Organization, which evolved from GATT in 1995, established an international framework for promoting trade liberalization. Cutting across this trajectory were other destabilizing forces, among them the digital communications revolution, climate change, and attacks on the Pentagon and the World Trade Center by Muslim extremists on 11 September 2001. Could the centre hold in such a context?

THE MARKET WELFARE STATE

Most Western nations had welcomed the enhanced power of the state in the decades following the Second World War, but there had always been critics of big government. In the United States sharp debates about economic policy had been churning since the 1950s, with Milton Friedman, an economist based at the University of

Chicago, championing the neoliberal cause and the Canadian-born Harvard economist John Kenneth Galbraith supporting a larger role for governments in maintaining economic stability and social well-being. Galbraith's perspective prevailed until the 1970s, when the oil crisis and stagflation opened the door to criticism of the welfare state. With corporate-sponsored think tanks predicting disaster if current policies continued and North American companies moving their operations to developing countries to avoid taxes, labour contracts, and environmental regulations, policymakers focused on economic restructuring to accommodate "a new world order."

In Canada the neoliberal turn was set in motion in 1982, when the Trudeau government established a Royal Commission on Canada's Economic Union and Development Prospects, chaired by former Liberal finance minister Donald Macdonald. The commission's report, submitted in 1985, supported corporate demands for a more flexible economy capable of adjusting to global trends, and recommended free trade with the United States to secure markets in a world increasingly divided into trading blocs. It also advocated a restructuring of welfare state policies to achieve greater efficiencies and an elected Senate to provide better regional representation.

Brian Mulroney's name is usually mentioned in the same breath as that of Ronald Reagan and Margaret Thatcher as a politician who helped to launch the neoliberal order in the Western world. Born to parents of Irish heritage in Baie-Comeau, a small community on Quebec's North Shore, Mulroney studied political science at St. Francis–Xavier University, earned a law degree at Université Laval, and became a successful labour lawyer for major Quebec corporations. He attracted national attention in 1974–75 with his membership on a commission investigating corruption in Quebec's construction industry. An active Progressive Conservative since his teenage years, he ran unsuccessfully for the party leadership in 1976. When Joe Clark stumbled in 1979, Mulroney worked behind the scenes to replace him, forcing a leadership convention in 1983, which he won by a close margin. He was more successful in taking down John Turner, Trudeau's successor as prime minister, winning 211 of the 281 constituencies in the September 1984 election. While scholars are divided on the merits of his administration, this much is clear: it transformed the political landscape. By the time Mulroney stepped down in 1993, the Progressive Conservative Party lay in ruins and two new regional parties – the Bloc Québécois and the Reform Party – made governing at the centre more difficult than ever.[1]

Following the Macdonald Commission's advice, the Mulroney government opened trade negotiations with the United States (Image 10.1). This initiative was supported by most sectors of the Canadian business community, including the Business Council on National Issues, a powerful lobby group founded in 1976 by the chief executive officers of major Canadian corporations. Free trade was welcomed by the Reagan administration as a means of gaining unfettered access to Canadian resources. In addition to sweeping away remaining tariff barriers to trade in goods and services, negotiators liberalized conditions for investment and established a mechanism of questionable efficacy for dealing with disputes. No attention was paid to issues relating to labour, social welfare, or the environment.

The Free Trade Agreement (FTA), concluded in the autumn of 1987, precipitated a year of heated debate in a country where relations with the United States invariably touched a sensitive nerve. When the Liberal majority in the Senate demanded that the government receive an electoral mandate before implementing the agreement, Canadians went to the polls in November 1988 in what was essentially a referendum on free trade. Leaders of the Liberal and New Democratic parties, supported by labour unions, feminist organizations, and a variety of nationalist coalitions, opposed free trade, but lost their cause by splitting their vote. With majority support only in Alberta and Quebec, and 43 percent of the popular vote, the Progressive Conservatives won 169 out of 295 seats. The FTA went into effect on 1 January 1989, and three years later Mexico signed a North American Free Trade Agreement (NAFTA) to take effect in 1994.

Restructuring became the order of the day as companies such as Varity Corporation (the former Massey-Ferguson) announced that they were centralizing their operations in the United States. By 1990 Canada was in the grip of a deep recession, which was followed by what in Orwellian newspeak was called a "jobless recovery."

Image 10.1. Brian Mulroney and American president Ronald Reagan were determined to thaw the frosty relationship between the two countries that prevailed under Trudeau's leadership. At a meeting in Quebec City in March 1985, dubbed the "Shamrock Summit," because it fell on St. Patrick's Day and both leaders had Irish roots, the Reagans and the Mulroneys joined Canadian contralto Maureen Forrester in singing "When Irish Eyes Are Smiling." Free-trade talks began later that year. (By permission of The Canadian Press/Scott Applewhite)

Exports to the United States increased over the next decade. As a logical extension of the long-term trend to continental economic integration, the agreement seemed to work to Canada's overall benefit, but only as long as the United States remained the world's economic juggernaut.

Workers – and some economists argued Canada as a whole – were less well served by neoliberal policies. Instead of implementing a program to soften the impact of restructuring – a guaranteed minimum income was suggested – the Mulroney government began replacing universal social programs with piecemeal policies that targeted those in need. The government also reduced corporate, personal, and estate taxes and in 1992 replaced the Manufacturers' Sales Tax with a Goods and Services Tax (GST), which registered in the pocketbook of every Canadian. Like the recession of the early 1980s, the economic slump of the early 1990s was exacerbated by high interest rates to discourage inflation. This policy increased the costs of servicing the national debt, which inevitably rose with higher rates of unemployment and lower taxes. In earlier times, the solution to the vicious cycle would have been the implementation of policies to get people back to work, but the neoliberal approach was to further reduce taxes and government services.

CONSTITUTIONAL CONUNDRUMS

Free trade was not the only controversial item on Mulroney's agenda. Taking most of the seats in his home province in 1984, he was determined to upstage Trudeau by "bringing Quebec into the constitution." Liberal premier Robert Bourassa, who had returned to power in 1985, was sympathetic to this goal but insisted on five conditions before signing any constitutional deal: a clause recognizing Quebec as a distinct society, a Quebec veto for constitutional amendments, a greater provincial role in setting immigration policy, the right to remain outside new cost-shared programs without financial penalty, and participation in the selection of Supreme Court judges. At a meeting with provincial leaders at Meech Lake, near Ottawa, in April 1987, a package that met Quebec's demands was approved after objections to Quebec's veto power were resolved by extending a veto to all provinces.

The Meech Lake Accord flew in the face of Trudeau's vision for Canada, not only by granting Quebec a poorly defined "distinct society" status but also by greatly strengthening the provinces at the expense of the federal government. To alert Canadians to these dangers, Trudeau emerged from retirement and denounced the accord. Others joined his crusade. The unanimity required for constitutional amendments drew criticism from many, including Aboriginal leaders, who despaired of ever achieving their goal of self-government if all provinces were obliged to approve. Outside Quebec, women's groups, trade unions, and antipoverty organizations criticized, among other things, the provision that allowed provinces to be exempted from new federal shared-cost programs, which would open the door to a patchwork of social services.

The three-year time limit set for debate provided ample opportunity for provincial support to unravel. In 1989 a new Liberal government in Newfoundland, led by Clyde Wells, rescinded the province's earlier approval of the accord, while Gary Filmon's minority Progressive Conservative government in Manitoba let the time limit on the accord lapse after Elijah Harper, the lone Aboriginal member in the legislature, used procedural measures to postpone the vote. The accord died in June 1990, leaving many francophones in Quebec outraged. As the anger mounted, Lucien Bouchard, a popular minister in Mulroney's cabinet, resigned to become leader of the Bloc Québécois, a group of nationalist MPs from Quebec, many of them Progressive Conservatives. The Bloc's raison d'être was to defend Quebec's interests in Ottawa until independence was achieved.

Determined to snatch victory from the jaws of defeat, Mulroney brought the premiers and Aboriginal leaders together at Charlottetown to produce a new accord in August 1992. Quebec received much of what it had been promised during the Meech Lake discussions, but the new agreement fell short of Quebec's growing list of demands, which now rested on the principle that Confederation was a partnership between Quebec and "the rest of Canada." With three provinces poised to hold a referendum on the agreement, Mulroney seized the initiative by holding a national referendum on 26 October 1992. The Charlottetown Accord suffered a defeat in a majority of the provinces and territories, including Quebec.

By this time, alienation in western Canada had coalesced in the Reform Party. Founded in 1987, it was led by Preston Manning, the son of a long-serving Social Credit premier of Alberta. The western provinces had been the bulwark of the Progressive Conservative Party since the 1950s, but under Brian Mulroney, the focus had shifted back to Quebec. As the price of oil collapsed in the mid-1980s, the mood in the west darkened. The tipping point came in 1986 when the Montreal-based firm Bombardier was awarded the contract for maintenance of Canada's CF-18 military aircraft, even though Winnipeg's Bristol Aerospace had submitted what, to many people, seemed to be a superior bid.

Positioning themselves to the right of the Progressive Conservatives, Reformers demanded a more rigourous neoliberal economic agenda and were prepared to let Quebec leave Confederation rather than receive special status. In 1988 the party campaigned with the slogan "The West Wants In," signaling their determination to set the national agenda. Other than lower taxes and balanced budgets, major planks in the party's platform included an elected Senate; privatization of Crown corporations such as the CBC, Canada Post, and Petro-Canada; and an immigration policy based "solely on economic need." The latter hinted that the party had also become home for social conservatives, people deeply troubled by everything that Canadian liberalism stood for: bilingualism, multiculturalism, feminism, and secular values. The Reform Party elected its first MP, Deborah Grey, in a 1989 bi-election in Alberta.

With public opinion turning resolutely against his government, Mulroney stepped down early in 1993. He was succeeded as party leader and prime minister by Kim Campbell, an MP from Vancouver who had proven her mettle as minister of Indian and northern affairs and minister of justice. Canada's first female prime minister had little hope of success, but few expected the outcome of the October 1993 election. When the votes were counted, the Progressive Conservatives were reduced to only 2 members, while the Bloc Québécois took 54 seats, two ahead of the Reform Party. The Liberals marched down the middle, taking 177 seats with only 41 percent of the popular vote.

THE LIBERAL PARTY REDUX

Jean Chrétien, dubbed "yesterday's man" when he lost the Liberal Party leadership to John Turner in 1984, proved more resilient than his detractors could ever have imagined. The eighteenth of nineteen children born to a family of modest means in Shawinigan, Quebec, he studied law at Laval and won a seat in the House of Commons in 1963 at the age of twenty-nine. Holding a variety of portfolios during his long parliamentary career, he was Trudeau's trusted lieutenant through the War Measures Act, the Quebec referendum, and the constitutional campaign. Chrétien resigned from the House of Commons in 1986 to work in the private sector but ran successfully for leadership of the Liberal Party after Turner stepped down in 1990.[2]

As heir to Trudeau's legacy, "the little man from Shawinigan" had more popular appeal than his rival for leadership, Paul Martin. Paul Martin Sr. had been a social welfare Liberal, but the younger Martin was cut from different cloth. Long-time president and CEO of Canada Steamship Lines, based in Montreal, he was in tune with neoliberal thinking in corporate boardrooms. Appointed minister of finance in the Chrétien cabinet, he continued along the path laid down by Mulroney, but much more successfully. Budget deficits were replaced by surpluses, the national debt was reduced, and Martin became the darling of the international business community.

The Liberal government, meanwhile, almost dropped the ball on Quebec. In the 1994 provincial election, the Parti Québécois, led by Jacques Parizeau, emerged the victor and proceeded with a promised second referendum on sovereignty, hoping to gain more support by expressing the question in convoluted wording. The campaign leading to the vote on 30 October 1995 got off to a sluggish start, but the pace quickened when Lucien Bouchard took charge. Alarmed by high unemployment rates in their province, francophone Québécois responded enthusiastically to Bouchard's message that the federal government, with its focus on the deficit, had abandoned constitutional reform and was to blame for hard times. An independent Quebec, he argued, would be free to pursue a more social democratic agenda.

Chrétien's decision not to take charge of the "non" campaign almost proved fatal. As polls began to show sovereignty forces taking the lead, the prime minister finally entered the fray, making an emotional plea to Quebec not to throw away the benefits of Confederation and promising constitutional reform. The final days leading up to the vote brought more drama as American president Bill Clinton delivered a message expressing his preference for a united Canada and First Nations in Quebec hinted that they might stage their own referendum if the "oui" forces won. Three days before the vote, a Unity Rally in Montreal, organized by the minister of fisheries, Brian Tobin, and sponsored in part by airline and railway companies offering deeply discounted fares, drew an estimated hundred thousand Canadians from outside Quebec to plead with the province not to break up the country.

Political theatre continued as the votes were counted. With the outcome uncertain until the early hours of the morning, the "oui" side failed by a razor-thin margin: 49.42 percent to 50.58 percent. Bitterly disappointed by the failure of a majority of anglophones and allophones (people of neither British nor French backgrounds) to support the sovereignty option, Parizeau declared: "It's true, we were beaten, yes, but by what? By money and the ethnic vote, essentially." He was correct in his analysis. More than half of francopones in Quebec voted "oui," and corporate funds were pumped into the "non" campaign, but this was Canadian democracy at work.

When Parizeau resigned in disgust, he was succeeded as premier of Quebec by Bouchard, and the sovereignty movement soldiered on. Instead of offering meaningful constitutional reform, the Chrétien government introduced a resolution declaring Quebec a distinct society, poured money into federal projects in Quebec, and passed the Clarity Act, which required any future referendum on sovereignty to be "clear," both in the wording of the question and the size of the majority. Critics noted that the legislation was itself ambiguous on what constituted a "clear question" and a "clear majority."

While the attention of Canadians focused on the Quebec referendum, Martin's budget-cutting efforts began to take their toll. Several provincial governments toppled as cuts in transfer payments forced them to pare back on support for education, health care, and social services. In the economically powerful provinces of Alberta and Ontario, Progressive Conservative administrations, led respectively by Ralph Klein (1992–2006) and Michael Harris (1995–2002), enthusiastically supported Martin's agenda. Nationally, the Progressive Conservatives limped along under Jean Charest (1993–1998), Joe Clark (1998–2003), and Peter MacKay (2003), but the days of "progressive" Conservatives were numbered. To lend support to the new face of conservatism, the Canadian-born newspaper baron Conrad Black founded the *National Post* in 1998. It championed a movement to unite the right in a coalition that would destroy the Chrétien government.

With the opposition divided, the Liberals managed to win majorities in 1997 and 2000, both times taking almost all of the 103 seats in Ontario. The Reform Party gained enough seats in 1997 to replace the Bloc as the official opposition and, shortly before the 2000 election, attempted to expand support by creating the Canadian Alliance, under the leadership of Stockwell Day, a former Pentecostal school administrator who had served as Alberta's provincial treasurer. The Alliance managed to gain only six additional seats in 2000, prompting yet another party reorganization. Early in 2004, the Canadian Alliance merged with the Progressive Conservatives to form the Conservative Party of Canada, led by Stephen Harper. The shedding of "Progressive" sent a clear message.

As the millennium approached, the Liberal Party took a different tack, trying to restore its image as a progressive force, a goal now made possible by budget surpluses. With Paul Martin snipping at his heels, Chrétien remained in office longer than he might have, hoping to keep his rival from becoming prime minister. Chrétien won the approval of a majority of Canadians when he refused to take Canada into George W. Bush's "coalition of the willing" to wage war on Iraq. In this decision he was influenced by Canadian popular opinion, especially in Quebec, where protests in Montreal against participation in the war drew two hundred thousand participants. Few people initially objected to Canada's support of the American invasion of Afghanistan in 2001 after its government refused to surrender Osama bin Laden, the leader of al-Qaeda, a terrorist organization deemed to be responsible for 9/11.

When Chrétien finally stepped down in 2003, Paul Martin succeeded him as Liberal Party leader and prime minister. His hopes of leaving a legacy worthy of his father were dashed by revelations of serious irregularities in the federal sponsorship program designed to raise the profile of the federal government in Quebec. After the June 2004 election, Martin found himself leader of a shaky minority government. With the support of the NDP, led by Jack Layton, the Liberal government provided additional funding to Medicare, introduced a federal-provincial agreement on child care, and took the lead in negotiating a \$5.1 billion program to improve the lives of Canada's First Nations. It also legalized same-sex marriage and flirted with the idea of legalizing the use of marijuana. Despite this progressive stance, the NDP wanted more concessions on social policy and withdrew its support. This opened the door for the Conservative Party to lead a minority government after the January 2006 election.[3]

HARPER AT THE HELM

Like Trudeau, Stephen Harper arrived in the prime minister's office by a circuitous ideological route. Born in Toronto, Harper excelled at school, where he joined the Young Liberal Club. After graduating, he moved to Alberta to work for Imperial Oil and quit the Liberal Party over Trudeau's National Energy Policy. He served briefly as an aid to Calgary Progressive Conservative MP Jim Hawkes but was disgusted with Mulroney's lack of fiscal restraint. An early recruit to the Reform Party, Harper became its chief policy officer, served as Deborah Grey's legislative assistant, and in 1991 received his second degree in economics from the University of Calgary, the Reform Party's intellectual power base. He won a seat in Calgary West in 1993, but, because of differences with Preston Manning, he refused to run in 1997 and became leader of the right-wing National Citizens Coalition. Like Manning, Harper is a member of the evangelical Christian and Missionary Alliance and is at heart both a neoliberal and a social conservative. He left little doubt during the 2006 campaign that he was determined to move Canada in a new direction.[4]

With the Bloc fearing another election and the Liberals in disarray under their leader, Stéphane Dion, Harper acted quickly on his campaign promises. Martin's national child-care program was scrapped, the GST was cut from 7 percent to 5 percent, the funding program for First Nations was abandoned, and military spending was increased. He even got away with calling a snap election in the fall of 2008, a decision that violated his own party's legislation fixing federal election dates. Although the Conservatives increased their number of seats from 124 to 143, they received less than 38 percent of the popular vote and remained in a minority position.

The failure of the Harper administration to respond energetically to the global financial crisis that erupted during the election campaign prompted the Bloc, Liberals, and NDP to come together to insist on a more vigorous response, but the idea of governing by coalition, typical of many European countries, failed to take root in Canada. Harper thus managed to stay the course, taking aim when he could at people he labeled "elites," who opposed policies such as scrapping the Canadian Firearms Registry and the compulsory long form census, both purported to be unpopular with the Conservative Party's core supporters. He also refused to champion a progressive environmental policy, which would be especially unwelcome in Alberta, where the exploitation of the tar sands, rebranded as "oil sands," had drawn international condemnation. When Canada failed to win a seat on the United Nations Security Council in 2010, losing in a secret ballot to Portugal and Germany, it came as a shock to many Canadians, who could remember when such an outcome would have been unlikely.

None of these concerns shifted enough votes to challenge the Conservative Party's ascendancy when Canadians returned to the polls on 2 May 2011. Targeting vulnerable ridings, the Conservatives won a majority of seats (166) with only 39.6 percent of the popular vote. The Liberals, led by Michael Ignatieff, were reduced to a 34-seat rump. Under the courageous leadership of Jack Layton, who was battling cancer, the NDP won 103 ridings, the majority of them in Quebec, where the Bloc Québécois salvaged only 4 seats. Layton died in August, leaving Canadians wondering how far Harper could go in pursuing his agenda now that all opposition parties seemed to be in disarray.

THE KNOWLEDGE ECONOMY

With support from governments at all levels, Canada managed to become a major player in the new economic order that emerged at the end of the twentieth century. Innovation became the goal as developed countries tried to keep one step ahead of the competition in producing value-added products. Despite the success of aerospace, defence, and mass transit industries in finding foreign markets, Canada remained primarily a resource-exporting country, much as it had always been. Energy, forestry, and mining did especially well.

Eying the massive government funding that went into education, pension plans, and social services, free-market advocates made efforts to insert private enterprise into these programs. Public-private partnerships were developed to deliver everything from school buildings and prisons to highways and senior care. Medicare remained so popular that changes to its structure proved difficult, but the campaign for "two-tier" medicine was persistent and well-funded. Inevitably, universities became the special targets of reform in the new Knowledge Economy. Business faculties expanded dramatically on most campuses and scholars in every discipline were urged to focus on "relevant" research. With governments trying to curb their financial outlays, the money required to transform universities into engines of economic growth came increasingly from higher tuition fees and corporate donations.

By the end of the twentieth century, all sectors of the economy and Canadians everywhere were obliged to adapt to the World Wide Web, a system of hyperlinked texts accessed through the Internet. The Web transformed not only the way people communicated (by e-mail) but also how they did research (by "Googling"), formed social networks (on Facebook and Twitter), and consumed everything from books and music to medical advice and pornography. With the shift from print to screen, many aspects of knowledge production, including notions of authority, authorship, and copyright, were called into question. Whole new industries developed around fibre-optic cables, cell phones, and the credit card, the latter having become an essential medium of consumption even before the Internet found ways to relieve people "virtually" of their money.

As media converged around the Internet, conglomerates such as Shaw Communications, Rogers, and BCE emerged to control a heady mix of newspapers, television, radio, movie production, and Internet services.[5] A Senate Commission reported in 2006 that only

1 percent of Canadian dailies were independently owned and that the concentration of media ownership threatened to limit both the diversity and the quality of reporting in Canada. With the Canadian Radio-television and Telecommunications Commission unwilling to slow the pace of media concentration, civil society organizations resorted to alternative ways to get their message to a public that was fragmented in a chaotic digital universe.

SWINGING IN THE ECONOMIC WINDS

The economic cycles that accompanied the neoliberal order broke many hearts and caused cynics to wonder if the stock market was designed only to relieve people of their hard-earned money. No sooner had Canada found its destiny as an energy-producing nation than the energy bubble burst in 1986, resulting in bankruptcies and foreign takeovers, especially in the Alberta oil patch. The digital revolution drew both public and private investment and brought major success for Nortel, a Canadian telecommunications equipment manufacturer, but the dot.com bubble burst in 2001, taking Nortel and many personal fortunes with it. At least oil and communications equipment were tangible commodities. The next big bubble resulted from speculation in mortgages by recently deregulated financial institutions in the United States. While the mortgaged houses were real enough, the financial dealings around them were outrageously fictitious.

When the New York–based financial firm Lehman Brothers filed for bankruptcy in September 2008, the whole wobbly mortgage edifice came tumbling down. As more banks crumbled and stock markets tanked, the world economy, now fully integrated into the American financial system, teetered on the brink of collapse. The Canadian banking system weathered the storm reasonably well, but a deep recession cut a swath through every economic sector. Despite the neoliberal mantra that less government was the best government, corporations were quick to turn to the state for assistance. The American government bailed out many of its failing financial institutions, as did European nations. When the North American automobile industry – running scared from more efficient Asian and European companies – seemed likely to be swept away by the tide of recession, both the American and the Canadian governments offered massive assistance to protect one of North America's core industries.

The thousands of workers who lost their jobs in the subsequent restructuring were not so well served. Even before the economic crisis of 2008, the determination of corporations to squeeze as much profit as possible from their operations had been taking its toll on wage earners, now commonly referred to as "human resources." While managers drew large bonuses for their efforts even when companies failed – Nortel was strongly criticized on this score – workers lost not only their jobs but often their pension benefits as well.[6] When they needed it most, workers' eligibility for Unemployment Insurance, rebranded Employment Insurance in 1996, was drastically cut, and the Canada Assistance Plan, one of the pillars of the welfare state, was abolished. In the new economic order, unions were targeted as villains in corporate efforts to make industries more efficient. By 2011, the proportion of workers belonging to unions in Canada dipped below 30 percent, helping to create what corporations demanded: a more "flexible" workforce.

Predictably, the gap between rich and poor in Canada widened. Social justice activists watched in dismay as Canada began to fall behind European nations in its poverty levels. Women, children, and the elderly proved to be especially vulnerable in a world where the values of caring and cooperation were trumped by competition and profits. Food banks, which had emerged as a temporary response to the recession of the early 1980s, served 867,948 individuals in March 2010. The shame of this reality in a country as rich as Canada prompted some politicians to revisit the idea of a guaranteed annual income, but the deficits racked up after 2006 made such a policy departure unlikely.[7]

In many respects, the trends associated with the new economic order were much like the old ones – only more so. Foreign ownership, a concern of many Canadians since the 1950s, was ignored for a time after Mulroney declared that Canada was "open for business," but as multinational corporations gobbled up all of Canada's steel companies, nearly half the oil and gas assets, much of the mining and publishing industries, and iconic corporations such as the Hudson's Bay Company and Molsons, even some corporate leaders became concerned. Closely attuned to popular opinion in the western provinces, Harper intervened to block foreign takeovers of the Vancouver-based satellite technology company MacDonald Dettwiler and Potash Corporation of Saskatchewan, but he resisted addressing the question that many people continued to ask: Was unregulated global capitalism really in the best interests of Canada and the world?

THE ENVIRONMENT IN QUESTION

By the beginning of the new century, political and economic uncertainty had swept away the optimism that characterized the three decades following the Second World War. Progress, it was clear, could no longer be taken for granted. In 2003 an outbreak of mad cow disease in Alberta, a failure of the power grid that brought activities in parts of eastern North America to a grinding halt, and the spread of a respiratory disease called SARS (severe acute respiratory syndrome) called into question the very survival of societies too complex to control. Two additional developments greatly added to the feelings of pessimism: climate change and the war on terror.

In the 1980s a string of environmental disasters convinced many of those in denial that the planet was desperately in need of life support. Incidents in Bhopal (1984) and Chernobyl (1986), along with ongoing concern about acid rain, global warming, nuclear winter, and ozone depletion, were compounded by a reminder from the United Nations in 1987 that the world's resources are finite.[8] These developments provided momentum for the Mulroney government to pursue a more ambitious environmental agenda, shaped with the help of activist Elizabeth May. In addition to adopting environmental assessment and protection acts, Canada concluded an acid rain treaty with the United States and was the first industrialized country to sign the Climate Change Convention and Biodiversity Convention proposed by the United Nations Earth Summit in 1992. The Chrétien government signed the 1997 Kyoto Protocol, agreeing to reduce emissions, but Canada's greenhouse gases actually rose in the following decade.

In this exigency, the Green Party of Canada, founded in 1983, gained a larger following. It fielded candidates in every riding in the

2004 election and, under its new leader, Elizabeth May, received nearly 7 percent of the votes in the 2008 election. Although the Green Party's popular vote was greatly reduced in the 2011 election, May won her riding of Saanich-Gulf Islands in British Columbia, thereby becoming the first elected Green Party MP.

Canada had many environmental disasters on its record, but none was as overwhelming as the collapse of the cod fisheries in the North Atlantic. Following the declaration of a two-hundred-mile limit in 1977, the east coast fisheries expanded dramatically. By the early 1980s Canada was the world's leading fish-exporting country, with the Atlantic provinces providing 65 percent of the national total. Initially, this seemed like a good-news story in an area of the country that lagged behind in economic development, but the outcome was uncompromisingly tragic: most of the fish were sucked out of the sea. In 1992 Fisheries Minister John Crosbie was obliged to announce a moratorium on the cod fishery and stringent controls on other fish stocks. More than twenty thousand people were thrown out of work in Newfoundland and Labrador alone, and many east coast communities faced their own extinction.

People living in Canada's northern territories were also shocked into recognizing the limits to growth. With airborne toxins poisoning the food chain in Arctic regions and rising temperatures threatening disaster to animals and birds dependent on the rapidly melting sea ice, a whole way of life was threatened. The Inuit Circumpolar Council, founded in 1977 to represent Inuit living in Canada, Greenland, Alaska, and Russia, quickly became a major player in the environmental movement. Led by Sheila Watt-Cloutier, northerners spearheaded a campaign that resulted in an international ban on persistent organic pollutants in 2001. Addressing the threat of global warming proved a more difficult challenge. Nominated in 2007 for a Nobel Peace Prize for her ongoing environmental activism, Watt-Cloutier lost to former American vice president Al Gore, who was the inspiration behind a highly influential 2006 documentary, *An Inconvenient Truth*, warning of the dangers of climate change.

Prime Minister Harper was concerned about developments in the Arctic, but his focus was Arctic sovereignty, now that melting ice made the Northwest Passage a viable transportation route and opened primary resources such as oil and gas to intense exploitation. Abandoning the Kyoto Accord as an impossible goal, Harper pledged $2 billion over five years to combat climate change, but the government's low profile at the 2009 United Nations Climate Change Conference in Copenhagen came as a deep disappointment to environmentalists everywhere.

A WARRIOR NATION

The "War on Terror" became an overriding concern in the wake of 9/11. While avoiding the war in Iraq, Canada participated in a NATO-led International Security Assistance Force to Afghanistan, contributing nearly 2,000 troops by May 2005. Casualties began to mount in the summer of that year when Canadian troops shifted their focus from Kabul to the Taliban stronghold of Kandahar. Pushing the timeline for involvement in the war to 2011, the Conservative government encouraged Canadians to "support their troops," but the war was a tougher sell. By the time that Canada officially withdrew from its combat role in July 2011, 157 soldiers had come home in body bags, more casualties than had been chalked up in the previous half century of peacekeeping.

The war on terror soon began to have a subtle but significant impact on how Canadians perceived themselves. As *Globe and Mail* columnist Michael Valpy noted in 2009, Canada had gradually become a military rather than a peacekeeping nation:

Not much more than a decade ago, Canada's armed forces were all but invisible, out of sight in remote bases and discreetly dressed in civilian clothes in the cities. Now, they march around Ottawa's streets in combat gear. They have become the heroes of middle Canada, celebrated at sporting events, re-mythologized as the new icons of nationalism and lionized by people such as Don Cherry, Rick Mercer and Wayne Rostad....[9]

The war in Afghanistan put an end to Canada's image as a peacekeeper, but that image had already lost much of its lustre. In the 1990s Canada's involvement in United Nations missions to Iraq, Somalia, Croatia, and Rwanda proved largely unsuccessful in what had essentially become "peacemaking" rather than peacekeeping efforts. Lieutenant General Roméo Dallaire, who led the UN force in Rwanda, lacked the resources to stop the bloodbath there, and the mission to Somalia was tainted by the murder of a young intruder in a Canadian camp, which led to the disbanding of the Canadian Airborne Regiment following a high-profile inquiry.

In a security-conscious world, Canada's commitment to human rights was also compromised. The Anti-Terrorist Act, passed three months after 9/11, increased the powers of the Canadian Security and Intelligence Service and the Royal Canadian Mounted Police to acquire information, detain suspects, and ban organizations believed to be supporting terrorism. When Canadian-born Omar Ahmhed Khadr was incarcerated by the United States at its prison in Guantanamo Bay for his involvement in attacks on American soldiers in Afghanistan, the Conservative government refused to repatriate him, even when the Supreme Court ruled in 2010 that his constitutional rights had been violated. Despite protests from civil society groups, the security state remained firmly in place and manifested itself with force during the G-20 (Group of Twenty Finance Ministers and Central Bank Governors established in 1999 at the suggestion of Paul Martin) meeting in Toronto in the summer of 2010.

Canada's liberal approach to multiculturalism also began to show its limits. In the wake of 9/11, some Muslims lost their jobs because they were deemed security risks and mosques were subject to desecration. Opposition to Muslim women covering their faces when they voted in a 2007 provincial election in Quebec prompted Premier Jean Charest to appoint a commission headed by respected scholars Charles Taylor and Gérard Bouchard to hold public hearings on what citizens believed to be a reasonable accommodation of cultural and religious minorities. Although extreme views were presented during the televised hearings, the final report was more restrained. It urged the government to promote "interculturalism" by providing more funding to diversity programs, training about best practices in cultural adjustments, and better protection to newcomers against all forms of discrimination.

SOCIETY IN TRANSITION

As the foregoing suggests, Canadians at the turn of the twenty-first century were undergoing a debate, much like the one that occurred a century earlier, about the impact of immigration on society. Canada's low birth rate, aging demographic profile, and demand for skilled workers combined to produce a policy encouraging immigration. Between 1986 and 2010, Canada became home to more than 6 million new immigrants, their numbers helping to bring the overall population to more than 34 million.

Nearly one in five Canadians in 2011 was an immigrant, a statistic that underscored a major transformation in the ethnic makeup of the country. In contrast to the post–Second World War period, when most immigrants came from Europe, half of the newcomers since the 1970s arrived from Asian countries – principally China, India, Pakistan, and the Philippines. The overwhelming majority of them settled in Toronto, Montreal, and Vancouver, making them some of the world's most multicultural cities. While the majority of new Canadians were classified as economic immigrants, because they met the high standards of education and skills demanded by the Immigration Act, as many as 20 percent each year were refugees from the growing number in a war-torn world. Canada was also home to illegal immigrants – estimates vary widely from 35,000 to 125,000 – who often risked life and limb to escape their homelands. In addition, Canada recognized a category of temporary immigrants, many of them recruited to work as live-in caregivers, truck drivers, software developers, miners, and seasonal agricultural workers. In 2010 Canada welcomed 182,322 temporary foreign workers and 96,147 foreign students.[10]

As was the case at the turn of the twentieth century, new immigrants brought their cultural baggage with them, creating concerns among Canadian-born citizens that their way of life would somehow be threatened. Hostility sometimes took the form of complaints about cultural practices, as when Baltej Singh Dhillon, a Sikh recruit to the RCMP, demanded that he be allowed to wear a turban, as his religious beliefs prescribed, rather than the traditional Stetson hat. The Supreme Court ruled in his favour in 1990. More often, the hostility was expressed by exclusion from employment opportunities, sports teams, voluntary organizations, and political parties.

Studies showed that the majority of those who experienced discrimination were members of visible minorities, who testified that, despite all the talk of multicultural accommodation, racism was still rampant in Canada. When a bomb exploded on an Air India flight operating on the Montreal-London-Delhi route in June 1985, it killed all 329 passengers and crew on board, most of them Canadian citizens. The slow and inadequate response prompted Indo-Canadians to wonder if the political and judicial system saw the tragedy as India's, not Canada's, problem.

While immigrants were sometimes the object of violent attacks in Canada, they were not alone in being targeted. Since the 1980s, neo-Nazi groups and white supremacists had been increasingly bold in expressing their hatred of Jews, blacks, and other minorities. In most major cities, youth gangs organized around ethnic identity reflected the presence of an underclass drawn to illegal activities such as drug dealing, robbery, and street fighting. The Mafia and biker gangs operated openly in some cities and often settled scores violently. Women also bore the brunt of physical abuse, both at home, where they were sometimes assaulted and killed by their partners, and in public settings, where violence against women remained a threat. On 6 December 1989 a deranged young man, claiming to be "fighting feminism," went on a shooting rampage against female engineering students at the École Polytechnique in Montreal, killing fourteen women and wounding others.

Aboriginal people were especially vulnerable to violence. In British Columbia Robert ("Willie") Pickton boasted to an undercover officer after he was arrested in 2002 that he had butchered forty-nine prostitutes, most of them from Vancouver's Downtown Eastside, on his farm in Port Coquitlam. Many of Pickton's victims were Aboriginal women. In 2010 Sisters in Spirit, a research institute established by the Native Women's Association, reported that it had the names of nearly six hundred murdered or missing First Nations, Métis, and Inuit women in its database.[11] Aboriginal men were also subject to violence, some of it perpetrated by police forces. In the winter of 1990 an inebriated Cree teenager, Neil Stonechild, was dropped on the outskirts of Saskatoon by the police, who left him there to die, a travesty that ultimately led to the discovery of other, similar "starlight tours."

Despite the decriminalization of homosexuality in 1969, many gays and lesbians were cautious about expressing their sexuality openly for fear of reprisals. This caution began to disappear in the 1980s, when the acquired immune deficiency syndrome (AIDS) pandemic descended on the world. While by no means confined to homosexuals, AIDS spread quickly in the gay community, encouraging an organized and public response. Lesbian, gay, bisexual, and transgendered (LGBT) Canadians came together to develop support networks for people infected with AIDS, to conduct education campaigns to encourage safe sexual practices, and to pressure governments for a wide range of reforms, which were gradually forthcoming. In 1992 the federal government lifted the ban on homosexuals in the armed forces, and three years later the Supreme Court ruled that "sexual orientation" should be read into the non-discrimination sections of the constitution. In 2003 Ontario became the first jurisdiction in North America to legalize marriage between same-sex couples, a right that the Martin government extended nationally in 2005. A year earlier, sexual orientation was added to the "hate propaganda" section of the criminal code. No longer confined to the closet, the LBGT community sponsored Gay Pride parades in many cities, published newspapers and magazines, and participated in a highly creative gay culture.

Opposition to the change in attitudes toward sexuality came from many directions, and included a variety of religious groups. While the United Church relaxed its injunction against homosexual clergy in 1988, the Roman Catholic Church joined many evangelical Protestant denominations and non-Christian religious groups in continuing to denounce homosexuality, along with abortion, birth control, and divorce, as threats to the traditional family. The strong stand taken by successive popes on these matters was ignored by most Canadians, but, for Roman Catholics who as young people had been the victims of sexual assaults by priests, the hypocrisy of the Church hierarchy became too much to bear. As people came forward to tell their stories, both the abuse and the Church's attempts to cover it up were widely condemned. Sexual abuse of children was not confined to the Catholic Church, of course, but its sanctimonious response to the matter prompted many people to abandon what had become unacceptably uncomfortable pews.

In the rampantly secular context of the second half of the twentieth century, weekly church attendance began to decline precipitously – from more than 60 percent in the late 1940s to 20 percent in 2000 – and some churches had difficulty finding enough clergy to minister to their declining membership. This trend then began to stall for a variety of reasons. Although Roman Catholicism in Quebec continued to lose followers, membership increased in Canadian cities where many new immigrants were practicing Roman Catholics. Evangelical churches that emphasized spiritual rebirth also showed marked increases in membership, and the counter-secularization movement had a significant following among the 8 percent of Canadians who subscribed to other religions, among them Orthodox, Jewish, Islamic, Hindu, Buddhist, Shinto, Sikh, and various New Age beliefs. Canadians nevertheless lagged well behind people in the United States in reporting in 2005 that their religion was "very important" to them (28 percent to 55 percent), and nearly one in five Canadians reported no religion at all.[12]

ABORIGINAL EMPOWERMENT

The empowerment of Canada's Aboriginal peoples, both spiritually and politically, is one of the major developments of recent decades. For the first time in more than five centuries, demography was on their side. Contrary to expectations, Canada's indigenous peoples did not die out or become assimilated. Instead, they grew in numbers and maintained their culture. According to the 2006 Census, Canada was home to 698,025 First Nations, 389,785 Métis, and 50,485 Inuit, together nearly 4 percent of Canada's total population. No longer confined primarily to reserves, more than half of the Status Indians lived off reserves, and half of the Aboriginal population was under the age of twenty-five, compared to about one-third for non-Aboriginals.[13]

As prescribed by the Constitution Act, Ottawa convened meetings with Aboriginal leaders to define the "existing aboriginal and treaty rights," but little was accomplished. The courts were more helpful. In 1984 the Supreme Court ruled that Ottawa had fiduciary responsibility for Aboriginal peoples; three years later, pre-treaty land rights were confirmed; and in 1997, in a landmark decision involving the Gitskan-Wet'suwet'en First Nation of British Columbia, the Supreme Court not only reconfirmed Aboriginal rights but argued that those rights went beyond hunting and fishing to the broader rights relating to their traditional lands. The ruling also validated oral testimony as a source of evidence in claims cases. For those who continued to think in the old imperialist framework, the world had turned upside down.

This seeming reversal of power relations brought complaints and sometimes violence. Following a 1999 Supreme Court ruling confirming that Donald Marshall Jr. had a treaty right to "make a moderate living" by catching and selling fish, violence erupted in the Maritimes, where Mi'kmaq and Maliseet suddenly had access to resources that had long been denied them. The Supreme Court moved quickly to clarify its ruling by stating that the fishery could be regulated, but this failed to prevent a nasty confrontation in Burnt Church, New Brunswick, where angry mobs destroyed lobster traps set by Mi'kmaq and trashed their boats.

Burnt Church was only one of a series of confrontations that brought international attention to Canada's "Aboriginal problem." In 1990 a long-standing dispute over land near Oka, Quebec, now being expropriated for a golf course, provoked a seventy-eight-day standoff between the Mohawk Warriors and the provincial police, who called in the Canadian army. The intensity of the conflict, which included the death of a police officer, prompted the Mulroney government to reestablish an Indian Claims Commission and appoint a Royal Commission on Aboriginal Peoples, which reported in 1996 (Image 10.2).

Violent confrontations between Aboriginal protesters and police at Gustafsen Lake in 1995 helped to convince the government of British Columbia to bear down on the long roster of land claims in the province. The Nisga'a, who had been pressing their claims since early in the twentieth century, were the first to sign a comprehensive agreement covering land; governance; rights relating to the forests, salmon fishery, and pine forest mushroom harvest; and the return of artifacts from the Canadian Museum of Civilization. In return, they relinquished much of the land they had originally claimed and agreed to phase out the Aboriginal exemption from sales and income taxes. Ratified by Parliament in 2000, the Nisga'a Treaty set the tone, but not necessarily the outcomes, for negotiations around the nearly thirteen hundred specific claims still outstanding.

Image 10.2. A Mohawk Warrior raises his weapon in triumph during the Oka crisis in 1990. (By permission of The Canadian Press/Tom Hansen)

By the end of the twentieth century, considerable progress had been made on Aboriginal rights and governance in northern Canada. The Inuit living in the Mackenzie Delta and the Yukon First Nations reached land agreements in 1984 and 1988, respectively, and in 1992 the Inuit of the eastern Arctic accepted an agreement that provided them with subsurface mineral rights to 350,000 square kilometers of territory and established a process for the eastern Arctic to become a separately administered territory. In March 1999 Nunavut (meaning "the people's land" in Inuktitut) became a separate territory with its own elected assembly. Unlike the Yukon and the now much smaller Northwest Territories, where non-Aboriginal residents were the majority of the population, Nunavut was dominated by Inuit, who made up about 80 percent of the approximately thirty-two thousand people living in a jurisdiction that encompasses more than one-fifth of Canada's landmass.

As was required by the Charter of Rights and Freedoms, the Canadian government amended the Indian Act in 1985 to remove most of the discrimination against Indian women who married non-Aboriginal men. Nearly a hundred thousand women and children had their Indian status reinstated by 1997. While a human rights victory, it created tensions on reserves and controversies over who was "Indian enough," culturally or genetically, to be reinstated. Concerns were also raised about the overcrowding and pressure on band resources that would result from the change in legislation. More than a century of patriarchal power under the Indian Act had greatly reduced the status of women in their communities. The Native Women's Association of Canada, founded in 1974, took the Canadian government to court for refusing to include them in the talks leading to the Charlottetown Accord, but they lost their case and remained excluded from constitutional negotiations.

The Métis were the fastest growing of all Aboriginal groups in Canada. After being ignored by federal and provincial governments for more than a century, the Métis, along with Status Indians and Inuit, were recognized in the constitution as Aboriginal people. Case law eventually followed, as did a debate, still not fully resolved, about how people of mixed heritage should be defined. In 2003 the Supreme Court ruled in *R. v. Powley* that three conditions must prevail to achieve Métis status: self-identification as a Métis individual, ancestral connection to a historic Métis community, and acceptance by a Métis community. The extent of Métis rights is still in contention, in part because it can easily be demonstrated that they were often involved in nineteenth-century treaty negotiations.

Canadian Aboriginals remain a diverse people, the majority of whom belong to more than six hundred bands attached to 2,633 reserves. For every story in the media about dysfunctional communities riven by disease, drug addiction, pollution, unemployment, and violence, there is another highlighting a success story such as Oujé-Bougoumou in Quebec, which has been named a model town by the United Nations. With the support of the Toronto-Dominion Bank, a First Nations Bank was established in Saskatoon in 1997, and a First Nations University was launched in Regina in 2003. Both of these initiatives emerged from the recommendations of the Royal Commission on Aboriginal Peoples, which made 440 specific recommendations and identified four key issues: the need for a new relationship between Aboriginal and non-Aboriginal peoples, self-determination through self-government, economic self-sufficiency, and healing for Aboriginal peoples and communities.[14]

Canadians still have a long way to go to achieve this ambitious agenda, and governments continue to have difficulty balancing Aboriginal rights and those of non-Aboriginal citizens. In June 2008 the Harper government formally apologized and offered compensation to former students of residential schools, but it dragged its heals in signing the 2007 UN Declaration on the Rights of Indigenous Peoples, a document that previous Canadian governments had helped to draft. Opposition parties in the House of Commons passed a resolution to endorse the declaration and fully implement its standards,[15] and in 2010 the government finally abandoned its position that the UN declaration was incompatible with Canada's constitutional framework. It nevertheless seems unlikely that Canadians will elect a prime minister of indigenous heritage in the near future.

WHERE ARE WE NOW?

Despite the tensions, Canada has managed its recent challenges better than most countries. Success has been purchased at the cost of devolving power to the provinces, territories, mega-cities, corporations, and First Nations, entities united only in their efforts to wrest power from the centre. While Canada is not unique in experiencing such pressures, they raise questions about how to proceed in a country where a consensus on national goals remains elusive.

What seems to be lost in this current "glocalization" process is an attachment to the larger nation-state. Even Ontario, which earlier played a leadership role in fostering a national framework for social welfare and equalization, is having second thoughts, concerned lest its own well-being be compromised. In Alberta, where investment in oil and gas now exceeds that in manufacturing in the industrial heartland, the idea that wealth from petroleum resources should be shared more broadly with other provinces continues to be publicly scorned. And it remains to be seen whether Quebec, which has abandoned concern even for francophones outside the province, will encompass all Canadians in its lingering commitment to the common good. Smarting from the failure of Canada to redress a badly conceived power contract with Quebec in the 1960s, the citizens of Newfoundland and Labrador fought successfully under Premier Danny Williams to become a major beneficiary of offshore oil development in 2005. After centuries of hardship and the recent collapse of the fisheries, how could they be blamed for wanting a larger share of the national economic pie? In such a context, producing a cohesive national policy seems beyond the capacity of any party or politician.

It has always been thus, of course. And although Canadians may well be divided on political choices, they collectively display a rather different image. Among their most popular heroes, at least in English Canada, is Terry Fox, a twenty-one-year-old Vancouver student who died of cancer in 1981 after attempting to run a Marathon of Hope across the country. Successful movie stars, recording artists, and sports figures tend to dominate the pantheon of Canadian heroes, but various surveys and popularity contests suggest that Tommy Douglas, the father of Medicare, environmentalist David Suzuki, and the long-time chair of the Council of Canadians, Maude Barlow, are admired by many Canadians for whom social justice is still a cherished ideal. When disasters strike, Canadians usually rise to the occasion, both at home and abroad. This tendency was reflected in Canada's quick response in 2009 to the disastrous earthquake in Haiti, the birthplace of nearly a hundred thousand people living in Canada, including former governor general Michaëlle Jean (2005–10). Her predecessor in this role was another immigrant, Adrienne (Poy) Clarkson, who arrived in Canada as a young refugee from Hong Kong in 1941. Both women developed high-powered careers in CBC/Radio Canada broadcasting, one of the few institutions devoted to explaining Canadians to each other and the world (Image 10.3).

Few would deny that Canadians are among the most fortunate people on the planet. Whether the country can sustain its relative good fortune is now in question. Close ties with the United States suggest a shared future of steady decline. With the balance of power tipping inexorably toward Asia, people living in Canada may well hitch their destiny to India and China, as their ancestors

Image 10.3. Women receiving their citizenship from dignitaries Linda Carvery, Geoffrey Regan, Michael Savage, and Leonard Preyra at a citizenship ceremony at Pier 21, 1 July 2010. (Copyright Azam Chadegnanipour, Canadian Museum of Immigration at Pier 21)

once did to France and Great Britain. Given its vast natural and human resources, Canada could become a global leader in its own right, but it is equally possible that the nation could dissolve into its constituent parts. Nowhere is it written that nation-states, a recent phenomenon in historical time, will last forever.

CONCLUSION

Canadians now face the latest challenges resulting from the processes of globalization that began five hundred years ago when Europeans began to export their people, technologies, institutions, and values around the world. In coming to terms with the country they have created, Canadians are confronted not only with old demons and divisions but also with new ones that require creative, and some would argue immediate, responses. The pace of political change in Canada, glacial by the standards defined by the Internet, creates anxiety and not a little cynicism.

The imponderables are many. Where *do* Canadians want to take their big lummox of a nation that lays claim to one-seventh of the earth's geography? Are the old political structures flexible enough to accommodate newly empowered Aboriginal peoples and the mass of new immigrants, who are moving Canada beyond the "two nations" template that prevailed in the twentieth century? Who should drive the political agenda? In a nation defined above all else by free-market capitalism, the Council of Chief Executives (the former Business Council on National Issues) often seems to wield more power than elected officials. Can it be any other way in a world dominated by multinational corporations that are now too big to be allowed to fail? Do nation-states even matter in a world experiencing unprecedented population growth and environmental collapse? And, more fundamentally, does the liberal framework have the capacity to bring life-affirming values honed by long experience through the current turmoil, or must it join the old aristocratic order on the scrap heap of history? How we address these questions will determine the next chapter in Canadian history.

NOTES

INTRODUCTION: A CAUTIOUS COUNTRY

1 Gerald Friesen, *Citizens and Nation: An Essay on History, Communication, and Canada* (Toronto: University of Toronto Press, 2000).

2 John Ralston Saul, *A Fair Country: Telling Truths about Canada* (Toronto: Viking Canada, 2008), 3.

3 Gordon W. Handcock, *"Soe longe as there comes noe women": Origins of English Settlement in Newfoundland* (St. John's: Breakwater Press, 1989).

4 Ian McKay, "The Liberal Order Framework: A Prospectus for a Reconnaissance of Canadian History," *Canadian Historical Review* 81, 4 (December 2000): 617–45.

5 Harold Adams Innis, "Great Britain, the United States and Canada," *in Essays in Canadian Economic History* (Toronto: University of Toronto Press, 1956), 405.

6 Margaret Atwood, *Survival* (Toronto: Anansi, 1972), 33.

1. SINCE TIME IMMEMORIAL

1 Cole Harris, *The Reluctant Land: Society, Space, and Environment in Canada before Confederation* (Vancouver: University of British Columbia Press, 2008), 16–18.

2 The research on origins, numbers, and cultural borrowing is summarized in Part 1 of Olive Patricia Dickason with David T. McNab, *Canada's First Nations: A History of Founding Peoples from Earliest Times*, 4th ed. (Don Mills, ON: Oxford University Press, 2008). See also James V. Wright, *A History of the Native People of Canada* (Ottawa: Canadian Museum of Civilization, 1995), and Bruce Trigger and Wilcomb Washburn, eds., *Cambridge History of the Native Peoples of the Americas*, 3 vols. (Cambridge: Cambridge University Press, 1996).

3 Robert McGhee, *The Last Imaginary Place: A Human History of the Arctic World* (Chicago: University of Chicago Press, 2007), 38.

4 Robert McGhee, "Canada Y1K: The First Millennium," *The Beaver* (December 1999–January 2000): 9–17.

5 Arthur J. Ray, *I Have Lived Here Since the World Began: An Illustrated History of Canada's Native People*, rev. ed. (Toronto: Lester/Key Porter Books, 2005), 33.
6 McGhee, *The Last Imaginary Place*, 38–39.
7 Nicolas Denys, *The Description and National History of the Coasts of North America*, ed. William F. Ganong (Toronto: Champlain Society, 1908), 401.
8 Elaine Keillor, *Music in Canada: Capturing Landscape and Diversity* (Montreal: McGill-Queen's University Press, 2006), 42; Jean-Jacques Nattiez, "Inuit Vocal Games," in *Encyclopedia of Music in Canada*, 2nd ed. (Toronto: University of Toronto Press, 1992), 633–34.
9 For an oral account of a female coming-of-age ceremony, see Kitty Smith, "Becoming a Woman," in Julie Cruikshank, *Life Lived Like a Story* (Vancouver: University of British Columbia Press, 1992), 214–15.

2. NATIVES AND NEWCOMERS, 1000–1661

1 Helge Kleivan, *The Eskimos of Northeast Labrador: A History of Eskimo-White Relations, 1771–1955* (Oslo: Norsk Polarinstitutt, 1966), 181, cited in Margaret R. Conrad and James K. Hiller, *Atlantic Canada: A History* (Don Mills, ON: Oxford University Press, 2010), 180.
2 Robert McGhee, *The Last Imaginary Place: A Human History of the Arctic World* (Chicago: University of Chicago Press, 2007), 54–55.
3 Alfred J. Crosby, *Ecological Imperialism: The Biological Expansion of Europe, 900–1900* (Cambridge: Cambridge University Press, 1986); Jared Diamond, *Guns, Germs, and Steel: The Fates of Human Societies* (New York: Norton, 1998).
4 Cole Harris, *The Reluctant Land: Society, Space, and Environment in Canada before Confederation* (Vancouver: University of British Columbia Press, 2008), 46–47.
5 Rony Blum, *Ghost Brothers: Adoption of a French Tribe by Beavered Native America: A Transdisciplinary Longitudinal Multilevel Integrated Analysis* (Montreal: McGill-Queen's University Press, 2005).
6 Cited in Arthur J. Ray, *I Have Lived Here Since the World Began: An Illustrated History of Canada's Native People*, rev. ed. (Toronto: Lester/Key Porter Books, 2005), 38.
7 "First Letters Patent granted by Henry VII to John Cabot, 5 March 1496," in *The Precursors of Jacques Cartier, 1497–1534*, ed. H. B. Biggar (Ottawa: Government Printing Bureau, 1911), 8–10 (cited in http://www.bris.ac.uk/Depts/History/Maritime/Sources/1496cabotpatent.htm). See also Peter Pope, *The Many Landfalls of John Cabot* (Toronto: University of Toronto Press, 1997).
8 George Calvert to King Charles I, 19 August 1629, in Gillian Cell, *Newfoundland Discovered: English Attempts at Colonization, 1610–1630* (London: Hakluyt Society, 1982), 295–96.
9 David Hackett Fischer, *Champlain's Dream* (New York: Alfred A. Knopf, 2008), 401–02, 515; Morris Bishop, *Champlain: The Life of Fortitude* (Toronto: McClelland and Stewart, 1963), 264.
10 Ramsay Cook, "1492 and All That: Making a Garden out of a Wilderness," in *Consuming Canada: Readings in Environmental History*, ed. Chad Gaffield and Pam Gaffield (Toronto: Copp Clark, 1995), 62–80.
11 Elizabeth Jones, *Gentlemen and Jesuits: Quests for Glory and Adventure in the Early Days of New France* (Toronto: University of Toronto Press, 1986), 92–93.

12 Peter E. Pope, *Fish into Wine: The Newfoundland Plantation in the Seventeenth Century* (Chapel Hill: University of North Carolina Press, 2004).

13 Sally Ross and Alphonse Deveau, *The Acadians of Nova Scotia, Past and Present* (Halifax: Nimbus, 1992), 16–21.

14 Luca Codignola, "Competing Networks: The Roman Catholic Clergy in French North America, 1610–1658," *Canadian Historical Review* 80, 4 (December 1999): 539–84.

15 S. R. Mealing, ed., *The Jesuit Relations and Allied Documents* (Toronto: McClelland and Stewart, 1963), 50.

16 Numbers relating to the Huron are difficult to fix. For the most recent estimates, see Gary Warrick, *A Population History of the Huron-Petun, A.D. 500–1650* (Cambridge: Cambridge University Press, 2008).

17 J. A. Brandão, *"Your fyre shall Burn no more": Iroquois Policy toward New France and Its Native Allies to 1701* (Lincoln: Nebraska University Press, 1997).

3. NEW FRANCE, 1661–1763

1 This chapter draws on a large literature on New France, much of it synthesized in Louise Dechêne, *Le peuple, l'État et la guerre au Canada sous le Régime français* (Montreal: Boréal, 2008); Cole Harris, *The Reluctant Land: Society, Space, and Environment in Canada before Confederation* (Vancouver: University of British Columbia Press, 2008); Jacques Mathieu, *La Nouvelle-France: Les Français en Amérique du Nord, xvie–xviiie siècle*, 2nd ed. (Sainte-Foy: Les Presses de l'Université Laval, 2001); Peter Moogk, *La Nouvelle France: The Making of New France – A Cultural History* (East Lansing: Michigan State University Press, 2000); Alan Greer, *The People of New France* (Toronto: University of Toronto Press, 1997); and Dale Miquelon, *The First Canada to 1791* (Toronto: McGraw-Hill Ryerson, 1994).

2 Yves Landry, "Gender Imbalance, Les filles du Roi, and Choice of Spouse in New France," in *Canadian Family History: Selected Readings*, ed. Bettina Bradbury (Toronto: Copp Clark Pitman, 1992), 14–32.

3 Hubert Charbonneau et al., "The Population of the St. Lawrence Valley, 1608–1760," in *A Population History of North America*, ed. Michael R. Haines and Richard H. Steckel (New York: Cambridge University Press, 2000), 99–142; Stephen A. White, "The True Number of Acadians," in *Du Grand Dérangement à la Déportation: Nouvelles perspectives historiques*, ed. Ronnie-Gilles LeBlanc (Moncton: Chaire d'études acadiennes, Université de Moncton, 2005), 21–56. See also Danielle Gauvreau, "Vingt ans des études sur la population pendant le Régime français," in *Vingt ans après Habitants et Marchands: Lectures de l'histoire des XVIIe et XVIIIe siècles canadiennes*, ed. Sylvie Dépatie et al. (Montreal: McGill-Queen's University Press, 1998), 31–51.

4 Bettina Bradbury, "Social, Economic, and Cultural Origins of Contemporary Families," in *Families: Changing Trends in Canada*, ed. Maureen Baker (Toronto: McGraw-Hill Ryerson, 2005), 71–97.

5 Moogk, *La Nouvelle France*, 114.

6 Benoît Grenier, "Gentilshommes campagnards: La présence seigneuriale dans la vallée du Saint-Laurent (xviie–xixe siècle)," *Revue d' histoire de l'Amérique française* 59, 2 (Spring 2006): 409–49.

7 Scholars have debated whether habitants were technically peasants. On this matter, see Allan Greer, *Peasant, Lord and Merchant: Rural Society in Three Quebec Parishes, 1740–1840* (Toronto: University of Toronto Press, 1985); Leslie Choquette, *Frenchmen into Peasants: Modernity and Tradition in the Peopling of French Canada* (Cambridge, MA: Harvard University Press, 1997); and Catherine Desbarats, "Agriculture within the Seigneurial Régime of Eighteenth-Century Canada: Some Thoughts on the Recent Literature," *Canadian Historical Review* 63 (March 1992): 1–29.

8 Richard White, *The Middle Ground: Indians, Empires, and Republics in the Great Lakes Region, 1650–1815* (Cambridge: Cambridge University Press, 1991), chap. 2.

9 W. J. Eccles, *The French in North America, 1500–1763* (Markham, ON: Fitzhenry and Whiteside, 1998), 33.

10 H. A. Innis, *The Fur Trade in Canada: An Introduction to Canadian Economic History* (Toronto: University of Toronto Press, 1927), 153–54.

11 Cited in John G. Reid, "Imperial Intrusions, 1686–1720," in *The Atlantic Region to Confederation: A History*, ed. Phillip A. Buckner and John G. Reid (Toronto and Fredericton: University of Toronto Press and Acadiensis Press, 1994), 100.

12 N. E. S. Griffiths, "The Golden Age: Acadian Life, 1713–1748," *Histoire Sociale* 17, 33 (May 1984): 21–34.

13 *Peter Kalm's Travels in North America*, vol. 2, ed. Adolph B. Benson (New York: Dover Publications, 1966), 558.

14 Yvon Desloges, *A Tenant's Town: Quebec in the Eighteenth Century* (Ottawa: National Historic Sites Parks Service, Environment Canada, 1991), 40.

15 Afua Cooper, *The Hanging of Angélique: The Untold Story of Canadian Slavery and the Burning of Montréal* (Toronto: HarperCollins, 2006), 291.

16 John Mack Faragher, *A Great and Noble Scheme: The Tragic Story of the Expulsion of the French Acadians from Their American Homeland* (New York: Norton, 2005), 469. See also Naomi Griffiths, *The Contexts of Acadian History, 1686–1784* (Montreal: McGill-Queen's University Press, 1992).

17 Details of the battle are outlined in René Chartrand, *Quebec 1759* (Oxford: Osprey Publishing, 1999), and C. P. Stacey, *Quebec 1759: The Siege and the Battle*, ed. Donald E. Graves (Toronto: Robin Brass Studio, 2002).

4. A REVOLUTIONARY AGE, 1763–1821

1 Richard White, *The Middle Ground: Indians, Empires, and Republics in the Great Lakes Region, 1650–1815* (Cambridge: Cambridge University Press, 1991), 288.

2 William C. Wicken, *Mi'kmaq Treaties on Trial: History, Land, and Donald Marshall Junior* (Toronto: University of Toronto, 2003), 190–209.

3 John C. Weaver, *The Great Land Rush and the Making of the Modern World* (Montreal: McGill-Queen's University Press, 2003), 4.

4 John Reid, "Pax Britannica or Pax Indigena? Planter Nova Scotia (1760–1782) and Competing Strategies of Pacification," *Canadian Historical Review* 85, 4 (December 2004): 669–93.

5 Alan Taylor, *The Divided Ground: Indians, Settlers, and the Northern Borderland of the American Revolution* (New York: Alfred A. Knopf, 2006), 112–13.

6 For a recent analysis of the numbers and experience of the Loyalists, see Maya Jasanoff, *Liberty's Exiles: American Loyalists in the Revolutionary World* (New York: Alfred A. Knopf, 2011).

7 James Walker, *The Black Loyalists: The Search for a Promised Land in Nova Scotia and Sierra Leone, 1783–1870* (1976; reprinted, Toronto: University of Toronto Press, 1992).

8 Peter A. Baskerville, *Ontario: Image, Identity, and Power* (Don Mills, ON: Oxford University Press, 2002), 47.

9 There is an extensive literature on the Loyalists in British North America. Historiographical issues are addressed in L. S. Upton, ed., *The United Empire Loyalists: Men and Myths* (Toronto: Copp Clark Pitman, 1967), and Norman Knowles, *Inventing the Loyalists: The Ontario Loyalist Tradition and the Creation of a Usable Past* (Toronto: University of Toronto Press, 1997). Overviews are provided by Christopher Moore in *The Loyalists: Revolution, Exile and Settlement* (Toronto: Macmillan, 1984), and Wallace Brown and Hereward Senior, *Victorious in Defeat: The Loyalists in Canada* (Toronto: Methuen, 1984).

10 Margaret Conrad, Toni Laidlaw, and Donna Smyth, *No Place Like Home: The Diaries and Letters of Nova Scotia Women, 1771–1938* (Halifax: Formac, 1988), 53, 55.

11 On the War of 1812, see G. F. G. Stanley, *The War of 1812: Land Operations* (Toronto: Macmillan, 1983); George Sheppard, *Plunder and Profit and Paroles: A Social History of the War of 1812* (Montreal: McGill-Queen's University Press, 1994); and Alan Taylor, *The Civil War of 1812: American Citizens, British Subjects, Irish Rebels, and Indian Allies* (New York: Knopf Doubleday, 2010).

12 J. R. Miller, *Skyscrapers Hide the Heavens: A History of Indian-White Relations in Canada*, rev. ed. (Toronto: University of Toronto Press, 1989), 87.

13 The details of this expansion are described and mapped in "The Northwest," in *Historical Atlas of Canada*, vol. 1, ed. R. Cole Harris and Geoffrey J. Matthews (Toronto: University of Toronto Press, 1987), 143–69.

14 Cole Harris, "Voices of Smallpox around the Strait of Georgia," in *The Resettlement of British Columbia: Essays on Colonialism and Geographical Change* (Vancouver: University of British Columbia Press, 1997), 11.

15 Elizabeth Vibert, *Traders' Tales: Narratives of Cultural Encounters in the Columbia Plateau, 1807–1846* (Norman: University of Oklahoma Press, 1997), 138–39.

16 Carolyn Podruchny, *Making the Voyageur World: Travelers and Traders in the North American Fur Trade* (Toronto: University of Toronto Press, 2006), 10.

5. TRANSATLANTIC COMMUNITIES, 1815–1849

1 The terms used for Lower and Upper Canada in this period are cumbersome. In 1840 the British Parliament passed legislation creating the United Province of Canada, and thereafter they become Canada East and Canada West. Although I try to use the term that fits the time period being discussed, this does not always work. The territory occupied by the Hudson's Bay Company was called Rupert's Land. Other areas under company domination were called the Northwest, which is a term often used to cover the entire western region in this period.

2 Phillip Buckner, "Whatever Happened to the British Empire?" Presidential Address, *Journal of the Canadian Historical Association*, n.s., 4 (1993): 3–32.

3 While the number of fugitive slaves is disputed, they made up at least 20 percent of the black population of Canada West in 1861, estimated at roughly twenty-three thousand. See Michael Wayne, "The Black Population of Canada West on the Eve of the American Civil War: A Reassessment Based on the Manuscript Census of 1861," *Histoire sociale/Social History* 28, 56 (Nov. 1995): 465–81.

4 Owen Beattie, *Frozen in Time: Unlocking the Secrets of the Franklin Expedition* (New York: Dutton, 1988); David C. Woodman, *Unravelling the Franklin Mystery: Inuit Testimony* (Montreal: McGill-Queen's University Press, 1991); Leslie H. Neatby, *The Search for the Franklin Expedition* (Edmonton: Hurtig, 1970).

5 On the immigrant experience in Upper Canada, see Elizabeth Jane Errington, *Emigrant Worlds and Transatlantic Communities: Migration to Upper Canada in the First Half of the Nineteenth Century* (Montreal: McGill-Queen's University Press, 2007).

6 Michael B. Katz, *The People of Hamilton, Canada West: Family and Class in a Mid-Nineteenth-Century City* (Cambridge, MA: Harvard University Press, 1975), 43.

7 Bettina Bradbury, *Wife to Widow: Lives, Laws, and Politics in Nineteenth-Century Montreal* (Vancouver: University of British Columbia Press, 2011). See also Constance Backhouse, *Petticoats and Prejudice: Women and the Law in Nineteenth-Century Canada* (Toronto: Osgoode Society, 1991).

8 Cole Harris, *Making Native Space: Colonialism, Resistance, and Reserves in British Columbia* (Vancouver: University of British Columbia Press, 2002), 10.

9 Two scholars pioneered the study of the Aboriginal women in the fur trade: Sylvia Van Kirk, *"Many Tender Ties": Women in Fur Trade Society in Western Canada, 1670–1870* (Winnipeg: Watson and Dwyer, 1980), and Jennifer S. H. Brown, *Strangers in Blood: Fur Trade Families in Indian Country* (Vancouver: University of British Columbia Press, 1980).

10 Peggy Bristow, "'Whatever you can raise in the ground you can sell it in Chatham': Black Women in Buxton and Chatham, 1850–65," in Peggy Bristow et al., *"We're Rooted Here and They Can't Pull Us Up": Essays in African Canadian Women's History* (Toronto: University of Toronto Press, 1994), 77.

11 Katherine Fierlbeck, *Political Thought in Canada: An Intellectual History* (Peterborough, ON: Broadview Press, 2006). See also Jeffrey L. McNairn, *The Capacity of Judge: Public Opinion and Deliberative Democracy in Upper Canada* (Toronto: University of Toronto Press, 2000).

12 For opposing views, see Fernand Ouellet, *Lower Canada, 1791–1840: Social Change and Nationalism* (Toronto: McClelland and Stewart, 1980), and *Economic and Social History of Quebec* (Toronto: Macmillan, 1981); and Allan Greer, *The Patriots and the People: The Rebellion of 1837 in Rural Lower Canada* (Toronto: University of Toronto Press, 1993).

13 A thoughtful treatment of these two important political figures can be found in John Ralston Saul, *Louis-Hippolyte LaFontaine and Robert Baldwin* (Toronto: Penguin, 2010).

14 Cited in Harris, *Making Native Space*, 18.

6. COMING TOGETHER, 1849–1885

1 Thomas C. Keefer, "Philosophy of Railroads," in *Philosophy of Railroads and Other Essays*, ed. T. C. Keefer (1850; reprinted, Toronto: University of Toronto Press, 1972), 10–11. Keefer's views are usefully contextualized in chapter 2 of R. Douglas Francis, *The Technological Imperative in Canada* (Vancouver: University of British Columbia Press, 2009), and in A. A. den Otter, *The Philosophy of Railways: The Transcontinental Railway Idea in British North America* (Toronto: University of Toronto Press, 1997).

2 Karl Polanyi, *The Great Transformation: The Political and Economic Origins of Our Times* (New York: Farrar and Rinehart, 1944).

3 Bettina Bradbury, *Working Families: Age, Gender, and Daily Survival in Industrializing Montreal* (Toronto: McClelland and Stewart, 1993).

4 Cited in Susan Houston, "Politics, Schools, and Change in Upper Canada," *Canadian Historical Review* 53, 3 (September 1972): 265.

5 Adele Perry, *On the Edge of Empire: Gender, Race and the Making of British Columbia, 1849–1871* (Toronto: University of Toronto Press, 2001).

6 Andrew Smith, *British Businessmen and Canadian Confederation: Constitution-Making in the Age of Anglo-Globalization* (Montreal: McGill-Queen's University Press, 2008).

7 There is an extensive literature on Confederation. A good introduction to the issues can be found in Ged Martin, ed., *The Causes of Canadian Confederation* (Fredericton: Acadiensis Press, 1990), and *Britain and the Origins of Canadian Confederation, 1837–1867* (Vancouver: University of British Columbia Press, 1995).

8 John A. Macdonald has attracted several talented biographers, including Donald Creighton, *John A. Macdonald*, 2 vols. (Toronto: Macmillan of Canada, 1952/1955); P. B. Waite, *Macdonald: His Life and World* (Toronto: McGraw-Hill Ryerson, 1971); Richard Gwyn, *John A.: The Man Who Made Us* and *Nation Maker* (Toronto: Random House, 2007/2011); and Ged Martin, *Favourite Son? John A. Macdonald and the Voters of Kingston, 1841–1891* (Kingston: Kingston Historical Society, 2010).

9 The huge literature on Louis Riel and the uprisings with which he is associated is assessed by Albert Braz, *The False Traitor: Louis Riel in Canadian Culture* (Toronto: University of Toronto Press, 2003).

10 The "dubious bargain" on Aboriginal matters is closely analyzed in Cole Harris, *Making Native Space: Colonialism, Resistance, and Reserves in British Columbia* (Vancouver: University British Columbia Press, 2002), 73.

11 Shelagh D. Grant, *Sovereignty or Security: Government Policy in the Canadian North, 1936–1950* (Vancouver: University of British Columbia Press, 1988), 5. See also Shelagh D. Grant, *A History of Arctic Sovereignty in North America* (Vancouver: Douglas and McIntyre, 2010).

12 Dale C. Thompson, *Alexander Mackenzie: Clear Grit* (Toronto: Macmillan, 1960).

13 The details, heroic and otherwise, of the construction of the CPR are chronicled in two volumes by Pierre Berton, *The National Dream* (Toronto: McClelland and Stewart, 1970), and *The Last Spike* (Toronto: McClelland and Stewart, 1971).

14 This debate and other aspects of Canadian economic history can be found in Kenneth Norrie and Douglas Owram, *A History of the Canadian Economy* (Toronto: Harcourt Brace Jovanovich, 1991); Graham D. Taylor and Peter Baskerville,

A Concise History of Business in Canada (Don Mills, ON: Oxford University Press, 1994); and Michael Bliss, *Northern Enterprise: Five Centuries of Canadian Business* (Toronto: McClelland and Stewart, 1987).

15 Sarah Carter, *Capturing Women: The Manipulation of Cultural Imagery in Canada's Prairie West* (Montreal: McGill-Queen's University Press, 2004), and *Aboriginal People and Colonizers of Western Canada to 1900*, 2nd ed. (Toronto: University of Toronto Press, 2004).

16 George McQueen to Jessie McQueen, 7 January 1888, Greenville. The McQueen Family Papers, Atlantic Canada Virtual Archives, no. 3347_05_02. University of New Brunswick, Fredericton, NB, Canada. On the McQueen family, see Jean Barman, *Sojourning Sisters: The Lives and Letters of Jessie and Annie McQueen* (Toronto: University of Toronto Press, 2003).

7. MAKING PROGRESS, 1885–1914

1 One of the best surveys on this period was published nearly four decades ago: Robert Craig Brown and Ramsay Cook, *Canada: 1896–1921: A Nation Transformed* (Toronto: McClelland and Stewart, 1974).

2 Carl Berger, *The Sense of Power: Studies in the Ideas of Canadian Imperialism, 1867–1914* (Toronto: University of Toronto Press, 1970).

3 Biographies of Laurier include Joseph Schull, *Laurier* (Toronto: Macmillan, 1965); Richard Clippendale, *Laurier: His Life and World* (Toronto: McGraw-Hill Ryerson, 1979); Réal Bélanger, *Wilfrid Laurier: quand la politique devient passion* (Quebec: Presses de l'Université Laval, 1986); and André Pratte, *Wilfrid Laurier* (Toronto: Penguin, 2011).

4 Cited in J. W. Dafoe, *Clifford Sifton in Relation to His Times* (Toronto: Macmillan, 1931), 142.

5 For a broader discussion of the arts, see Maria Tippett, *Making Culture: English-Canadian Institutions and the Arts before the Massey Commission* (Toronto: University of Toronto Press, 1990).

6 Carl Berger, *Honour and the Search for Influence: A History of the Royal Society of Canada* (Toronto: University of Toronto Press, 1996), 32.

7 J. R. Miller, *Shingwauk's Vision: A History of Native Residential Schools* (Toronto: University of Toronto Press, 1996).

8 Borden's administration is discussed in Robert Craig Brown, *Robert Laird Borden*, 2 vols. (Ottawa: Carleton University Press, 1969), and John English, *The Decline of Politics: The Conservatives and the Party System, 1901–1920* (Toronto: University of Toronto Press, 1977).

8. HANGING ON, 1914–1945

1 Desmond Morton and J. L. Granatstein, *Marching to Armageddon: Canadians and the Great War, 1914–1919* (Toronto: Lester and Orpen Dennys, 1989).

2 The military historian J. L. Granatstein, who earlier in his career argued that conscription had failed in its objectives, has more recently concluded that conscripts "kept units up to strength, allowed the Canadian Corps to function with great effectiveness and efficiency in the final decisive battles of the Great War, and helped to minimize casualties." J. L. Granatstein, "Conscription in the Great War," in *Canada and the First World War: Essays in Honour of Robert Craig Brown*, ed. David

Mackenzie (Toronto: University of Toronto Press, 2005), 75. The earlier argument is made in J. L. Granatstein and J. M. Hitsman, *Broken Promises: A History of Conscription in Canada* (Don Mills, ON: Oxford University Press, 1977).

3 Cited in James W. St. G. Walker, "Race and Recruitment in World War I: Enlistment of Visible Minorities in the Canadian Expeditionary Force," *Canadian Historical Review* 70, 1 (March 1989): 1–26.

4 Mark Osborne Humphries, "The Horror at Home: The Canadian Military and the 'Great' Influenza Pandemic of 1918," *Journal of the Canadian Historical Association*, n.s., 16 (Ottawa 2005): 235–61. On the fortunes of the expeditionary force sent to Russia, see Benjamin Isitt, *From Victoria to Vladivostok: Canada's Siberian Expedition, 1917–1919* (Vancouver: University of British Columbia Press, 2010).

5 On the experience of Canadians soldiers in war, see Tim Cook, *At the Sharp End: Canadians Fighting the Great War, 1914–1916* (Toronto: Viking Canada, 2007), and *Shock Troops: Canadians Fighting the Great War, 1917–1918* (Toronto: Viking Canada, 2008). See also Desmond Morton, *When Your Number's Up: The Canadian Soldier in the First World War* (Toronto: Random House, 1993).

6 Robert J. Sharpe and Patricia I. McMahon, *The Persons Case: The Origins and Legacy of the Fight for Legal Personhood* (Toronto: University of Toronto Press, 2007).

7 The diaries are available online at http://www.collectionscanada.gc.ca/databases/king/index-e.html. King has a attracted many biographers. A good place to start is H. Blair Neatby's entry in the *Dictionay of Canadian Biography* (http://www.biographi.ca).

8 E. R. Forbes, *Maritime Rights: The Maritime Rights Movement: A Study in Canadian Regionalism* (Montreal: McGill-Queen's University Press, 1979); David Frank, *J. B. McLaughlin: A Biography* (Toronto: Lorimer, 1999).

9 John Boyko, *Bennett: The Rebel Who Challenged and Changed a Nation* (Toronto: Key Porter Books, 2010); P. B. Waite, *The Loner: Three Sketches of the Personal Life and Ideas of R. B. Bennett, 1870–1947* (Toronto: University of Toronto Press, 1992).

10 Cited in P. B. Waite, "Bennett, Richard Bedford," *Dictionary of Canadian Biography* (http://www.biographi.ca).

11 Two monographs bring postwar values into perspective: Jonathan Vance, *Death So Noble: Memory, Meaning, and the First World War* (Vancouver: University of British Columbia Press, 1997), and Veronica Strong-Boag, *The New Day Recalled: Lives of Girls and Women in English Canada, 1919–1939* (Toronto: Copp Clark, 1988).

12 See, for example, Denyse Baillargeon, *Making Do: Women, Family, and Home in Montreal During the Great Depression* (Waterloo, ON: Wilfrid Laurier Press, 1999).

13 Cynthia Comacchio, *The Infinite Bonds of Family: Domesticity in Canada, 1850–1940* (Toronto: University of Toronto Press, 1999); Denyse Baillargeon, *Babies for the Nation: The Medicalization of Motherhood in Quebec, 1900–1970* (Waterloo, ON: Wilfrid Laurier Press, 2009); Daniel Dagenais, *The (Un) Making of the Modern Family*, trans. Jane Brierley (Vancouver: University of British Columbia Press, 2008).

14 General surveys of Canada's role in the Second World War include J. L. Granatstein and Desmond Morton, *A Nation Forged in Fire: Canadians and the Second World War* (Toronto: Lester and Orpen Dennys, 1989);

J. L. Granatstein, *Canada's War: The Politics of the Mackenzie King Government, 1939–1945* (Don Mills, ON: Oxford University Press, 1975; and Jeffrey A. Keshen, *Saints, Sinners, and Soldiers: Canada's Second World War* (Vancouver: University of British Columbia Press, 2004). Canadian-American relations during the war are contextualized in Norman Hillmer and J. L. Granatstein, *For Better or for Worse: Canada and the United States into the Twenty-first Century* (Toronto: Thomson/Nelson, 2007).

15 Timothy Snyder, *Bloodlands: Europe between Hitler and Stalin* (New York: Basic Books, 2010). The Canadian figures are drawn from Desmond Morton and J. L. Granatstein, *Victory 1945: Canadians from War to Peace* (Toronto: HarperCollins, 1995), 19.

16 The controversy surrounding a critical treatment of Bomber Command in the 1992 film *The Valour and the Horror* is discussed in David J. Bercuson and S. F. Wise, eds., *"The Valour and the Horror" Revisited* (Montreal: McGill-Queen's University Press, 1994).

17 Olga Rains, Lloyd Rains, and Melynda Jarratt, *Voices of the Left Behind: Project Roots and the Canadian War Children of World War Two* (Fredericton: Project Roots, 2004).

9. LIBERALISM TRIUMPHANT, 1945–1984

1 Eric Hobsbawm, *Age of Extremes: The Short Twentieth Century, 1914–1991* (London: Abacus, 1995), 6.

2 Mark Mazower, *No Enchanted Place: The End of Empire and the Ideological Origins of the United Nations* (Princeton: Princeton University Press, 2009).

3 The Universal Declaration of Human Rights (http://www.un.org/en/documents/udhr). On human rights in Canada, see Ross Lamberton, *Repression and Resistance: Canadian Human Rights Activists* (Toronto: University of Toronto Press, 2005); Christopher MacLennan, *Towards the Charter: Canadians and the Demand for a National Bill of Rights, 1929–1960* (Montreal: McGill-Queen's University Press, 2003); and Dominique Clément, *Canada's Rights Revolution: Social Movements and Social Change, 1937–1982* (Vancouver: University of British Columbia Press, 2008).

4 Andrew Armitage, *Social Welfare in Canada: Ideas, Realities and Future Paths*, 2nd ed. (Toronto: McClelland and Stewart, 1988), 22.

5 Robert Bothwell, "Louis-Stephen St. Laurent," *Dictionary of Canadian Biography Online* (http://www.biographi.ca); Dale C. Thomson, *Louis St. Laurent: Canadian* (Toronto: Macmillan, 1967).

6 Denis Smith, *Politics of Fear: Canada and the Cold War, 1941–1948* (Toronto: University of Toronto Press, 1988); Reginald Whitaker and Steve Hewitt, *Canada and the Cold War* (Toronto: James Lorimer, 2003).

7 David Jay Bercuson, *Blood on the Hills: The Canadian Army in the Korean War* (Toronto: University of Toronto Press, 1999).

8 Military policy and much about this period in Canadian history are usefully summarized in Robert Bothwell, Ian Drummond, and John English, *Canada since 1945: Power, Politics, and Provincialism* (Toronto: University of Toronto Press, 1981), and in Robert Bothwell, *Alliance and Illusion: Canada and the World, 1945–1984* (Vancouver: University of British Columbia Press, 2007). A sharper critique of federal policy in this period can be found in Alvin Finkel, *Our Lives: Canada after 1945* (Toronto: Lorimer, 1997).

9 Denis Smith, "John George Diefenbaker," *Dictionary of Canadian Biography Online* (http://www.biographi.ca). See also Smith's magisterial biography, *Rogue Tory: The Life and Legend of John G. Diefenbaker* (Toronto: Macfarlane, Walter and Ross, 1995).

10 See John English, *The Life of Lester Pearson*, 2 vols. (Toronto: Random House, 1989/93), and his entry, "Lester Bowles Pearson," *Dictionary of Canadian Biography Online* (http://www.biographi.ca).

11 In 1953 Colonel Robert S. McCormick, the editor of the *Chicago Tribune*, confided in his diary that Pearson was "the most dangerous man in the English-speaking world" because of his perceived left-leaning sympathies. English, *Life of Lester Pearson*, vol. 2, *The Worldly Years, 1949–1972* (Toronto: Vintage Books, 1993), 88.

12 Jeffrey Cormier, *The Canadianization Movement: Emergence, Survival, and Success* (Toronto: University of Toronto Press, 2004).

13 Bruce Hutchison, *The Unknown Country* (Toronto: Longmans, Green, 1942).

14 Michael Behiels, *Prelude to Quebec's Quiet Revolution: Liberalism versus Neo-Conservatism, 1945–1960* (Montreal: McGill-Queen's University Press, 1985).

15 Claude Bélanger, "The Quiet Revolution," http://faculty.marianopolis.edu/c. belanger/quebechistory/events/quiet.htm/.

16 William Coleman, *The Independence Movement in Quebec, 1945–1980* (Toronto: University of Toronto Press, 1984); Sean Mills, *The Empire Within: Postcolonial Thought and Political Activism in Sixties Montreal* (Montreal: McGill-Queen's University Press, 2011).

17 Doug Owram, *Born at the Right Time: A History of the Baby-Boom Generation* (Toronto: University of Toronto Press, 1996); Bryan D. Palmer, *Canada's 1960s: The Ironies of Identity in a Rebellious Era* (Toronto: University of Toronto Press, 2009).

18 For a summary of developments on the status of women in this period, see Ruth Roach Pierson et al., eds., *Canadian Women's Issues*, 2 vols. (Toronto: James Lorimer, 1993/1995), and Joy Parr, ed., *A Diversity of Women, Ontario, 1945–1980* (Toronto: University of Toronto Press, 1995).

19 For the Trudeau years, see John English's award-winning biography, *Just Watch Me: The Life of Pierre Elliott Trudeau, 1968–2000* (Toronto: Vintage Canada, 2010).

20 José Igartua, *The Other Quiet Revolution: National Identities in English Canada, 1945–71* (Vancouver: University of British Columbia Press, 2006).

10. INTERESTING TIMES, 1984–2011

1 Raymond Blake, *Transforming the Nation: Canada and Brian Mulroney* (Montreal: McGill-Queen's University Press, 2007); William Kaplan, *A Secret Trial: Brian Mulroney and the Public Trust* (Montreal: McGill-Queen's University Press, 2008).

2 Lawrence Martin, *Iron Man: The Defiant Reign of Jean Chrétien* (Toronto: Penguin, 2003); Edward McWhinney, *Chrétien and Canadian Federalism: Politics and the Constitution, 1993–2003* (Vancouver: Ronsdale Press, 2003).

3 Paul Wells, *Right Side Up: The Fall of Paul Martin and the Rise of Stephen Harper's New Conservatism* (Toronto: McClelland and Stewart, 2006).

4 Lawrence Martin, *Harperland: The Politics of Control* (Toronto: Penguin, 2010); William Johnson, *Stephen Harper and the Future of Canada* (Toronto: McClelland and Stewart, 2006).

5 Standing Senate committee on transport and communications, *Final Report on the Canadian News Media*, 2 vols. (Ottawa, 2006). Available at http://www.parl.gc.ca/39/1/parlbus/commbus/senate/com-e/tran-e/rep-e/repfinjun06vol1-e.htm.

6 The salaries of Canada's highest-paid CEOs increased by 444 percent between 1995 and 2007, while the income of the average worker stalled. Susan Mohammad and Duncan Hood, "Cashing In: Canada's CEO salary surge," *Macleans*, 1 May 2009 (http://www2.macleans.ca/2009/05/01/the-rising-salaries-of-canadas-top-50-ceos/). See also The Conference Board of Canada, *How Canada Performs: A Report Card on Canada* (2011), http://www.conferenceboard.ca/HCP/default.aspx.

7 On Canadian food banks, see Food Banks Canada, *HungerCount 2010*, http://smr.newswire.ca/en/food-banks-canada/count-study. The guaranteed annual income is discussed in the *Globe and Mail*, 20 November 2010, sections F1 and F5.

8 United Nations World Commission on Environment and Development, *Our Common Future* (Oxford: Oxford University Press, 1987).

9 Michael Valpy, "Canada's Military: Invisible No More, *Globe and Mail*, 20 November 2009, http://www.theglobeandmail.com/news/politics/canadas-military-invisible-no-more/article1372117/. This theme is expanded in Ian McKay and Jamie Swift, *Warrior Nation? Rebranding Canada in a Fearful Age* (Toronto: Between the Lines, 2011).

10 The statistics cited here can be found at Citizenship and Immigration Canada, Facts and Figures 2008, http://www.cic.gc.ca/english/resources/statistics/facts2008/index.asp; and Statistics Canada, Projections of the Diversity of the Canadian Population, 2006 to 2031, http://www.statcan.gc.ca/pub/91-551-x/91-551-x2010001-eng.pdf.

11 Native Women's Association of Canada, Sisters in Spirit, http://www.nwac.ca/programs/sisters-spirit.

12 The statistics reported here are derived from Reginald Bibby, *Restless Gods: The Renaissance of Religion in Canada* (Toronto: Novalis, 2004), and Lydia Saad, "Can a 'Reagan Revolution' Happen in Canada?" http://www.gallup.com/poll/20986/Can-Reagan-Revolution-Happen-Canada.aspx.

13 Statistics Canada, Aboriginal Peoples of Canada, 2001 Census. http://www12.statcan.ca/english/census01/Products/Analytic/companion/abor/canada.cfm.

14 *Royal Commission Report on Aboriginal Peoples*, http://www.ainc-inac.gc.ca/ap/rrc-eng.asp. The five-volume, 3,537-page report is usefully summarized and discussed in Olive Patricia Dickason with David T. McNab, *Canada's First Nations: A History of Founding Peoples from Earliest Times*, 4th ed. (Don Mills, ON: Oxford University Press, 2008), 417–20.

15 Dickason and McNab, *Canada's First Nations*, 431–32.

GUIDE TO
FURTHER READING

There is a vast literature on Canadian history in English and French, only a small portion of which is cited here and in the notes to each chapter. Those interested in Canadian studies generally would do well to consult John D. Blackwell and Laurie Stanley-Blackwell, *Canadian Studies: A Guide to the Sources*, available online at http://www.iccs-ciec.ca/Blackwell.html. The following reference works and surveys offer a place to start for further reading and research.

REFERENCE SOURCES

Burcuson, David J., and J. L. Granatstein. *Dictionary of Canadian Military History*. Don Mills, ON: Oxford University Press, 1992.

The Canadian Centenary Series. 19 vols. Toronto: McClelland and Stewart, 1963–1986.

The Canadian Encyclopedia. 4 vols. Edmonton: Hurtig, 1988. Updated version available online at http://www.thecanadianencyclopedia.com.

Canadian Institute for Historical Microreproductions. http://www.canadiana.org/cihm.

The Champlain Society Digital Collection. http://www.champlainsociety.ca.

The Dictionary of Canadian Biography. 15 volumes to date. Toronto: University of Toronto Press, various years. Available online at http://www.biographi.ca.

Hallowell, Gerald, ed. *The Oxford Companion to Canadian History*. Don Mills, ON: Oxford University Press, 2004.

The Historical Atlas of Canada. 3 vols. Toronto: University of Toronto Press, 1987, 1990, 1993.

Kellmann, Helmut, et al., eds. *The Encyclopedia of Music in Canada*. 2nd ed. Toronto: University of Toronto Press, 1992.

Library and Archives Canada. http://www.collectionscanada.ca.

GENERAL SURVEYS

Bothwell, Robert. *The Penguin History of Canada*. Toronto: Penguin Canada, 2006.

Brown, Craig, ed. *The Illustrated History of Canada*. Rev. ed. Toronto: Key Porter, 2007.

Bumsted, J. M. *A History of the Canadian Peoples*. 4th ed. Don Mills, ON: Oxford University Press, 2011.

Conrad, Margaret, and Alvin Finkel. *History of the Canadian Peoples*. 2 vols. 5th ed. Toronto: Pearson Longman, 2009.

Francis, R. Douglas, Richard Jones, and Donald B. Smith. *Origins: Canadian History to Confederation,* and *Destinies: Canadian History Since Confederation*. 6th ed. Toronto: Nelson Education, 2010.

Friesen, Gerald. *Citizens and Nation: An Essay on History, Communication, and Canada*. Toronto: University of Toronto Press, 2000.

Harris, Cole. *The Reluctant Land: Society, Space, and Environment in Canada before Confederation*. Vancouver: University of British Columbia Press, 2008.

Morton, Desmond. *A Short History of Canada*. 6th ed. Toronto: McClelland and Stewart, 2008.

Nelles, H. V. *A Little History of Canada*. Don Mills, ON: Oxford University Press, 2004.

REGIONAL, PROVINCIAL, AND TERRITORIAL SURVEYS

Barman, Jean. *The West Beyond the West: A History of British Columbia*. Rev. ed. Toronto: University of Toronto Press, 1995.

Baskerville, Peter. *Ontario: Image, Identity, and Power*. Don Mills, ON: Oxford University Press, 2002.

Buckner, Phillip A., and John G. Reid., eds. *The Atlantic Region to Confederation: A History*. Toronto and Fredericton: University of Toronto Press and Acadiensis Press, 1994.

Cadigan, Sean T. *Newfoundland and Labrador: A History*. Toronto: University of Toronto Press, 2009.

Coates, Kenneth, and William Morrison. *Land of the Midnight Sun: A History of the Yukon*. Montreal: McGill-Queen's University Press, 2005.

Conrad, Margaret R., and James K. Hiller. *Atlantic Canada: A History*. Don Mills, ON: Oxford University Press, 2010.

Dickinson John, and Brian Young. *A Short History of Quebec*. 3rd ed. Montreal: McGill-Queen's University Press, 2008.

Forbes, E. R., and D. A. Muise, eds. *The Atlantic Region in Confederation*. Toronto: University of Toronto Press, 1993.

Friesen, Gerald. *Canadian Prairies: A History*. Toronto: University of Toronto Press, 1987.

Linteau, Paul-André, René Durocher, and Jean-Claude Robert. *A History of Contemporary Quebec.* 2 vols. Toronto: Lorimer, 1983/1989.

MacDonald, Edward. *If You're Stronghearted: Prince Edward Island in the Twentieth Century.* Charlottetown: Prince Edward Island Museum and Heritage Foundation, 2000.

Morrison, William R. *True North: The Yukon and Northwest Territories.* Don Mills, ON: Oxford University Press, 1998.

Roy, Patricia E., and John Herd Thompson. *British Columbia: Land of Promise.* Don Mills, ON: Oxford University Press, 2002.

Thompson, John Herd. *Forging the Prairie West.* Don Mills, ON: Oxford University Press, 1998.

Waiser, Bill. *Saskatchewan: A New History.* Calgary: Fifth House, 2005.

TOPICAL SURVEYS

Berger, Carl. *The Writing of Canadian History.* 2nd ed. Toronto: University of Toronto Press, 1986.

Bliss, Michael. *Right Honourable Men: The Descent of Canadian Politics from Macdonald to Mulroney.* Toronto: HarperCollins, 1994.

Bliss, Michael. *Northern Enterprise: Five Centuries of Canadian Business.* Toronto: McClelland and Stewart, 1987.

Boutelier, Beverly, and Alison Prentice, eds. *Creating Historical Memory: English Canadian Women and the Work of History.* Vancouver: University of British Columbia Press, 1997.

Brandt, Gail Cuthbert, Naomi Black, Paula Bourne, and Magda Fahrni. *Canadian Women: A History.* Toronto: Nelson Education, 2011.

Dickason, Olive Patricia with David T. McNab. *Canada's First Nations: A History of Founding Peoples from Earliest Times.* 4th ed. Don Mills, ON: Oxford University Press, 2008.

Duke, David Freeland, ed. *Canadian Environmental History: Essential Readings.* Toronto: Canadian Scholars' Press, 2006.

Fleming, Patricia Lockhart, et al., eds. *A History of the Book in Canada.* 3 vols. Toronto: University of Toronto Press, 2004, 2005, 2007.

Fierlbeck, Katherine. *Political Thought in Canada: An Intellectual History.* Peterborough, ON: Broadview Press, 2006.

Gaffield, Chad, and Pam Gaffield, eds. *Consuming Canada: Readings in Environmental History.* Toronto: Copp, Clark, 1995.

Gauvreau, Michael. *The Evangelical Century: College and Creed from the Great Revival to the Great Depression.* Montreal: McGill-Queen's University Press, 1991.

Granatstein, J. L. *Canada's Army: Waging War and Keeping the Peace.* 2nd ed. Toronto: University of Toronto Press, 2011.

Heron, Craig. *The Canadian Labour Movement: A Short History.* 2nd ed. Toronto: James Lorimer, 1996.

Hillmer, Norman, and Granatstein, J. L. *For Better or for Worse: Canada and the United States into the Twenty-first Century.* Toronto: Thomson/ Nelson, 2007.

Kalman, Harold. *A History of Canadian Architecture.* 2 vols. Don Mills, ON: Oxford University Press, 1994.

Kinsman, Gary. *The Regulation of Desire: Homo and Hetero Sexualities.* Montreal and New York: Black Rose, 1995.

MacEachern, Alan, and William J. Turkel, eds. *Method and Meaning in Canadian Environmental History.* Toronto: Nelson Education, 2009.

Mahant, Edelgard E., and Graeme S. Mount. *An Introduction to Canadian-American Relations.* Rev. ed. Toronto: Metheun, 1989.

Miller, J. R. *Skyscrapers Hide the Heavens: A History of Indian-White Relations in Canada.* Rev. ed. Toronto: University of Toronto Press, 1991.

Morrow, Don, and Kevin B. Wamsley. *Sport in Canada: A History.* Don Mills, ON: Oxford University Press, 2010.

Morton, Desmond. *A Military History of Canada.* Toronto: McClelland and Stewart, 2007.

Murphy, Terrence, et al., eds. *A Concise History of Religion in Canada.* Don Mills, ON: Oxford University Press, 1996.

Norrie, Kenneth, and Douglas Owram. *A History of the Canadian Economy.* Toronto: Harcourt Brace Jovanovich, 1991.

Palmer, Bryan. *Working Class Experience: Rethinking the History of Canadian Labour, 1800–1991.* 2nd ed. Toronto: McClelland and Stewart, 1992.

Ray, Arthur J. *I Have Lived Here Since the World Began: An Illustrated History of Canada's Native People.* Rev ed. Toronto: Lester/Key Porter, 2005.

Reid, Dennis. *A Concise History of Canadian Painting.* 2nd ed. Don Mills, ON: Oxford University Press, 1988.

Rubin, Don. *Canadian Theatre History: Selected Readings.* 2nd ed. Toronto: Playwrights Canada Press, 2004.

Taylor, Graham D., and Peter A. Baskerville. *A Concise History of Business in Canada.* Don Mills, ON: Oxford University Press, 1994.

Thompson, James Herd, and Stephen Randall. *Canada and the United States: Ambivalent Allies,* 4th ed. Montreal: McGill-Queen's University Press, 2008.

Vance, Jonathan. *A History of Canadian Culture.* Don Mills, ON: Oxford University Press, 2009.

Voyageur, Cora J., et al. *Hidden in Plain Sight: Contributions of Aboriginal Peoples to Canadian Identity and Culture.* Toronto: University of Toronto Press, 2005/2011.

Warner, Tom. *Never Going Back: A History of Queer Activism in Canada.* Toronto: University of Toronto Press, 2002.

INDEX

Titles in the Series

A Concise History of Australia, 3rd edition
STUART MACINTYRE

A Concise History of Austria
STEVEN BELLER

A Concise History of the Baltic States
ANDREJS PLAKANS

A Concise History of Bolivia, 2nd edition
HERBERT S. KLEIN

A Concise History of Brazil
BORIS FAUSTO, TRANSLATED BY ARTHUR BRAKEL

A Concise History of Britain, 1707–1975
W. A. SPECK

A Concise History of Bulgaria, 2nd edition
R. J. CRAMPTON

A Concise History of Canada
MARGARET CONRAD

A Concise History of the Caribbean
B. W. HIGMAN

A Concise History of Finland
DAVID KIRBY

A Concise History of France, 2nd edition
ROGER PRICE

A Concise History of Germany, 2nd edition
MARY FULBROOK

A Concise History of Greece, 2nd edition
RICHARD CLOGG

CPSIA information can be obtained
at www.ICGtesting.com
Printed in the USA
LVOW04s2331061115
461517LV00017B/619/P